Parental Participation in Children's Development and Education

Special Aspects of Education

A series of books edited by Roy Evans, Roehampton Institute, London, UK, and Herman Green, Northern Illinois University, De Kalb, Illinois, USA.

Volume 1
Disadvantaged Post-Adolescents:
Approaches to Education and Rehabilitation
Reuven Kohen-Raz
The Hebrew University

Volume 2
Israelis in Institutions:
Studies in Child Placement, Practice and Policy
Eliezer D. Jaffe
The Hebrew University

Volume 3
Parental Participation in Children's Development and Education
Sheila Wolfendale
North East London Polytechnic

Other volumes in preparation

ISSN:0731–8413

This book is part of a series. The publishers will accept continuation orders which may be cancelled at any time and which provide for automatic billing and shipping of each title in the series upon publication. Please write for details.

Parental Participation in Children's Development and Education

SHEILA WOLFENDALE
North East London Polytechnic

GORDON AND BREACH SCIENCE PUBLISHERS
New York   London   Paris   Montreux   Tokyo

Copyright © 1983 by Gordon and Breach, Science Publishers, Inc.
All rights reserved

Gordon and Breach Science Publishers

P.O. Box 786
Cooper Station
New York,   NY 10276
United States of America

P.O. Box 197
London,   WC2E 9PX
England

58, rue Lhomond
75005 Paris
France

P.O. Box 161
1820 Montreux-2
Switzerland

14–9 Okubo 3-chome
Shinjoko-ku
Tokyo,   160
Japan

First Printed 1983
Reprinted 1984, 1985, 1985

Library of Congress Cataloging in Publication Data
Wolfendale, Sheila, 1939
Parental participation in children's development and education

(Special aspects of education, ISSN 0731–8413; v. 3)
Includes index.
1. Home and school.   2. Community and school.
I. Title.   II. Series.
LC225.W69   1983   380.19'31   82–11946
ISBN 0–677–06060–2
ISBN 0–677–06065–3 (pbk.)

For Trevor

Contents

Introduction to the Series

Increasingly in the last 10 to 15 years the published literature within the field of care and education has become more specialised and focused: an inevitable consequence of the information explosion and the improved standards of theoretical and practical knowledge being required of students in both the traditional and developing areas of professional training. Students within initial and post-initial training evidently need to have ready access to specialist theoretical and pedagogical resources relevant to the context of future professional involvements which also develop special aspects of an area of study in a critically evaluative way.

In the study of education and pedagogy, the analytical and experimental approaches of psychology, philosophy, sociology, social anthropology, etc., have provided insights to teaching and learning, to schooling and education. Historically these disciplines have focused their attention on relatively homogeneous populations. Increased worldwide mobility has created a need for a more pluralistic approach to education – particularly in Western countries – and a more broadly based concern for educational issues related to particular contexts. Hence, *further* literature has developed in recent years which is concerned with the pedagogical and curriculum issues, raised for example, in connection with the "urban school", minority ethnic groups, disadvantaged and handicapped groups, and children who live apart from their families.

What is frequently missing from discipline-orientated studies is a real appreciation of context beyond the "general". What is often not present in the contextual study is an inter-disciplinary analysis of the issue, to provide a framework for practice.

The present series – "Special Aspects of Education" – is intended to bridge the gap between the problems of practice as perceived in a variety of contexts, and the theory as derived from a variety of disciplines. Books accepted or commissioned for inclusion in the series will be expected to manifestly acknowledge the inter-disciplinary nature of issues and problems in the field of education and care, and in addressing themselves to particular contexts, provide a conceptual framework for identifying and meeting special educational needs.

ROY EVANS
HERMAN GREEN

Preface

This book has been in preparation during a period in time when parents and their place in their children's development and education have been the objects of scrutiny and a focus for politicians and professionals in child services. Whether parents' rights to be closely involved in educational and child care services should or should not be extended can be a passionately debated issue that cuts across political and ideological boundaries. By no means are the issues clearcut, and it may in part be a reflection of their complexity that progress towards an extension of parental involvement in the provision and delivery of child-focused services in Britain has been slow compared to a number of other countries.

I have not set out to offer a definitive blueprint for one viable way in which parents' views and expertise can be reflected and represented in educational and child service settings. Rather, I have tried to suggest what policy guidelines could be adopted which would enable proponents and advocates of a partnership with parents to explore possibilities and test the feasibility of a number of optional models.

That I am finally, after considering the evidence, in favour of the greater encompassment of parents into the daily lives and concerns of their children will not be doubted by a reader who finishes this book. However, the odyssey that comprised the study on which this book is based was no idyll. The inherent and practical difficulties that lie along a path to eventual partnership between parents and professionals concerned with children were glimpsed or evident in reports and articles I read and places I visited as part of the information-gathering exercise. I have talked, too, with colleagues from various spheres of the education and child services and am under no illusion that entrenched attitudes constitute stumbling blocks and that the practical problems of implementing policies into practice are daunting. But for those who believe that anything less than open, frank and equal dialogue between the adults who share responsibility for the rearing and nurturing of children is prejudicial to children's welfare, it is heartening to report that there is, too, tremendous enthusiasm and optimism that sharing and partnership policies can work.

I have attempted to provide illustrations of work mostly in Britain that demonstrates the potential. What emerges as a dominant theme is that the concept of partnership is defined and interpreted in a variety of ways, as best suits the purposes of particular groups of people.

There is as yet no widely accepted or acceptable definition of what constitutes a partnership – perhaps there is no need for it – and therein lies much scope. I have consequently had in mind a potential readership of teachers, advisers, psychologists in education, special education and social services, child-care workers of all kinds, and those with responsibilities for the initial and in-service training of those personnel.

Although parents are the prime audience for the book, I have addressed myself more to the hearts and minds of professionals many of whom at times may have been guilty of regarding parents as less than equal to them in terms of expertise and unique insights. Now there are signs, embedded in legislation or by example, that parents are emerging from their twilight zone to take their place alongside people equally but differently versed in child development expertise, for children's benefit. I feel that it behoves professional child workers to redress the uneven power-sharing status quo and to acknowledge and act upon the contribution parents can and want to make.

This book has its origins in a study[†] undertaken during 1980–1981 when I was Research Associate at Homerton College, Cambridge. I should like to acknowledge the interest in the topic shown by John Robertson at Homerton College and the unfailing courtesy and

---

† Wolfendale, S. (1981) 'Parental participation in the development and education of children', unpublished dissertation leading to the award of Research Associate of the Cambridge Institute of Education

support extended to me by the principal, Alison Shrubsole. I have received too, much encouragement from Roy Evans, editor of this series.

At this point, too, I should like to single out and acknowledge the constructive interest in my venture shown by Alastair Macbeth from the Department of Education, University of Glasgow, who saw the manuscript in draft form and made valuable suggestions.

Especial and loving thanks go to Trevor, and to Daniel and Rachel for their enduring support. Without their acceptance of the restrictions and pressures imposed by such a lone and self-centred activity, this book would not have been written.

SHEILA WOLFENDALE
LONDON

CHAPTER 1

Aims and Scope

1. Introduction

The original impetus for this study stemmed from professional interest in the concept of special educational needs recommended by the Warnock Committee (1978) to replace the terminology relating to handicapping conditions within special education. The committee, set up by the British Government and comprising child development and educational experts, some eminent in their fields, was given a brief to review special educational provision in England, Scotland and Wales and to make recommendations. One of the key recommendations was that parents should be partners in special education procedures.

These areas of interest and concern led the author to wider consideration of the extent of parental involvement with the development and education of children, since the Plowden Report of 1967 had unequivocally called for 'a closer partnership between the two parties to every child's education' (Ch. 4, para. 102, p. 37). The Plowden Report also commissioned by the government considered the whole subject of primary education in Britain.

Examples abound of post-Plowden ventures involving parents in the early development of their pre-school children via the fostering of home school links in the educational priority areas designated after the Report; the provision of educational home visitors, and the setting up of community and school-focussed mothers' and parents' groups to promote support and guidance.

Reference will be made to certain of these past and currently operating projects in an attempt to assess whether or not the philosophies upon which they were based still constitute a viable basis for wider adoption by many more schools. There is recent evidence that, by and large, mainstream schools do not have an articulated policy of parental involvement that exemplifies in practice all the principles of a clearly-formulated philosophy along the lines of the Plowden and Warnock Reports.

Since the original area of concern in this enquiry was that of special educational needs and parental involvement, it became a relevant exercise, along with that of reviewing post-Plowden developments, to attempt a survey of contemporary approaches in the specific area of participation by parents in the development and education of their pre- and post-school handicapped children. Some of this work is only now beginning to be chronicled. It has been part of this enquiry to examine the principles upon which the practice of parent-professional partnership has been based within special education, particularly now that parental rights are extended in the provisions of the Education Act 1981.

Further investigation into the rationales underlying the 'compensatory' approaches within educational priority areas, and the development/training emphasis of work with young handicapped children and their parents led to the conclusion that, in order to present a synthesis of all this work that might have special relevance to future directions within education, it would be necessary to broaden the notion of special educational needs and its Warnock-style connotations, (that up to one child in five is likely to require special educational provision at some point during his/her school career) to a view that embraced all children and their developmental and educational needs.

The Court Report into Child Health Services in Britain (1976) took this view, maintaining that the appraisal of particular children's needs should be set within the overall premise that all children have a commonality of needs that can be defined and detailed, and over and above this some children will have special transient or enduring needs to be met by parents and professionals within the community. 'Future improvements in the health of children will depend as much on the beliefs and behaviour of parents as on the services provided' (p.3).

The aims of this book are:

— to present an account of recent developments in parent–professional collaboration in the areas of child development and the learning process;

— to examine the relationship between parents and schools and the potential for enhanced parent–teacher collaboration, on behalf of children and their developmental and educational needs;

— to encompass the wider aspects of educational provision, in terms of support services and related agencies, so that schools, though the central formal agent for the enhancement of children's learning, can be viewed as being part of a wider community network, within which exist other institutions and resources capable of meeting children's educational and learning needs;

— to explore the extent to which parents are agents of change in the enhancement of their children's development and learning, and whether they are central in the process. The outcomes of this particular exploration will not be in quantitative terms but it is hoped that it will be possible to illuminate some of the crucial areas.

Finally, it is intended to present a synthesis of these areas, the central purpose of which will be to articulate some features of a proposed policy for parental partnership in education.

Along the way, several significantly related issues will recur and be dealt with in their specific contexts. Amongst these are: whether or not parents are active partners or recipient clients in the delivery of services, including education; whether or not there are models for practice in parent–school partnerships in various settings that are firmly based on established precedent, or which, by being carefully formulated, are amenable to hypothesis testing and measurement; whether or not the philosophical tenets adhered to in all the contemporary literature on the topic that closer collaboration between parents and schools is positive and to be welcomed stands up to closer scrutiny; whether or not, in reality, there is an irreconcilable clash of interest and perceptions between parents and the teachers of their children.

2. Format

The rest of the book is outlined as follows.

Chapter 2 *Preamble – definitions and delineations* introduces the terms and concepts to be used throughout, presents working definitions and raises the major themes.

Chapter 3   *Parents and schools – innovation and initiative* aims to place developments in home–school links within a post-Plowden chronological context, examining various initiatives, amongst which are descriptions of various ways of involving parents, teachers and children in beginning-reading and remedial reading programmes – a rapidly expanding area.

Chapter 4   *Parents and schools – an evolving relationship?* continues to explore related issues as well as raising questions to do with parents' rights and schools' accountability, teachers' and parents' attitudes. Reference is made to research and survey evidence of recent years into home–school links and the present position is assessed.

Chapter 5   *Intervention in the community – focus on families* widens the brief in attempting to appraise notable innovations that have sought to meet the social, emotional and educational needs of families, where the focus is on community provision, with links with educational institutions. The rationales and outcomes of some key initiatives are examined and the implications for an intervention policy that encompasses educational and community provision are discussed.

Chapter 6   *Parents in the pre-school.* Although pre-school collaborative ventures will have already been referred to, it is considered necessary to include a chapter that concentrates on issues raised in a discussion of recent examples of parent–professional cooperation, in nursery or other pre-school settings. This will include some speculation as to whether there are models which are applicable to educational practice with older age-groups.

Chapter 7   *Special educational needs, and the place of parents.* Some of the main recommendations of the Warnock Report (1978) will be used as referents, and particularly those endorsed by the Government in the White Paper *Special Needs in Education* of August 1980, which, as a discussion document, preceded the 1981 Education Act referred to above. It is proposed to examine the term 'special educational needs' and explore the parameters of 'a partnership with parents' of children with identifiable handicaps and parents of children with a variety of learning and behaviour problems. Work with families in school and community settings will be referred to, and the feasibility of these ventures for replication discussed.

Chapter 8   *Schools, support services and the place of parents.* This continues the theme of the previous chapter. The existence of support services employing professionals with a brief for home contact raises questions about schools' responsibilities towards children presenting problems and their families. Professional practice *vis à vis* home liaison will be discussed in an attempt to illuminate the contribution of the supporting agencies to the alleviation and resolution of problems in childhood. Fundamental issues pertaining to parents being recipients of services, rather than decision-makers or instigators of action will be linked to a constructive view that an equally balanced parent–professional partnership is possible. Recent development in the areas of school–agency links, and agency–home links will be examined.

Chapter 9 *The craft of parenting and the place of parents in child development.* There is a long tradition of professionals writing books and other treatises for parents on how to effectively rear their infants. These writers have hopefully presupposed a take-up of their exhortations, but the effects of this advice on actual child-rearing practice are not known. The precise skills involved in 'successful' parenting have not yet been adequately researched, thus the 'education for parenthood' programmes and curriculum elements have been founded on a pragmatic concensus of what appears to work, i.e., what *seems* to promote positive relationships, rounded personalities. This chapter will look at some of the assumptions that have been made in this area and discuss the scope of parents' potential to foster development and enhance educational opportunities.

Chapter 10 *Parental Partnership in Education – a case for policy.* This chapter is split into two sections. The first gives a theoretical overview and synthesis of the areas under scrutiny in an attempt to provide a coherently argued policy statement for a parent–professional partnership. This will include consideration of some possible underlying principles. The second section sets out a case for parent partnership policies in education, examines a possible range of objectives and outcomes which teachers and parents might want from increased cooperation, and provides a taxonomy for a partnership based on a principle of reciprocity. The part that research and evaluation techniques could play in policy implementation is considered.

Appendix *Children of multi-ethnic origin and home–school links.* Although all children have been the focus of the report, it is felt that there is enough current social, public and educational concern over children from multi-ethnic backgrounds to warrant consideration being paid as to whether or not reported problems of adjustment, 'disaffection', relevance of curricula, underachievement could be alleviated by closer home–school links, and a more systematic or determined move towards a partnership with parents of multi-ethnic children. All recent reports support the explicit adoption of such policies, on behalf of children's distinctive needs, as well as of their parents.

References

Court, D. Prof. (Chairman) (1976) *Fit for the Future*, the Report of the Committee on Child Health Services, Volume I, HMSO.
Plowden, Lady B. (Chairman) (1967) *Children and their Primary Schools*, a report of the Central Advisory Council for Education, Volume I, HMSO.
Special Needs in Education (1980) White Paper, command 7996 August.
Warnock, M. (Chairman) (1978) *Special Educational Needs*, the Report of the Committee of Enquiry into the Education of Handicapped Children and Young People, HMSO.

CHAPTER 2

Preamble – Definitions and Delineations

1. A National Context

Chapter 1 contained reference to several recent reports commissioned by the British government on education and services for children. Though the remits of the Plowden, the Court and the Warnock Reports were within three quite separate and distinct frameworks, one theme unifies them, and that is the insistence that optimisation of children's developmental and learning potential is a realistic goal only if parents are involved in the formal processes of education and the delivery of child services. Furthermore, the role of parents is regarded in the reports to be that of partners and equals in these activities.

The Bullock Report (1975) was also set up by the government, with a main brief to consider 'all aspects of teaching the use of English including reading, writing and speech'. In a chapter on 'Language in the Early Years' the report endorsed the idea of parents (usually mothers) coming into school to participate in language and beginning-reading activities, gave examples of such ventures and expressed the view that 'there is room for many more such initiatives' (para. 5.37, p. 70). Furthermore, the Bullock Report concluded that educational visitors or home liaison teachers were a valuable resource for schools and parents in developing language and cognitive skills in early childhood and for encouraging and supporting parents to be involved in activities which can be tried out at home.

On a different educational matter, that of school management and government, but still related to the theme of parent participation, the Taylor Report (1977) also commissioned by the British government echoed the spirit evident in the previously cited government-instigated reports. Some of its key recommendations were for increased numbers of parent governors and a clearer statement of parental rights to knowledge about organisational and curricular processes. These reports will be referred to again in subsequent chapters, where it will be pertinent to set recent pronouncements in the context of practice.

At present there are examples of attempts to follow up and try out recommendations. These are within particular conceptual frameworks according to an individual report's influence and professional orientation. Thus, one venture involving parents might take place in a special ESN(S) school, another in a primary school in an EPA which runs groups for mothers. An infants' school could have been inspired by the Bullock Report to introduce a scheme for maternal involvement in language and reading activities. There are marked regional variations in the take-up and implemention of principal recommendations, many of which are suggestions for improving practice, rather than being mandatory and binding upon local education authorities.

It is argued that the value of these ventures would be enhanced if there were a coordinated policy, within an agreed conceptual framework, based on analysis of the (locally) perceived issues and areas for development. Jennings (1977) provides a useful six-stage process model for policymaking within local education authorities, which allows for educational committee members, officials, professionals, laypersons with vested interests, to participate at one or more stages. This is not to pre-empt either the arguments contained in this book nor its conclusions, but rather to direct attention to the vacuum that is perceived to exist in this area and to make the observation that there are many assertions and speculations contained in official reports that could be hypothesis-tested.

It could be argued that it is not the responsibility of reports such as those cited to do more than put forward general ideas, but that the onus is an professionals and administrators to interpret these and instigate action.

So the national scene regarding parental participation in any of the many areas of education can be seen to consist of patchy application of official prescriptions. It is not surprising, therefore, that in the spate of post-Plowden reports of ventures tried out here and there, there are not enough clear guidelines for future developments based on these undoubtedly innovative schemes – too few were replicated and the concept of action research in education (Gregory 1981) has not yet been correspondingly established.

2. The Concept of Parental Participation

The terms 'parental involvement' and 'parental participation' have tended to be used synonymously and interchangeably. Involvement can range from a parent being a member of a school's parent–teacher association, to turning up to parents' evenings, to representation as a parent governor, to direct collaboration in the learning process and the curriculum.

It has been generally agreed that varying forms and degrees of parental involvement with the educational process is, in the most lay of terms, 'a good thing' with these assumptions usually invoked:

— that a forging of home–school links is beneficial to an individual child and to children collectively;
— that the benefits lie in the cognitive and affective realms of functioning.

It would be invidious to single out particular books from the avalanche of American Head Start or British EPA project reports, especially since the intention is not to destructively challenge the foundations and raison d'être of the work, but rather to take the baseline premises as a starting point for discussion. Much of the thinking behind Head Start and Follow-Through (Lazar 1979) has rested on the contention that direct parental (usually maternal) participation in many facets of early childhood education programmes achieves a dual purpose. The child benefits, in terms of evidently boosted attainment, and the mother benefits by being alerted to different and more effective ways of handling her child, and by becoming aware of ways in which she can create or develop learning opportunities and stimulating experiences for her child. The intention to 'compensate' for economic disadvantage and its alleged deleterious consequences is echoed in the British projects (Halsey 1972, Woodhead 1976).

In latter years the base may have broadened to encompass home–school links in general (Craft, Raynor, Cohen, eds 1980) and equal-partner parental involvement in developmental and training programmes for young handicapped children (Pugh 1981), but the hypothesis remains the same, that if parents are manifestly involved to any extent, then their children's development and educational progress are promoted and enhanced.

This may be an irrefutable humanitarian hypothesis, and one based on a seemingly impregnable logic of 'common sense'. However, it will be argued in this book that for the future, various kinds of analytical and evaluative tests (using qualitative and quantitative information) ought to be applied to establish sound principles for parent–school collaboration with clearly enumerated short and longer term objectives. In short, what has been lacking has been an overall theory of parental participation, established and tested by proper investigation in the tradition of the behavioural sciences. Of course the methodology applied in 'real life' situations would be vulnerable and questionable (Dalin 1978) but now there needs to be an articulated concensus over the areas of enquiry rather than a perpetuation of unrelated small-scale projects.

The term 'parental participation' will be used in this report along with that of 'parental involvement' as an umbrella term to describe all the models and types of liaison between parents, schools and other community institutions that provide for children. 'Parents' in this context will refer, in the dictionary sense, to 'a father or mother as one who brings forth or produces' (Collins Dictionary, Oxford Concise Dictionary) as well as to the 'in use' sense that a parent figure is that person or persons who has care, custody and control over and concern for a child. This can include any combination of adult caretakers (two parents, a lone parent, adoptive parent, step-parent, foster-parent, and so on). It is hoped that the reader will understand and accept the use of the generic term in this book with its apparently conventional connotations, knowing that it embraces accepted contemporary variations on a basic theme.

3. The Use of Terms 'Development' and 'Education'

The inclusion of the words 'development' and 'education' in the title is intended to widen the scope of the enquiry beyond that of (simply) examining or making a case for fostering home–school links because this is thought to be on the whole beneficial to children, parents and teachers.

'Development' will here refer to the informal, incidental process of learning, whether at home or in school, gradual skill acquisition, and the evolving of techniques for social and emotional survival on the part of the chronologically young. Williams (1969) expresses the dissatisfaction with the term 'child development' that other writers have had, in doubting it as a viable construct, and comes up with 'development...referring to increase in extent, complexity and integration of an individual's attributes' (p. 32).

'Education' is referred to here as the formalised, intentional processes of learning, knowledge acquisition, and subject mastery. Most societies explicitly institutionalise the processes, via schools as communities that are formal-learning centred, within an education system.

The academic controversy continues as to whether or not early child development is marked by continuity or discontinuity (Clarke and Clarke 1976) and whether or not the effects of early experience profoundly influence, even irreversibly, later functioning. Kagan, in an essay entitled *The Primacy of Early Experience* (Kagan 1979) outlines in detail several bases for the view that the early experiences of the child 'cast a special shadow on early development' (p. 14) and shows how these views are culture-bound and value-laden. So intervention in the course of children's development via the process of formal education and compulsory attendance at school is deemed, by common consent in most societies, to be justified in promoting learning and preparing children for eventual adult citizenhood. What part parents might play in these processes is the subject matter of this book.

4.   The Purpose of Learning – Future Directions

The debate over the *effects* of early learning could be linked with recent discussion over the *purpose* of formal learning. Botkin *et al.* (1979) denounce 'maintenance' learning which is the traditional learning prevalent in most schools and contend that 'innovatory' learning is the key to survival in a world threatened by destructive forces. Innovatory learning is 'problem formulating ... problem-solving' (p. 43). Wolfendale (1980) took this formulation as a starting point for suggesting a reappraisal of the purpose of learning and a view of the curriculum which would go further than at present in equipping children with survival and coping techniques in an uncertain world (see Chapter 10). Raven (1980) has drawn attention to the predicted change, by the end of this century, from 'teaching of subject content toward the facilitation of personal learning' (p. 65).

If there is to be a policy towards radical change in our schools rather than the *laissez faire* evolution that so often characterises educational developments, whose is the responsibility for agreeing the objectives and the means by which these are achieved? Should these be the proper concerns of parents as well as of the teachers of their children?

It could be argued that traditional subject-centred curricula are the rightful preserve of specialist pedagogues, trained in methods by which to impart content, mainly geared to examination success as an ultimate criterion; whereas the different orientation that is being proposed, by the writers cited above and others, presupposes school curricula with reduced elements of rote-learning material and passively received information. Since the curriculum would contain a significantly greater number of socially and personally relevant elements, the argument continues, curriculum formation cannot then remain in the control of teachers and educationalists (whether local or central). The responsibility of equipping children with cognitive and practical means for personal competence and survival is a collective one. Might not parents, with their life and job experience, their own developed areas of skill and expertise, as well as their intimate knowledge of their own children, be able to contribute to the formulating of educational learning programmes that bridge schools and communities?

5. International Perspectives

At a seminar, held at Sèvres, Paris (March 1981) organised by the International Federation for Parent Education, and attended by delegates from 25 nations, one of the key themes was that schools and parents have shared common aspirations for academic success. A resulting effect, particularly marked in the latter part of the twentieth century, is that many children, caught between teachers and parents, often resort to undue emotional reliance upon and investment in the peer group and its subculture. In so doing, they reject the aspirations and mores of the adult-dominated culture. One speaker spoke of this phenomenon as a 'flight into marginality' (Sèvres 1981) describing the attendant features in behavioural terms, of 'disequilibrium' and 'disaffection'. It was suggested that it is high time that formal education and its cultural contexts were realigned and reconciled, with common goals spelled out between parent communities and educationalists. Priorities for the future have to include a *rapprochement* between the world of work and that of education.

These themes, expounded by several speakers at the seminar, appear to have universal relevance in many 'advanced' and 'less advanced' countries. In pluralist and fragmented societies, the child can exist uneasily on the fringes of several 'worlds' – his family setting, his peers, the locality, school, the world of his parents' work. Thus a reconciliation between these worlds was called for as part of a changing curriculum and a school-focussed ethos, to include parents and the wider community.

The 'bridging' that is envisaged is also endorsed by Lüscher (in Doxiades 1979) in these words:

In view of recent historical developments and foreseeable trends, it seems less and less adequate to strictly separate 'education' from other – more care-related – societal actions for children (p. 241).

The Athens symposium of 1978 on the theme *The Child in the World of Tomorrow* took a global perspective. Psomopoulos (in Doxiades 1979) in a paper on 'The Natural and Manmade Physical Environment of Tomorrow' starkly declared 'There is ample evidence . . . that the period between now and the year 2000 is likely to be the most difficult one for humanity' (p. 23). He goes on to present a list of insuperable problems and threats to survival common to all men – what Botkin *et al.* (1979) refer to as the 'world problematique'. So Doxiades in the Foreword to the published report of the Athens Symposium (Doxiades 1979) reminded the participants that, as the problems are universal – ergo – the responsibility is a collective and universal one. He pleads for all people to become involved in 'political activity' which he defines in the spirit of ancient Greece, as being interested 'in all things which are of concern to the community, not only to the individual' (p. xiii).

It follows that the proper exercising of citizens' rights would extend to parents having a greater share in educational decision-making on behalf not only of their own children, but in true community spirit on behalf of all the adult citizens of tomorrow. The accumulating evidence from sober academic reports as well daily raucous reminders from the press, television and radio is that mankind is heading for disaster and that averting action is a paramount priority. Education, in its formal sense, or learning, to use its widest sense, becomes, therefore, too important and vital a commodity to be left to schools.

6. Views Concerning Parents

Having presented a particular stance and argued a case for extended participation in education and learning by the citizenry, and especially those with the care of children, it must be acknowledged that it is difficult to write about an entity or collective force called *parents*.

Britain does not have a juggernaut National Union of Parents. The views of most parents are refracted variously through schools, governors, political parties, both local and central. (Bourne, *The Guardian*, 12 May 1981).

On educational and child welfare issues, professional voices have traditionally been more clamorous and vociferous than those of parents, precisely because there has never been a united forum from which to present a parental standpoint, if this were in reality, possible. At worst, this means that well-organised professionals, sophisticated at self-representation and lobbying, exclude parents totally from decision making. At best, parents still remain ignorant of the ramifications and convolutions which are part of the processes of wielding and exercising power, and if presented with *faits accomplis*, could not begin to unravel the complex sequences that precede eventual decisions.

This portrayal of the status quo is at the bleakest end of a spectrum where involvement is least. The other end represents full parental participation in the many aspects of education: subsequent chapters of this book aim to present many examples of the varying degrees and extent of parental involvement.

An appraisal of work with parents in educational and community settings reveals that parents have been regarded and treated in a variety of ways. A summary of these views will be introduced as part of the scene setting for this chapter.

Parents have traditionally been viewed and dealt with as *clients*, and only recently as *partners*.

The client concept incorporates these characteristics:

— parents are dependent on experts' opinions (paid professionals, books, official sources of information);
— parents are passive in the receipt of services;
— parents are apparently in need of redirection;
— parents are peripheral to decision-making;
— parents are perceived as 'inadequate', 'deficient'.

In contrast, the partner concept includes these characteristics:

— parents are active and central in decision making and its implementation;
— parents are perceived as having equal strengths and equivalent expertise;
— parents are able to contribute to as well as receive, services (reciprocity);
— parents share responsibility, thus they and professionals are mutually accountable.

Having outlined the characteristics that pertain to both categories, these will now be exemplified by reference to traditional and innovatory ways of working with parents. The dichotomy is followed through (below).

Parents as Clients

Traditional home–school relationships:

Parents are in receipt of information, reports, services; marginal parental involvement with curriculum, i.e., 'helping out' (listening to reading, clearing away); peripheral or temporary involvement with activities, i.e., fund-raising.

Development and training programmes (school and/or community focus) :

EPA projects, including home visiting, where eventual aspiration may be towards partnership or self-help, but where a 'deficit' model and professional intervention provides the initial framework.

Child care and welfare services (Child Guidance Clinic, School Psychological Service, Education Welfare Service, Social Services) :

Offering support and redirection. Advice, support, treatment start from a 'premise' or assumption of inappropriate or inadequate handling of children, with the eventual aim of imparting insights, changing handling techniques, and increasing understanding of the mechanics involved.

Parents as Partners

'*New style*' *home–school relationships*:

Some choice of school parents as governors (Education Act 1980); Parental involvement with curriculum and learning (*viz* reading projects); contributory expertise and imparting skills (as in community school ideal); parents' group activities, including self-help, sometimes based in schools.

Development and Training Programmes: (for pre-school, young handicapped children and children with special needs) parent-run and parents as co-partners working in conjunction with professionals, often in multi-disciplinary settings.

A number of these examples are explored in greater depth in subsequent chapters.

7. Models of Parental Participation

There is general agreement in the literature as to the desirability of developing and applying models of participation by parents in the development and education of their children, of which the main characteristics are those outlined above. Some writers (Deitchman, Newman and Walsch 1977, Kushlick, Felce and Lunt 1978, Bricker, Selbert and Casuso 1980) are scrupulous in spelling out the format of their programmes, the manner of their implementation, and the outcomes matched against aims. In so doing, they are cautionary, pointing out the pitfalls inherent in any action-based system that is an hypothesis-testing exercise derived from theoretical principles.

Other writers have presented the issues discursively, even abstractly. For example, Blackstone (1979) presents a case for parental involvement in education and analyses evident 'sources of resistance' to the straightforward adoption of such a policy, concluding that we need to find out 'what the various parties regard as legitimate subjects on their agenda and whether and how they can shift their position to reconcile the interests of other parties' (p. 95). Datta (1975) outlines a taxonomy of parent involvement in early childhood education in the United States, examines the feasibility of various models (parents as staff, parents as resources, parents as tutors, parents as paid employees, parents as advisors and decision makers) and points to the main issues that need further exploration and resolution. She sees some of these as the specific role that parents want and seek; costs of parental involvement; whether or not 'induced changes have the same effects as naturally occurring differences' (p. 45); who should educate parents; methodological concerns.

A highly detailed exposition of a model of parent–teacher partnership is given in Rutherford and Edgar (1979). At the outset they present prerequisites for cooperation:

1) 'teachers must believe that parents have a role in the education process' (p. x). The authors back up this assertion;

2) 'Parents and teachers... must trust each other' (p. x). This could sound like a homily, but the authors go on to say what techniques can be utilised to capitalise upon and promote these prerequisites in practice.

Morrison (1978) presents differing models for use with different child–client populations, first defining his terms. The most thorough treatment of the issues comes from United States writers, for professionals and parents in the USA have a longer history of

B

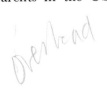

collaborative ventures, and parents' rights, *vis à vis* special education, are now enshrined in legislation (see Chapter 7).

A perusal of the literature reveals that the usage has tended to define the terms 'parental involvement', 'parental participation', depending on the locus of action (school, clinic, community base), and the extent of both professional and parental input. Grotberg (1979) reviews a number of parental involvement programmes in varying settings, each with a distinctive focus (e.g., parents as the major focus of training, children as the main focus of training) and concludes 'parents in fact have been discovered as critical to the education and development of their children' (p. 217) and 'research which helps determine new relationships of families with a variety of services and professionals is already highlighting some ways to improve the relationship' (p. 217 and see Chapters 8 and 9).

8. Towards a Principle of Reciprocity

The notion of mutual benefit which Grotberg highlights, has to be one of the cardinal principles embedded in a rationale of parent–professional partnership, on behalf of the child or children who are the joint concern. Writers, such as Blackstone, referred to above, and the Tizards (1979, and Tizard *et al.* 1981) have addressed themselves to the issues of vested interests, disparate expectations and differing overall aspirations, concepts of professionalism versus responsibilities of parenthood and so on.

Certainly these are *issues* in the sense of needing to be explored and preferably resolved. But the question of inherent problems must remain, for the moment, separate from the ideological principles that constitute an agreed policy for parent–professional cooperation which is predicated on the theme of reciprocity. By this is meant the evolution of agreed aims that takes into account the differing aspirations of professionals (teachers, representatives from welfare and support services) as well as the professed needs of the parents; a statement of the means by which the contributions of parents and prefessionals can be made; concensus regarding the criteria for success or failure of the collaboration.

But reciprocity – mutual involvement, mutal accountability, mutual gain – must be viewed within the wider contexts of the community, the society, the culture, on behalf of the child. Earlier discussion in this chapter sought to demonstrate how strategies to cope with contemporary world dilemmas could be incorporated into the curriculum. In fact, there is a wealth of evidence, from people's informal personal experience and from formal studies, to show that learning in its widest sense does not and should not only take place in school (Illich 1973).

To optimise that learning therefore, a partnership which reduces the gap between community institutions and their provisions would, in theory, do more good than harm. But it is the larger-scale application and testing of this theory that is called for by the advocates of greater involvement by parents in the development and education of their children. Furthermore, Taylor (1980) cautions that the pursuance of home–school links, parent–professional collaboration 'can only be performed within the context of a complex set of traditions, value assumptions and attitudes regarding the roles and relationships of family and society, individual and State' (p. 17). And

The whole business of home-school relationships cannot be discussed realistically if our context is merely that of providing more educational opportunity for the individual child, of satisfying certain needs which the individual child is believed to possess, or removing handicaps to his or her educability. We are concerned here with a fundamental social relationship between the primary socializing role of the family and the inducting function of the school. (Taylor 1980, p. 4)

This quotation serves as a summary statement on this chapter and a lead-in to the next.

References

Blackstone, T. (1979) Parental involvement in education, *Education Policy Bulletin*, Vol. 7, No. 1.
Botkin, J., Elmandjra, M. and Malitza, M. (1979) *No limits to learning: bridging the human gap*, a report to the Club of Rome, Oxford: Pergamon Press.
Bricker, D., Seibert, J. and Casuso, V. (1980) 'Early intervention' in Hogg, J. and Mittler, P. (eds) *Advances in Mental Handicap Research*, Vol. I, Chichester, Sussex: John Wiley and Sons.
Bullock, Lord A. (Chairman) (1975) *A Language for Life*, report of the Committee of Inquiry, HMSO.

Clarke, A. D. B. and Clarke, A. (eds) (1976) *Early Experience*, Shepton Mallet, Somerset: Open Books.
Craft, M., Raynor, J. and Cohen, L. (eds) (1980) *Linking Home and School*, a new review, 3rd edition, London; WC1: Harper and Row.
Dalin, P. (1978) *Limits to educational change*, London, WC2: Macmillan.
Datta, L. (1975) 'Parent involvement in the United States', in *Developments in Early Childhood Education*, OECD/CERI.
Deitchman, R., Newman, I. and Walsh, K. (1977) 'Dimensions of parental involvement in pre-school programmes', in *Child: Care, Health and Development*, Vol. 3, No. 3, pp. 213–225, May/June.
Doxiades, S. (ed.) (1979) *The Child in the World of Tomorrow*, Oxford: Pergamon Press.
Gregory, P. (1981) 'Educational psychologists and innovation', Chapter 4 in McPherson, I. and Sutton, A. (eds) *Reconstructing Psychological Practice*, London. SW11: Croom Helm.
Grotberg, E. (1979). 'The parental role in education and child development', in Doxiades, S. (ed.) *The Child in the World of Tomorrow*, Oxford: Pergamon Press.
Halsey, A. H. (ed.) (1972) 'Educational Priority', *EPA. Problems and Policies*, Vol. I, HMSO.
Illich, I. (1973) *Deschooling Society*, Harmondsworth, Middx: Penguin Educational.
Jennings, R. (1977) *Education and Politics, Policy-making in Local Education Authorities*, London; W1: Batsford Ltd.
Kagan, J. (1979) *The Growth of the Child: Reflections on Human Development*, London, EC4: Methuen.
Kushlick, A., Felce, D. and Lunt, B. (1978) 'Monitoring the effectiveness of services for severely handicapped people: implications for managerial and professional accountability', in *Report of the Sixth National Conference of the National Council for Special Education*.
Lazar, T. (ed.) (1979) *Lasting Effects after the school*, Washington: US Government Printing Office.
Morrison, G. (1978) *Parent Involvement in the Home, School and Community*, Wembley, Middx: Charles E. Merrill.
Pugh, G. (1981) *Parents as Partners*, intervention schemes and group work with parents of handicapped children, National Children's Bureau.
Raven, J. (1980) *Parents, Teachers and Children, a Study of an Educational Home Visiting Scheme*, Sevenoaks, Kent: Hodder and Stoughton for the Scottish Council for Research in Education.
Rutherford, R. and Edgar, E. (1979) *Teachers and Parents, a Guide to Interaction and Cooperation*, Boston, Mass.: Allyn and Bacon, Inc.
Sèvres, (1981) *Family and School*, seminar organised by the International Federation for Parent Education March (details from the author).
Taylor, T. (Chairman) (1977) *A New Partnership for our schools*, Report of the Committee on School Management and Government, HMSO.
Taylor, W. (1980) 'Family, School and Society', Chapter I in Craft, M., Raynor, J., Cohen L. (eds) *Linking Home and School*, 3rd edition, London, WC2: Harper and Row.
Tizard, J. and Tizard, B. (1979) 'Parents and teachers as educators', in Doxiades, S. (ed.) *The Child in the World of Tomorrow*, Oxford: Pergamon Press.

Tizard, B., Mortimore, J. and Burchell, B. (1981) *Involving Parents in Nursery and Infant Schools*, London: Grant McIntyre.
Williams, N. (1969) *Child Development*, London W1: Heinemann Educational Books.
Wolfendale, S. (1980) 'Learning difficulties: a reappraisal', *Remedial Education* Vol. 15, No. 3., August.
Woodhead, M. (1976) *Intervening in Disadvantage*, National Foundation for Educational Research.

CHAPTER 3

Parents and Schools – Innovation and Initiative

The main intention in this chapter is to describe recent initiatives in the development of home–school relationships, particularly focussing on small or large-scale ventures, where the aim has been to involve parents (as ever, usually mothers) in school-based activities, or collaborative learning projects.

Green (1969) points out that prior to the mid 1960's, there was a dearth of investigative work and informed writing on the topic of parent–teacher interaction and the potential for collaboration. He refers to a seminal study into teachers' opinions on the matter carried out by Wall (1947) and compares the results with what appeared to be the situation by the mid to late 1960's. By that time there appeared to be a lack of articulated policy regarding the fostering of home–school links, and the examples of such cooperation in practice were still rare.

Two notable attempts at reducing the gap between the home and the school were the Education Shop experiment run by The Advisory Centre for Education in the Cooperative Store in Ipswich, Suffolk over a period of a few days, and the experiment carried out by Green himself. The parents, children, teachers and other citizens who visited the Shop during the course of a week, either out of general interest or with specific queries, were overwhelmingly in favour of the idea of there being a forum where a universally relevant topic like education was accessible to all.

Green (1968) gave an account of 'an attempt at improvement' whereby differing forms of school–parent contact were explored and the results evaluated. These appeared to be positive: teachers felt they had learned more about home circumstances, parents felt they had gained understanding of teachers' aims, teaching and learning processes. The main means used to effect this change were new-style school reports, interview with parents, informal contacts.

The Plowden Report (1967) is regarded by writers in education and related disciplines as having been highly influential, regarding the philosophy of a partnership with parents and subsequent action that could be taken to bring this about. In fact, two main themes, treated separately in two different chapters of the Report became fused. Chapter 4 is entitled 'Participation by Parents'. It refers to survey evidence indicating a high level of interest by parents in their children's education and concludes, without going into more profound argument, that 'by involving the parents, the children may be helped' (p. 43, para. 114). On the basis of that hypothesis, the chapter ends with a set of recommendations for promoting home–school links. These cover an increased provision for parent–teacher contact, receipt of information booklets by parents about schools, improved forms of report-writing, and access to the school and its resources by the community. These were prescriptions which were to apply to all schools and all parents.

Chapter 5, on Educational Priority Areas, does not mention parents explicitly; rather it concentrates on drawing attention to the *effects* on children's learning and well-being of disadvantageous homes and neighbourhoods. Thus was the notion of 'positive discrimination' born: 'The schools must supply a compensating environment' (p. 57, para. 151). Nowhere in the recommendations at the end of Chapter 5 is there mention of work with parents of children in Educational Priority Areas. However, the two themes – participation by *all* parents in the education of their children, and 'positively to discriminate' in favour of *some* children – came together in practice in the several years following the publication of the Plowden Report. Most of the innovatory EPA action-research projects (Halsey 1972, Poulton and James 1975, Woodhead 1976) included schemes involving parents (mothers in the main) in the development and learning of their young children, either by school-focussed contact or by a linked system of home visiting by educational visitors, often a teacher.

The concept and rationale of 'disadvantage' will be examined in Chapter 5 and issues specifically relating to pre-school involvement will be highlighted in Chapter 6.

Whether or not the projects in five EPA-designated areas (Deptford in London, Liverpool, Balsall Heath in Birmingham, West Riding of Yorkshire, and Dundee in Scotland) led to measurable short or longer term cognitive advances by children has been discussed in the accounts of the projects cited above as well as by other authors (Kelsall and Kelsall 1971, Berthoud 1976, Bell 1976). Whatever the criteria for evaluating the success or failure (including a 'nil-gain' criterion) of the EPA and Urban Aid programmes, all the writers have in principle endorsed the involvement of parents in their children's education from pre-school onwards. Berthoud puts it simply: 'A new cooperation between mother and teacher must be found, but it will not be easy' (p. 117). Halsey writes

It must be significant advance if schools could be encouraged to run child–parent projects attempting to make sure that every parent has at least one chance of such an experience during the child's time at school (1972).

And, in a later comment, he says

The schools can be asked, in partnership with the families they serve, to bring up children capable to exercising their political, economic and social rights and duties in such a society (Halsey, in Field, ed., 1977).

So, with the only reservation that the issue of disparate cultural and moral values between (some) teachers and (some) parents has to be faced, there has been unanimous agreement that increased co-operation between parents and schools is positive and believed to be beneficial.

The Plowden Report bequeathed this philosophy, yet the application and testing out of what has certainly remained a hypothesis has been erratic within educational practice. Even the Plowden Report in asking 'Can more schools do so [involve and influence parents] and on a bigger scale?' cautioned and advised 'Only experience sieved by discussion and research, will show how effective it can be' (p. 37, para. 103).

EPA itself died, with the mandate and the grants coming to an end, but it has left a legacy of ideas, some of which have been implemented in practice. The guiding twin themes of educationally combating depriving backgrounds and forging closer home–school links to a greater or lesser extent is evident in some recent and continuing ventures and attention will now turn to these, where the focus is on schools and education, and on children's learning whether or not there is also a community involvement.

1. Contact and Collaboration with Parents – Innovations and Initiative

Some of the projects which will be referred to in this chapter were set up in the wake of the EPA studies, within those localities designated as needing forms of positive discrimination. Others were 'one-off' investigations, designed to test a particular hypothesis under certain controlled conditions. Yet others have evolved pragmatically to meet the perceived local need. All the projects, no matter how formal or informal, theoretically based or pragmatic, constitute models of the parent–school–community relationship in its many guises and forms. All have been reported upon, the manner of this varying in length and sophistication from page-long accounts in newspapers, magazines, journals, to traditional-type articles in academic journals, and sometimes via reports intended for local and therefore limited consumption. Most of the work would be amenable to replication as this has not happened on any significant scale. Some of the ventures are characterised by unique and imaginative features, which have not been endorsed or refuted by replication in other settings.

The necessarily brief descriptions of a number of these studies will adopt for clarity of presentation a loose format covering name/title; reference; aims (including background, rationale, target or focus); methods (approach, structure, implementation); outcomes (evaluation and results). Some studies have a pre-school component, which are included in this chapter because in them there is a linked school element (nursery and/or infant). Likewise, the wider community provides the backcloth to some of the projects; again the criterion is the school-focussed element.

In the bibliography at the end of this chapter, the work referred to is indicated by a 'dagger' (†). The order is alphabetical by place or author – no significance should be attributed to the ordering.

1.1. Belfield Community School   (Jackson and Hannon 1981)

This primary school in Rochdale, Lancashire, was opened in 1973 with a brief for community and parental involvement. Parents were encouraged to help in the classrooms. There was an attached nursery unit, in which it was hoped to work more closely with pre-school children and their families, via a home visiting scheme where parents and teachers discussed once a week the educational use of toys left with the family.

In recent years Belfield School has involved parents directly in the reading process (see the section on reading later in this chapter). The system is described by Jackson and Hannan (1981):

Every night, Belfield children each take home a reading book and card. The child reads for 10–15 minutes to a parent, who then initials the card and makes comments about the child's progress. Next day in school, the teacher goes over the same passage with the child if he is having difficulties or moves to a new one if he is making good progress. That evening the child takes home a new passage to read.

The experiment is being monitored by Hannan and colleagues from Sheffield University. Preliminary reports are encouraging in terms of enthusiastic responses by teachers and parent–participants.

1.2. Cornwall   (Wilton 1975)

A mother-helper scheme had been in operation for several years in a Cornish infant school. A mother-helper's role was to share in her child's school life. Her subsidiary role in helping the class teacher included practical help and basic care with all the children. The aim of Wilton's study was to describe the system and evaluate it via a questionnaire given to the participant mothers. The analysed data indicated positive benefits as perceived by the mothers, in terms of gaining knowledge of school routines, teachers' expectations, their own children's learning and perceived advantages by the teacher. A rationale is provided 'that the worlds of home and school interact positively, rather than unintentionally oppose each other in isolation' (p. 4).

1.3. Coventry – Education Visiting   (Feeley, Rennie and Robinson 1980)

The booklet entitled Education Visiting (1980) describes what the role and function is of the education visitor as it has developed generally post EPA, and with particular relevance to work in Coventry as part of the Community Education Project. Nine major objectives of educational visiting are listed, the main one summarised as 'an education visitor is an outreach member of a school staff, who aims to promote better understanding between parents and school ... the education visitor finds ways for parents and teachers to work together for their mutual benefit and for the benefit of children' (p. 2). The idea is perceived to work successfully in practice, and in the preface to the booklet the view is expressed 'it is hoped that the reasons for the success of the work will become apparent and to be more capable of replication elsewhere'.

1.4. *Cleveland Home–School Liaison Teachers*   (Centre for Educational Disadvantage, CED 1978)

Cleveland local education authority appointed ten home–school liaison teachers to nine infant, nine junior and two secondary schools in 1974, at first on an experimental basis with an Urban Aid grant. The aims of the project are to build a link between home and school, and to foster in parents an appreciation of their role in the education of their children. The account in the CED journal assesses success on various criteria: parents becoming more educationally aware; greater understanding by teachers of children's home circumstances. An appraisal of the scheme elicited areas of concern, such as the proper delineation of the home–school–liaison teacher's role and need for preliminary in-service training.

1.5. *Cradley, W. Midlands*   (Rathbone 1977)

The experiment reported by Rathbone introduced working-class mothers into the nursery unit to act as collaborators in implementing a language intervention programme for their children. One main aim was to ensure that 'parents and teachers ... see education as a community undertaking' (p. 81). The study conformed to pre- and post-testing and control-group requirements, and the results were said to be positive and encouraging. The teachers found contact with parents easier than they had anticipated and the author concludes 'objective proof in one area of the nursery curriculum of the value of parent participation is ... an indicator that such programmes would promote the child's cognitive and social development as a whole if parents and teachers worked together through every aspect of nursery education' (p. 84).

1.6. Donachy 'Parent participation in pre-school education'   (in Clark and Cheyne, eds. 1979)

This is similar to Rathbone's study in being an experimentally-designed, controlled investigation with inbuilt pre- and post-testing. The aim was to investigate the effects on three- and four-year-old children of exposure to a four month programme administered by mothers at home and organised through a local primary or nursery school. Again, broad-based positive gains were reported.

1.7. Froebel Institute   (Athey 1980)

In this study, which took place within the nursery unit at the Froebel Institute in South London during the period 1973–1978, results from American pre-school projects involving parents were invoked as the initial rationale. The exploratory nature of the project was several-fold: to narrow the gap between 'practical know-how of the professional' (teachers) and research on the nature of improvement (cognition and learning); in the tradition of recent nursery-focussed research, to see what constitutes good nursery practice; to gauge the effects of maternal involvement.

Twenty experimental and twenty control children were selected; both groups pre- and post-tested. The project aimed at 'describing, documenting, summarising, finding commonalities and continuities in the behaviour of the twenty experimental children who attended'. Parental participation was categorised in four types. Athey's article goes into some detail concerning the activities covered and parental response. Overall, gauged by follow-up measures carried out on all the children one to two years after the project ended, the results were positive, i.e., cognitive gains were maintained.

1.8. The Govan Project   (Wilkinson and Williamson 1980)

The authors of the report state that their first aim was to 'improve the education of the children in Moorpark, Govan (Strathclyde) by working with all the significant adults in the child's environment. The further aim is to clarify those procedures which turn educational theory into good practice, and to articulate the findings in a co-ordinated framework'. The work of the three year (1976–1979) action–research project, funded by the Scottish Office and the region, was carried out by seven full-time workers, a neighbourhood tutor, a literacy worker, two primary school 'link' teachers, a pre-school co-ordinator and an evaluator.

Parental interest in the education and development of their children was stimulated in various practical ways, one main impetus of which was to establish direct links between parents and their children's schools. The report gives an account of all the initiatives, pointing to inherent difficulties in working with professionals and non-professionals within a scheme that sought to draw together many elements of the community. The authors in their conclusions assert that 'education is wider than schooling and that schooling needs to be more community oriented – not simply in terms of curriculum but also in terms of participation and control' (p. 34). They point to the Project's success in bringing teachers and parents closer together, and suggest that the teacher's role should include a home-contact brief. In short, they advocate a partnership which includes 'genuine parental participation in a community-based carriculum' (p. 38).

1.9. Centre for Educational Disadvantage, CED   (Hull 1978, and other examples)

A short description in the CED journal of a parent-involving approach in a junior school in Hull, Humberside, illustrates how a policy can work in practice, without necessarily needing to be evaluated beyond the ad hoc appraisal of those involved. Involvement is of the traditional type where parents help in the classrooms, though there are planned opportunities for the head-teacher and parents to discuss results and observations.

Similar parental involvement in school activities is now established practice in schools in Crosby, Liverpool, and in Bury, near Manchester. These are reported upon in the same issue of the CED journal (1978). In another issue of the CED journal (1979) the Headteacher of Halton Bank Primary School, Salford, Manchester, describes 'an exercise in cooperation between parents and teachers' which came about with the creation of a summer play-scheme jointly organised by teachers and parents. The Head felt that amongst the successful aspects of the scheme were 'spin-offs in terms of improved relationships... these spin-offs are as important as the planned objectives and eventually they help in rethinking play-scheme policy and can be written into the objectives'.

1.10. Newham Parents' Centre   (Newham Parents' Centre Annual Report 1981)

The Parents' Centre has sought to 'evolve a radical programme of parent support in local education', and operates in three main areas – provision for the under-fives, reading help (for adults) and careers advice. It has been in operation since 1973 and is housed in high street premises in London's dockland area. This provides the base for the Centre's activities: selling educational and informational material to parents and others, storage of resource material, providing a centre for meetings. The Parents' Centre receives funds from Newham local education authority and grants from various trusts and foundations. It sees itself as a local self-help organisation offering various services, which are: support and information to parents regarding education and community matters; secretarial services to teachers and organisations; adult literacy classes; under-fives services; careers' advice; self-evaluation exercises and research monitoring activities; running a holiday play-scheme. The proper title of Newham Parents' Centre is the Newham Education Concern Services Association (NECSA). It now appears to be a firmly established feature of local education and community provision.

1.11. Sandwell   (Times Educational Supplement 1 May 1981)

A scheme which links five-year-old children at infant school, their younger siblings and parental involvement is described in this article. Parents of five-year-olds at school with poor scores on vocabulary tests were contacted and those with younger children still at home were then visited for about an hour a week. Teachers took toys and aimed to improve the parents' attitudes to education and the language development of their children. On later testing, the younger siblings scored higher than their older brothers or sisters on vocabulary measures; however, the older children's school work and attitudes improved noticeably, and parents developed confidence and self-esteem. Overall the scheme has led, 'not just to self-help but better communities. Some of the mothers visited earlier now supported others going through the same crises.'

1.12. South Yorkshire (Hubbard and Wellings 1978)

The authors describe several mothers' groups based in primary schools which have been in existence for over seven years. They say that over time the rationale and objectives gradually became clearer. Subject matter is seen as having two components:

(a) extending the experience and the educational skills of the mothers by devising and using with them and their children language and concept materials;

(b) discussion and analysis of aspects of child behaviour and development and child rearing and education, starting from the basis of the mothers' own experience with their children (p. 41).

Hubbard and Wellings conclude that as a result of the work with the groups, there is an increase in:

1) the number of different adults (rather than just mothers) attending;

2) parent–teacher 'face to face' participation;

3) requests for guidance and consultation about support services for such groups received from LEAs;

4) the demand for education courses in which adults from various in-service experiences may meet and study.

1.13. Wandsworth (Bennett and Stobart 1981)

The Family Workshop Unit was established in 1974 by Community Education and Careers Branch of the Inner London Education

Authority. Its brief was to 'develop community education projects in which parents and children could take part together in educational activities' (p. 1). After its inception as a community provision, the two community education lecturers who were centrally involved felt that a priority exercise should be to develop school-based projects involving adults and children.

The 1977-1981 report describes the workshops based in eight schools in one Inner London borough. These take place during the day, usually for one afternoon a week and last two hours. Activities include crafts, cookery, music and attenders comprise mothers, pre-school children, grandmothers, neighbours and some children from the school, whose mothers may be regular participants. The staff teams comprise two or three family workshop tutors. In addition teaching staff from one or more of the schools form part of the team, in one case the parent-liaison teacher, in another the deputy head.

The report's authors present a list of what they perceive to be the educational benefits of the project. Overall these are bringing into school traditionally non-participating parents; school providing a focal place where teachers, parents and children can meet informally; teachers having the opportunity to learn about families and see parent-child interaction; teachers and parents being able to communicate mutual aspirations and concerns; pre-school children gaining familiarity with school settings and concepts of learning through play. One of the conclusions is 'a school can in this way become a learning centre for the whole community'.

The types of evaluation of all the projects reported above vary, some relying on verbal reports, subjective estimates, and continued participation as evidence of an criteria for 'success', others employing stringent pre- and post-test measures, and sophisticated quantitative means by which to gauge the reported gains. There could be no one blueprint or formula applicable to such a variety of local schemes; yet an appraisal of the strengths and weaknesses of these unique ventures and their relevance to future replication in other settings seems long overdue. They all 'work', i.e., they all report benefits and advantages, but in the absence of comparative information, it would not be easy to generalise with confidence as to which features are known to guarantee 'success' and which would be less effective if used as models elsewhere.

2. Parental Involvement in the Reading Process

Mostly the initiatives described above have not been concerned centrally with curriculum; curriculum involvement by parents has been incidental or tangential. However there are recent examples of collaboration between teachers and parents where the child's acquisition of reading and literacy skills is the main target activity in a joint school – home enterprise. Some of this work will be described. One system, at Belfield School has already been referred to in this chapter.

Educational folklore says that teachers do not approve of parents teaching their children to read before going to school, nor indeed, of parents augmenting at home school-based reading activities. In reality, professional opinion would probably be divided, with a concensus view that teachers have reservations about parents cutting across their teaching methods and, at worst, reducing the effectiveness of teaching reading by well-established approaches.

Yet the Bullock Report (1975) endorsed the principle that parents have a part to play in fostering language development and communication skills in early childhood and it may only be a short and entirely logical step from this contention to the 'belief' that parents could also be facilitators in their children's learning to read. This 'belief' is currently being translated into theoretical propositions which are used as the starting point for some hypothesis-testing initiatives. Woodhead (1981) feels that 'the mysteries attributed to teaching the skill (of reading) still remain beyond the grasp of most interested but bewildered parents, thereby serving to retain the distance between the lay and the professional'. He quotes the Newsons' (1977) assertion that 'a revolution in literacy could be sparked off and fuelled by parents and teachers in determined cooperation.'

Publications have attempted to bridge the gap or blur the role demarcation between teachers and parents. Books have been written for parents on how to teach their children to read, to master various techniques, to supplement school-based instruction, even to recognise and combat early-appearing reading difficulties (Gillham 1974, Clarke 1974, Mackay and Sims 1976, Thompson 1978, Baker 1980, and Pickarts and De Franco 1972, who wrote two books aimed respectively at teachers and parents).

Reading and teachers' centres have published booklets for parents-Nicholls from the Reading Centre in Reading provides one example, Townsend (1979) from the Northamptonshire Reading and Language Development Centre another. These booklets are full of practical advice and suggestions to parents (and teachers).

Several of the recent systematic attempts to involve parents in their children's reading will be briefly described below, in alphabetical order.

2.1. Bushell, Miller, Robson (1982)

A paired-reading project was carried out by three educational psychologists in Derbyshire, with junior school failing readers and their parents. The authors drew on the small-scale study by Morgan and Lyon (1979) which is described later in this chapter. The reading programmes lasted for eight weeks, with each child (there were twenty-two in the project) pre- and post-tested on reading tests. Substantial gains in reading attainment were reported. Parents completed questionnaires and, in general, appeared to be enthusiastic and endorsed the scheme. At present the educational psychologists are engaged upon a follow-up study. They have been encouraged by the results as well as by the considerable local interest in the scheme.

2.2. Fry (1977) 'Remedial reading using parents as behaviour technicians.'

This experiment set out to evaluate the effectiveness of the systematic use of token reinforcement by parents teaching reading to their children (thirty in the sample) who were retarded by two to four years, and aged between seven and ten years. The study was of a reversal design type in which reading ability was assessed (via the revised Burt Graded Reading Test) at the beginning and end of a two month baseline. The experimental phase lasted two months and was followed by a further two months return to baseline with assessments at the conclusion of these phases. The amount and type of cooperation shown by the parents was reported to be highly encouraging and to exemplify the potential of parental help in children's learning activities.

2.3. Glynn, T (1980 and 1981 'Parent–child interaction in remedial reading at home')

The following abstract describes similar programmes.

A home-based remedial tutoring programme was introduced to parents of eight- to twelve-year-old boys in Auckland, New Zealand, and four ten-year-old boys in Birmingham, UK. The boys had reading deficiencies of between two years and five years. The tutoring programme trained parents to delay their attention to errors, to use context prompts and letter-sound prompts, and use praise contingent upon independent reading behaviours, such as correct reading, self-correction and prompted corrections following errors. All parent training took place at home where a therapist provided written instructions and explicit feedback to each parent. Both child and parent behaviour were recorded under baseline, untrained tutoring and trained tutoring conditions.

Data indicated that target tutoring behaviours occurred at generally low or zero levels during baseline tutoring and that increases in all tutoring behaviours occurred in all parents with the introduction of the training programme. Data from the Auckland study showed further that gains in specific tutoring behaviour generalised from training sessions with the therapist present to sessions with the therapist absent. In the Birmingham study, it was found that the effectiveness of parents' prompting improved dramatically with the training programme.

Parents changed from displaying a baseline pattern of support for tutor-dependent behaviour in their children to displaying a pattern of support for independent reading, during the parent training programme. Gains in reading at home occurred for all children in both studies. Gains in reading at school occurred (without additional school tutoring) for two of the eight Auckland boys and for all four of the Birmingham boys.

Glynn, in summarising his detailed account of the two programmes and reference to other work, expresses the view that the 'effectiveness of the schools in teaching academic skills will be enhanced and not hindered, by a working partnership between parent and teacher' (p. 79).

2.4. Haringey Reading Project (Hewison 1982)

This project attracted considerable attention from the non-educational media as well as from educational publications. The impetus for the project grew out of earlier work into wider aspects of the relationship between the child's home background and his success in school (Hewison and Tizard 1980). There was evidence that 'parents who displayed attitudes and behaviour which appeared to favour the development of reading ability in their children were also more likely to have the habit of hearing the child read', referred to in the article as 'coaching' (p. 210).

The apparent correlations were explored in a second study in the London Borough of Barking, and were confirmed. A further (re-plication) study attempted to assess the amount of coaching children were currently receiving or had received in the past. This time detailed questionning of the parents in the sample (of 104 children) made it possible to classify the amount of help they gave their children, into 'regular', 'or occasional' (or none). Data analysis revealed that the relationship between amount of help given and reading performance was statistically highly significant and positive.

Following these explorations, the Haringey Reading Project was started as a collaborative venture between research workers from the Thomas Coram Unit (London University Institute of Education) and advisory and teaching staff in the London Borough of Haringey. Parents of primary-age children (aged from six years) were asked to hear their children read several times a week over a period of two years from reading material sent home from school. The reading progress of the children who received help from their parents was compared with that of control children who received no help at home. Another group of children were given regular supplementary reading tuition from a specially appointed teacher in school. Six schools participated; all were situated in the same multi-ethnic inner city area, where reading standards were well below the national average.

The results, on testing, were that the children who had received help from their parents were superior in reading attainment to the children who had not been given help. A one-year later follow-up confirmed continuing leads and sustained gains. Hewison observes that most parents are willing and able to help their children with reading at home. She elaborates some points in Tizard *et al.* (1981).

2.5. Inner London Education Authority 'A description of a homework reading scheme, 1976–1977' (Ebbutt and Barber 1979).

This was a scheme aimed at developing reading and literacy skills in retarded secondary school girls. It was designed to 'improve the children's literacy, involve parents and link reading which was regularly practised at home with that at school, on a structured basis' (p. 7). The report by Ebbutt and Barber outlines the mechanics of the scheme, choice of materials, reading techniques that were used (comprehensions, cloze procedure, sequencing) record-keeping and some of the problems experienced by the girls in addition to and consequent upon their markedly lowered reading attainment.

The results were interpreted by staff as being positive and successful in terms of pupil enjoyment, value of structure, improvement in attainment, and parental response. The authors are well aware that because they did not (for 'ethical reasons') employ any kind of control or comparison groups, then the results cannot with confidence be attributed to the specific home-help link with reading instruction, though this was the intention and hope. Nevertheless, they believe the outcomes are sufficiently encouraging to be used as inspiration for similar schemes elsewhere.

2.6. Inner London Education Authority 'Family Cooperation in the Development of Literacy' (Centre for Urban Education Studies (CUES) 1980)

The basic hypotheses of the project were

1) that parents were interested in their children's education and would like to be more involved in it;

2) that parents had insights to offer teachers about their children's developing literacy. The project ran from 1978–1980 and took place

in four primary schools in the London boroughs of Hackney and Lewisham. The research team of three from the CUES initially established that there was indeed a high degree of parental interest, though often teachers tend to discount this, seeing no apparent signs. This mismatch, between teachers' perceptions and *evident* parental interest was explored by the team.

They identified a range of working which they believe to be critical in establishing active home-school links. Amongst these were: making a video film with teachers on their approaches to the teaching of reading and showing this to parents; supporting teachers in establishing a lending library; inviting parents and teachers to jointly prepare teaching–learning materials for use at school and at home; releasing teachers from the classroom to talk to parents. In due course, the project results will be reported on more fully by the team.

Influenced by this and other work in the field of parental involvement and the reading process, a team of teachers and psychologists (led by Alex Griffiths) in the Inner London Borough of Hackney is currently extending its remit of intervening with learning difficulties into the area of securing parental participation in reading. Another example of parental involvement in reading in a junior school in London is described by Heath (1981) who reports that a group of children aged seven to nine years, who were involved with their mothers in a paired-reading programme, made significant gains in their reading attainment. Attitudes of mothers and children, their active participation, the certainty offered to them by the technique as well as what Heath refers to as 'the mum effect', together with reinforcement and modelling are all offered as explanations for the results.

2.7. *Morgan and Lyon* (1979) 'Paired Reading – parental tution of reading-retarded children.'

The paired reading technique, the authors explain, draws upon behavioural learning theory and aims to affect reading performance directly, rather than indirectly through the mediation of its underlying skills. Two components of the tuition process are simultaneous reading and reinforced individual reading. In simultaneous reading parent and child read in close synchrony 'any adjustments to pace being made by the parent'. This is 'participant modelling' and Morgan and Lyon explain how these techniques were applied in an investigation carried out on four children (three aged eight years, one aged eleven years) who were in need of extra help with reading. The mothers of the four children attended several training sessions, during which the techniques were imparted, including conveying the importance of praise as reinforcement.

The length of the tuition period was approximately twelve weeks and consisted of fifteen-minute sessions at home with mother and child engaged upon reading activities along the prescribed lines. They received a once weekly, thirty minute supervising and monitoring session. All the children made noticeable gains in reading attainment, and the authors point to the general effectiveness of the tuition scheme. Of course, this was a tiny sample from which to draw conclusions and the authors are aware that further investigation is essential.

Two projects already referred to in this chapter contain reading-focussed elements. The Govan Project (Wilkinson and Williamson 1980) established a Reading Workshop, aimed at helping parents to understand the process of learning to read. The Coventry Community Education Project publishes booklets, such as, 'Reading: what every parent should know' and 'Reading: involving Parents' (Pritchard and Rennie 1978) which is a handbook containing ideas and suggestions for activities involving teachers, parents and children in the reading process. These include workshops, helping at home, school bookshops, parents' evening on reading, and the use of audio-visual aids.

The area of parental involvement in reading is burgeoning rapidly. A number of the experimental studies described in this section are seminal and have inspired teachers and educational psychologists to work together. There are local and unreported examples of intervention approaches for reading-retarded secondary school pupils including parent-involving reading programmes, and local examples, too, of enhancing the initial acquisition of reading skills in younger children by involving their parents. Thus educational practice is reflecting social–educational philosophies regarding parental participation – and at a time of economic retrenchment, *all* resources are being maximised.

3. Concluding Remarks

The final example in this overview of recent and current ventures is characterised by its unusual nature. It is an account of a highly systematic, closely-focussed attempt to involve parents in the curriculum, on the premise that parents should be seen 'to be more truly partners in the education process than has traditionally been the case'. The work was carried out by Wood (1974) as part of a doctorate study. He identified a Parental Involvement Factor and delineated four levels of educational cooperation: observational, instructional, practical, formal. The activities within the levels range from open-days and concerts, to educational meetings with speakers, parents' groups, to parents helping in school in and out of school hours. The formal level includes parents being involved in parts of the formal school curriculum.

Wood outlined four hypotheses of the study. These were:

1) school performance of children whose parents were drawn into part of the curriculum improve more than those parents who are not involved;

2) responsiveness of parents is independent of their child's academic status and of parental social class;

3) a high degree of parental involvement in the curriculum is associated with a favourable change in the attitudes of parents to school and education generally;

4) school performance of children whose parents' attitudes become more favourable improve more than those children with parents whose attitudes remain static or regress.

His criteria of a good home assignment were:

a) it grows from and contributes to the school curriculum;
b) it successfully involves the parent and child in some meaningful activity.

Wood concluded from his elaborated study that there is an area of untapped potential for parental involvement in the curriculum and he invoked an action-research formula to try out various forms, including the provision of a home-liaison teacher as a catalyst. One direct and optimistic outcome of Wood's study was that one school in his sample planned, when the study was finished, to introduce a through-school programme involving parents in the curriculum and to employ a liaison teacher.

This chapter has attempted to convey a flavour of British work during recent years in the area of school–parent cooperation and to demonstrate a variety of models. Whether or not any or all of these constitute 'good practice' is left as an open question, although this author has already commented here, and the previous chapter, that some features in many of the projects described are amenable to replication is similar settings in other parts of the country. If the concept of 'good practice' implies generalisability, it is to be deplored that there has not been a greater 'take-up' of the ideas generated in any one single study (Wolfendale 1981).

All the projects identified an initial problem area or area of concern; all outlined short and long term aims and objectives; all specified the means by which these were to be achieved; and all assessed outcomes in some form. Some of the work was put into a theoretical context; and some workers perceived the problem totally within the local context and devised problem-solving strategies accordingly, without recourse to abstract principles.

Yet a perusal of the reports from many of these projects leaves a pot-pourri impression. There is no overall 'scheme of things', acceptable bodies of theory into which the published accounts could fit and appear compatible. It has to be reiterated, pace Chapter 2, that the effects of well-intentioned and imaginative endeavours described in this chapter must not be dissipated and lost through lack of follow-up, and that it is timely to draw together common ideologies, common elements and to chart the potential for development.

References

(†denotes projects referred to)

† Athey, C. (1980) 'Parental involvement in nursery education', *Early Childhood*, Dec.
Baker, C. (1980) *Reading through Play*, London, EC2: Macdonald Educational.
Bell, L. (1976) *Underpriviledged Under Fives*, London, W1: Ward Lock Educational.
† Bennett, D. and Stobart, T. (1981) *A Paper About our Work with Schools 1977–1981*, Family Workshop Unit, Wandsworth, London.

42 PARENTAL PARTICIPATION

Berthoud, R. (1976) *The Disadvantages of Inequality, a Study of Social Deprivation*, a PEP Report, London, EC2: Macdonald.
Bullock, Lord A (Chairman) (1975) *A Language for Life*, HMSO.
† Bushell, R., Miller, A. and Robson, D. (1982) 'Parents as remedial teachers, *Journal of the Association of Educational Psychologists* Vol. 5, No. 9, Summer.
CED (Centre on Educational Disadvantage) (1978) 'Action by an LEA' in 'Parents as Partners', *Disadvantage in Education*, No. 9, Vol.
CED (1979) *Disadvantage in Education*, Vol. 2, No. 1.
Clarke, L. (1974) *How to Recognise and Overcome Dyslexia in Your Child*, Harmondsworth Middx: Penguin.
† CUES (Centre for Urban Educational Studies) (1980) *Family Cooperation in the Development of Literacy*, 34 Aberdeen Park, London N5 2BL., February.
† Donachy, W. (1979) 'Parental participation in pre-school education', in Clarke, M. M. and Cheyne W. M. (eds) *Studies in Pre-school Education*, Sevenoaks Kent: Hodder and Stoughton.
† Ebbutt, C. M. and Barber, E. J. (1979) *A Description of a Homework Reading Scheme 1976–1977*, Inner London Education Authority.
Feeley, G., Rennie, J. and Robinson, F. (1980) 'Education visiting', No. 3 in the series *Community Education in Action*, Coventry Education Committee.
Field, F. (1977) *Education and the Urban Crisis*, London, WC1: Routledge and Kegan Paul.
† Fry, L. (1977) 'Remedial reading using parents as behaviour technicians', *New Zealand Journal of Educational Studies*, 12 (1) 29–36.
Gillham, W. (1974) *Teaching a Child to Read*, University of London Press.
† Glynn, T. (1980) 'Parent–Child Interaction in Remedial Reading at Home', in Clarke, M. M., and Glynn, T. (eds) Reading and writing for the child with difficulties, *Educational Review*, Occasional Publications No. 8, University of Birmingham.
† Glynn, T. (1981) 'Behavioural research in remedial education: more power to the parents', in Wheldall, K. (ed.) *The Behaviourist in the Classroom, Educational Review*, Offset Publications No. 1, University of Birmingham.
Green, L. (1969) *An Examination of Some Teachers' Attitudes to and Experience of Home-school Cooperation*, unpublished Child Development Thesis, (Eltringham School, London SW16).
Halsey, A. H. (ed.) (1972) 'Educational Priority', *EPA Problems and Policies*, Vol. 1, HMSO.
† Heath, A. (1981) *A paired reading programme*, Inner London Education Authority, March.
Help your Child, ( ). A series of four books, Collins.
† Hewison, J. and Tizard, J. (1980) 'Parental involvement and reading attainment', *British Journal of Educational Psychology*, 50, 209–215.
Hubbard, D. and Wellings, A. (1978) '"Mother" groups in the school setting', *Education*, Vol. 3. No. 13.
† Jackson, A. and Hannon, P. W. (1981) *The Belfield Reading Project, Rochdale Lancashire*. Belfield Community Council.
Kelsall, R. K. and Kelsall, H. (1971) *Social Disadvantage and Educational Opportunity*, Eastbourne, Sussex: Holt, Rinehart and Winston.

Mackay, D. and Sims, J. (1976) *Help Your Child to Read and Write and More*, Harmondsworth, Middx: Penguin.

† Morgan, R. and Lyon, E. (1979) 'Paired reading – a preliminary report on a technique for parental tuition of reading-retarded children', *Journal of Child Psychology and Psychiatry*, Vol. 20, No. 2.

† Newham Parents' Centre, Annual Report (1981). 747 Barking Road, London, E13.

Newson, J., Newson, E. and Barnes, P. (1977) 'Perspectives on School at 7 years old', London WC1: George Allen and Unwin.

Nicholls, R. (undated) *Helping Your Child to Read*, Reading, Reading Centre, University of Reading, Berkshire.

Pickarts, E. and DeFranco, E. (1972) *Parents, Children and Reading: a Handbook for Teachers* and *Dear Parents – Help Your Child to Read*, American Book Co., Los Angeles. City Schools.

Plowden, Lady B. (Chairperson) (1967) *Children and Their Primary Schools*, HMSO.

Poulton, G. and James, T. (1975) *Pre-school Learning in the Community*, London WC1.: Routledge and Kegan Paul.

Pritchard, D. and Rennie, J. (1978) *Reading: Involving Parents*, Coventry Community Education Project.

† Rathbone, M. (1977) 'Parent participation in the pre-school', *Educational Studies*, Vol. 3, No. 1.

† Sandwell Scheme (1981) 'Children and parent benefit from regular home visits', Times Educational Supplement, p. 9.

Thompson, B. (1978) *Learning to Read*, London, WC1: Unwin Paperback.

Tizard B., Mortimore, J. and Burchell, B. (1981) *Involving Parents in Nursery and Infant Schools*, London, WC1: Grant McIntyre.

Townsend, D. (1979)
Reading: The School and Parents,
Reading: How can I help my child?,
Language and Learning: How can I help my child?,
Northamptonshire Reading and Language Development Centre, Boughton Green Road, Northampton, NN2 7AL.

Wall, W. D. (1947) 'The Opinions of teachers on parent–teacher cooperation', *British Journal of Educational Psychology*, Vol. XVIII, Part 2, pp. 97–113.

† Wilkinson, E. and Williamson, D. (1980) *Education and the Community – a Policy for School–Community Relations: The Govan Project*, Department of Education, Glasgow University.

† Wilton, V. (1975) 'A mother helper scheme in the infant school', *Educational Research*, Vol. 18, November.

Wolfendale, S. (1981) 'Editorial comment', *Early Child Development and Care*, Vol. 7, Nos. 2 and 3.

† Wood, A. J. (1974) *Parents and the Curriculum – a Study of Academic Cooperation and its Effects on Children, Parents and Teachers*, unpublished D. Phil Thesis p. 550, University of Southampton.

Woodhead, M. (1976) *Intervening in Disadvantage*, NFER.

Woodhead, M. (1981) 'Cooperation in early education. What does it mean? Why does it matter?', *Early Child Development and Care*, Vol. 7, Nos. 2 and 3.

CHAPTER 4

Parents and Schools – An Evolving Relationship?

The previous chapter presented an overview of recent developments in school–home links. This chapter will deal with other recent developments and current thinking on topics associated with the relationship between parents, schools and the education process, and will try to demonstrate that it is a relationship that is evolving in positive, closer directions, if fairly slowly, and in an ad hoc fashion.

Chroniclers of the historical origins of any kind of unofficial or formalised association between educational institutions and the parents of children in the state schools in Britain have usually pointed to the post Second World War period as being the most active in this regard (Bate 1978).

Bryans and Wolfendale (1981) in charting changing attitudes towards children over a several hundred year period, draw attention to the increasing influence of the state, in terms of greater statutory provision of education and child services. Correspondingly, as British state education spread pervasively during the latter part of the nineteenth and the first part of this century, parents' rights were not explicitly spelled out or delineated, beyond an initial clear duty to send their children to school daily. The historical analysis by David (1980) amply demonstrates the equivocal attitudes to parents and family by educators and legislators.

As was emphasised in Chapter 2, the Plowden Report of 1967 was an agreed landmark, even a turning point, in the history of education–family relationships, since it explicitly elaborated a philosophy and thus paved the way for policy-into-practice systems. Not only did the Plowden Report generate ideas and schemes designed to compensate children for depriving, 'inadequate' environments and to incorporate parental participation in these schemes, but the publication of the Report stimulated much public and academic discussion during the 1970s about the purpose and quality of home–school links, parental access to the educational process, accountability of schools to parents and a wider public, and other issues.

In the author's view, the central issue of parental entitlement to have knowledge of, and some access to, educational decision-making was obscured in recent times by a professional fixation on notions of social class. It seemed to be important to know whether or not middle-class parents were more interested in their children's education then were working-class parents, rather than starting from the reverse basic assumption that parents *are* interested in their children's welfare and educational progress until or unless there is contrary proof (Pilling and Pringle 1978). This view should not imply criticism of worthwhile attempts to ascertain factors hindering the educational progress of children from working-class backgrounds, such as Douglas (1967), Jackson and Marsden (1962) as earlier seminal studies, and more recent survey evidence, including the National Child Development Study (Concern 1980) and the work reported by Halsey and colleagues (Halsey *et al.* 1980). The empirical value of these studies in determining or influencing educational policy in present or future times is undoubted.

It *is* important to know of survey evidence as to the relationship between 'origins and destinations' and to search for solutions within or without the framework of political ideologies; however, this debate must not divert attention from considering the proposition that *all* parents ought to have a greater number of rights within, and increased access to, the education process, since it is another community resource, and the major one. We now have 'harder', first-hand evidence than the earlier suppositions relied on as to the reason and/or explanations why initial parental interest in and concern for their children's welfare appears to dissipate (Newsons 1977, Wilson and Herbert 1978). To create a structure for the provision and manifestation of these rights would be one formal way of ensuring support and encouragement for parents whose enthusiasm and motivation are sapped by adverse domestic or occupational circumstances.

Returning to the theme that there has been in the last few years an upsurge of interest into the actual relationship between parents and schools, and into the areas of desired and potential growth, what particular aspects have received attention?

One immediate post-script to Plowden was the Department of Education and Science (DES) publication *Parent Teacher Relationships in Primary Schools* (DES 1968) which was intended to stimulate discussion and action. Likewise the Inner London Education Authority put out a booklet *Home and School* (revised version 1974) which was prescriptive and exhortatory, but the basic commonsense approach can neither be denied nor decried. It represented a forward-looking move and approximated to an informal policy document, linking ideas with suggestions for action. Heads and teachers from nursery, infant and junior schools were urged in the pamphlet to involve parents in all sorts of ways.

Sharrock (1970) reviewed the position *vis à vis* home–school relations in the late 1960s and identified four areas of change that were positive and encouraging of better links: changes in teachers' attitudes, including improvements in communication between home and school; increasing individualisation of contacts; the provision of information about modern educational trends; the greater involvement of parents in the life of the school (p. 59). But Sharrock also acknowledged the disappointingly slow progress evident on some fronts at that time, and the theme of discrepant or inconsistent attitudes by teachers and parents towards each other's role and potential for dialogue comes out clearly in Sharrock's book, as well as in Goodacre's (1970) published at around the same time and covering similar ground. These attitudes will be examined towards the end of this chapter.

A 1972 publication (Cluderay, ed. 1972) drew attention, as had other writers from the early 1960s to the dearth of research in the area of home–school links, and took the optimistic line that much could be done in schools to foster these links and draw parents into school. The emphasis in contributions to this journal issue seemed to be on maximising opportunities for parental contact, utilising the client model (see Chapter 2) rather than invoking the partnership model, which indeed has only received serious consideration recently.

In 1972, too, there was a report of a survey (Hubbard and Salt 1972) of current practice in home–school relationships, based on a sample of 40 primary (twenty junior, twenty infant) schools. The reporting of the results is prefaced by a discussion of the issues and problems, taking the Plowden recommendations as a starting framework. The authors refer to difficulties in communicating, mismatches between the values and cultures of the home and those of school, and the child's task of adjusting to and feeling comfortable within both milieus. The results encourage the authors to conclude that 'in many cases the minimal proposals set out in Plowden have been realised and extended' (p. 40).

A concurrent investigation was the Schools' Council project *Parents and Teachers*, (Lynch and Pimlott 1976). The aim was simply to seek to improve home–school relations in three secondary schools, and the objectives were four-fold:

1) to seek to foster a critical awareness in teachers and parents of the importance of the home environment in successful child education;

2) to attempt to clarify for parents the values and objectives of formal education;

3) to seek to foster a wider community interest in educational values and objectives and to assist schools to play an active and vigorous role in the life and development of the community;

4) to provide teachers and parents with information, instruction and guidance.

This was a limited pilot study, along action-research lines. Ending on a sober note of reality, despite positive outcomes from their endeavours, Lynch and Pimlott in a retrospective analysis (in Craft *et al.* 1980) say 'at the moment and in spite of all the talk and writing, parents are very far from being recognised as partners by schools' (p. 85).

The most recent and widespread survey into the extent and type of parental involvement in primary schools in England and Wales is that carried out by Cyster and colleagues for the National Foundation for Educational Research (Cyster *et al.* 1979). The research took place in 1977 and 1978 and took its bearing from the Plowden Report that parents should be welcomed into schools, should regularly meet teachers, and should receive information about the school and the child's progress. The team elicited an 80% response rate from 1700 schools contacted. The main findings are presented below.

59% of headteachers said they wanted more parental involvement

52% of headteachers said they wanted parents involved in a wider variety of activities

20% of headteachers thought that the limits of desirable parental involvement had been reached

63% of headteachers felt that parents' attitudes had changed markedly as a result of greater involvement

33% approximately of primary schools have formal Parent–Teacher Associations (PTAs)

95% of primary schools hold parents' evenings and open days (attendance levels of over 75%)

65% of primary schools send written information to new parents

92% of primary schools invite new parents to visit before their children start school

50% of primary schools send written reports to parents (mainly seven to thirteen age-range)

The observation is made that as their children proceed into senior classes, parents feel progressively less knowledgeable and less able to help their children directly (also see Johnson and Ransom 1981 for similar feedback from a secondary schools' survey). The Cyster survey examines a number of factors which were thought to constrain greater involvement by parents in school activities. The authors summarise their results by saying 'parental involvement...seems generally to be on the increase' (p. 149). However, it is acknowledged that post-Plowden progress in general has been slow, tentative and conservative, that is, there are areas of school life with considerable potential for continued teacher–parent collaboration.

The survey by Her Majesty's Inspectors (HMI) 'Primary Education in England' (1978) an account of the work of seven, nine and eleven year-old children in 1,127 classes in 542 schools, includes some information on parental involvement as follows:

Parents helped teachers in nearly a third of the seven-year-old classes and in just under a fifth of nine and eleven-year-old classes. The proportion of classes receiving parental help was lower in the inner city areas than in 'other urban' or rural areas. Typically, where parental help was given, an average of two parents a week visited the class.

In over three quarters of the classes where help was given parents assisted teachers in matters concerning the children's welfare and in the supervision of children on visits outside the school.

Teachers reported that parents were also involved with children's learning in over two-thirds of the classes where help was given. This type of involvement most commonly took the form of assisting with practical subjects or hearing children read (p. 26, para. 3.16).

Policies of home–school relations, then, vary from locality to locality in the degree of sophistication and the care and consistency with which they are implemented.

At a national level, various professional and parent–professional organisations sprang up during the 1950s, 1960s and 1970s which have aimed to collect and disseminate information on home–school links, and to propagate the idea that the pursuance of a parent–teacher partnership is a worthwhile major aim. In 1967 three of the main organisations came together to form the Home and School Council. These three are:

1) the Advisory Centre for Education, formed in 1960;

2) the Campaign for the Advancement of State Education, formed in 1962;

3) the National Confederation of Parent–Teacher Associations, formed in 1954.

The Home and School Council (see references) is concerned to disseminate information about good practice, to help parents and to support the extension of parents' rights within state education.

A recent addition to the number of organisations whose *raison d'être* is the improvement of home–school relations via a variety of means was the National Home–School Liaison Association, established in 1976, but which is currently in abeyance. One of the most recent appraisals of the home–school liaison teacher idea is by Bailey (in Craft *et al.* 1980) who himself is a past chairperson of the NHSLA.

1. Parents' Rights: The Education Act 1980

1.1. Parent Governors

The Taylor Committee was set up by the Government in 1975 to look into the existing arrangements for management and government of schools in England and Wales and to make recommendations. In its report (Taylor 1977) it suggested a format for the composition of

C

governing bodies of schools, which was to include parents (and older pupils). This proposal was to formalise the situation of the 1970s, in which parent representation on governing bodies of schools varied in different parts of the country. A survey carried out by Sallis (1979) confirmed current practice in 108 areas.

The Taylor Committee was concerned that the new-style partnership would extend beyond mere formal representation to effective relationships between the groups concerned.

So Taylor and his colleagues suggested that parents should be allowed to form associations based in the school. Sallis, a member of the Taylor Committee later amplified much of the thinking behind the report's recommendations (1977). She expresses the rationale behind an evolving policy for partnership ('Nor can one demand more responsible behaviour without giving parents a status in the process' (p. 83), but makes it clear what the demarcations should be between parents' right to have greater accessibility and teachers' professional rights to role delineation which would not be encroached or eroded).

Now some of the Taylor recommendations are enshrined in British law, in the provision of the 1980 Education Act. Section Two requires that all state schools have parents and teachers as elected representatives on the governing body. Reservations are expressed by Fowler (in Craft *et al.* 1980) who asserts that in practice the 'balance of interests' proposed by Taylor will not come about since, as the law stands, the 'power of the local education authority' will be 'in essence undiminished' (p. 30) so the elections of parent governors 'must usually prove little more than a cosmetic exercise, not serving effectively to provide a link between the school and the families which it serves' (p. 31). As Fowler comments, parents' choice of representatives to approach with queries or problems is extended, but it is not made clear which person or which channel would be the most appropriate for which purposes – a representative parent governor, a local committee member (who might also be a governor), the class teacher, the head teacher, or anyone else.

This rather gloomy view of what the reality will be, as against the intention, is substantiated with data supplied by Bacon (1978). Research into the role of parent governors in Sheffield elicited the following evidence: that public knowledge of parent governors' functions was abysmally limited; that turnout to vote for school governing bodies was low and unrepresentative; and that parent-candidates did not specify policies, but confined themselves to generalist aspirations concerning their interest in helping the school. Bacon questioned elected parent governors and formed the impression that since new parent governors were dependent upon experienced governors (who included professional and lay educators) for information regarding procedure, administration, finance, their vulnerability and susceptibility were reinforced.

Since the legislation is only now being implemented, it is too early to know conclusively whether or not these are steps, faltering or firm, in the direction of increased parent participation (Brunel University School Governing Bodies Project 1980–1983).

1.2. Choice of School

The range of options as to which aspect to become involved in has increased for parents with legal mandation, and one particular area, which has long been contentious, is that of parental choice of school. The provisions of the 1980 Education Act, in Section 6 stipulate that parents will have a right to express a preference for the school they wish their child to attend and to state reasons. Local education authorities have to comply with this preference unless to do so would 'prejudice the provision of efficient education or the efficient use of resources...' Appeals committees have to be set up for parents who are refused their preferred school.

The Advisory Centre for Education (ACE) has published a revised edition of its guide for parents on choosing a school (Taylor 1981). The legal framework of the Act is spelled out and parents are urged to exercise their now-extended rights to choose and to appeal, the procedures for which are clearly set out. The main section of the 49-page guide is in the form of *Questions to ask the Headteacher* and *Questions to ask Yourself* – these cover all the components which are referred to in the following section of this chapter under Information, in addition to which it is suggested (in the ACE guide) that parents ask about schools' policies for a partnership with parents.

Of course, in reality the now-established choice of school will expose and aggravate a number of problems – falling rolls and local education authority policy for closing or rationalising some schools and criteria for 'good' or 'bad' schools. These and other issues are examined by Fowler (in Craft *et al.* 1980).

1.3. Information

The third area of extended parental rights within education is the right to be in receipt of information about local schools and educational provision. Section 8 of the Education Act 1980 compels local education authorities to publish their rules governing admission to schools, the arrangements for parents to express a preference and the appeals procedure. They must also publish details of the number of places available at schools, in the age groups in which pupils are admitted.

In a Government discussion paper on the topic circulated in August 1980 by the Department of Education and Science (DES 1980) the Secretary of State set out his aims in requiring the publication of a basic minimum of information about each school. These are:

to enable parents, now that they are to have a statutory right to express their preference as to the school they wish their child to attend, to make an informed decision and to contribute towards the early establishment of an informed and mutually supportive relationship between parents and the schools their children attend (p. 2).

The discussion paper outlines some basic information which schools should include apart from basics pertaining to name, address, and number on roll.

These should incorporate: details of the curriculum, subject options, examination results (secondary schools), teaching organisation, arrangements for pastoral care and discipline, extra-curricular activities, school uniform.

The Schools Council, in conjunction with its Parents' Liaison Group recently completed a study of a wide range of brochures providing parents with information about individual schools. The brochures varied widely in presentation, and the features which the Parents' Group most endorsed were clear and logical presentation, inclusion of an index, plain language, uncluttered style and explanation of educational terms that might not be familiar to parents. In its summary leaflet (School Council 1981) the Council presents a list (no. B) which is additional to the Statutory requirements of the Act. Information on list B gives details on school layout; list of names of teaching and non-teaching staff and governors; assessment procedures used by the school; medical facilities and arrangements in the event of illness; provision for school or packed lunch; likely incidental costs; schools' policies for home–school links.

The Advisory Centre for Education has produced a guide to help schools provide information for parents and their children (Taylor 1980). It includes sections on purpose, layout, categories of information, which it lists as nine-fold: basic information; parents and the school; admission and transfer; teaching and learning; assessment, tests and examinations; pastoral care and discipline; careers and work experience; health and welfare; extra-curricular activities. The guide is illustrated with examples from existing 'good practice' in British schools.

On the question of openness of school records to parents, the Department of Education and Science review of curriculum arrangements (DES 1979) gives some details about the increasing number of schools which make available school records for parental perusal, and a number of schools which are currently redesigning theirs with that purpose in mind.

In a consultative document which considered the communication between schools and home, the DES (1977) suggested 'more comprehensive and comprehensible school reports as a means of meeting parents' requirements for more information, and drew attention to those in current use. Soon after the publication of the DES document, the National Foundation for Educational Research embarked upon a three year research project *School Reports to Parents – an Evaluation of Policy and Practice in the Secondary School*. There had never been an indepth enquiry into school reports, their function, their content and their effectiveness as a means of conveying basic or detailed information to parents about their children's progress. The findings of the study will include suggestions for initial and in-service training and a checklist for schools to carry out an evaluation of their own reporting procedure.

Two other investigations into forms of communication between home and school have already made public their results. One, which is part of the Cambridge Accountability Project referred to later in this chapter, is a detailed case study of one secondary school (Gibson

1980) which bases its practice implicitly on the three beliefs that Gibson puts forward:

1) that parents have a right to know what goes on in the schools their children attend;

2) that such knowledge makes for good relations between parents and teachers;

3) that good communications will result in improvement in pupils' learning and attitudes.

The examples given of the school's written communications to its parents, are characterised by careful attention to detail and an unfailing degree of courtesy towards the recipients, who are informed of the syllabus, curriculum-content, tutoring, options for further and higher education, all via booklet or newsletter. Gibson sampled parents' views about the school's communication system and this feedback, he feels, constitutes a form of evaluation. Overall, the parents were totally endorsing of the school's efforts and highly appreciative. Criticism was rare and confined to minor quibbles. Thus, the 'policy made practice' works in this case, that is, both school and parents perceive it to be effective in maintaining a satisfactory flow of information.

The other investigation is that of Bastiani and colleagues into various kinds of written communication between school and home (reports, brochures, newsletters). They propose four models or types of school brochure (Bastiani, ed., 1978) discuss each, and give examples. They are fairly critical of some aspects of the many brochures they examined in a sample sent to them. 'Faults' ascribed include an unduly prescriptive tone, weak on context, too verbose, lack of clear intention. However, trends identified on an impressionistic basis, seemed to be emerging, among which were higher standards of design and layout, and a generally more thoughtful approach. A 'check list' in the form of key questions that teachers should ask themselves when planning brochures is suggested.

The 1980 Education Act specifies what local education authorities must publish concerning admissions, list of schools, and addresses. Beyond this, however, local education authorities 'are free to publish such other information, if any, as they wish' (DES August 1980). In practice, this resource varies from locality to locality. The author came across examples of parent-oriented, publicly available material put out both by the Ontario (Canada) Ministry of Education, and the City of Toronto (Ontario) School Board. The Ministry issues a series of booklets, among which are titles such as *Parents and Teachers Working Together, Helping Your Child Learn, The Community and its School, Guidance Services, Education Services,* and *Your School Board : Get in Touch.* The Toronto Board of Education provides a booklet for parents *Student Services and Special Education,* and separate pamphlets on *School Social Work Services,* and *Psychological Services.*

In the main, in Britain, parents have had to rely on published paperback books for sources of information on education, and their rights (Bagnall 1974, Pedley 1967, Stone and Taylor 1976, O'Connor 1977, Croall 1978). The present government could argue that, via recent developments now enshrined in the 1980 Education Act, parents' rights and access to schools have increased. Undeniably this is so, taking the Statute Book as the yardstick, but there are those who would argue that not only does this not go far enough, but that Britain still lags behind other countries on these issues. Chapter 7 will present information pertaining to recently-increased parental rights in the United States of America in the area of special education. In West Germany and other European countries, there are parents' forums and pressure groups of long standing with the established power to intervene far more directly in policy and curriculum affairs than we are even beginning to move towards (Kellmer Pringle in Doxiades, ed., 1979).

An article in the *Times Educational Supplement* (Rogers 1980) points to developments in 'child advocacy' and extension of children's and parental rights in other countries such as Sweden, Norway and America, and considers the possibility of the creation of ombudsmen on behalf of children, their needs and rights. Rogers widens the scope by proposing 'a permanent focus for children's affairs to make the right connexions and draw together various and disparate disciplines, themes and policies'.

In fact the Children's Committee was set up in October 1978, following a recommendation by the Court Committee on Child Health Services (Court 1976). The Children's Committee advised the government on 'the coordination and development of health and personal social services for children', and its brief was to keep children's needs under review and monitor and check upon statutory and voluntary provision for meeting needs. The Committee is now disbanded, though the government continues to receive advice from child experts.

A move to initiate better ways of representing children – in care proceedings, court hearings, schools, hospitals, hostels – was the impetus in the newly-created Children's Legal Centre (for address, see end of chapter). It is an independent organisation working to 'clarify, develop and improve children's law'. It grew out of concern expressed by child-focussed groups which came together for the International Year of the Child in 1979. The Children's Legal Centre will advise and support parents and children in problems to do with housing, employment, health, environment and education (school suspension appeals and procedures for assessing children's need for special educational provision).

2. Accountability

A pivotal aspect crucial to an evolving relationship between schools and the families and communities they render service to is their accountability to these external institutions. To put it another way, 'in exchange for the public having delegated responsibility for educational decisions to the professional group, the teachers in return owe the public an accurate account of their activities' (Ebbutt 1980). In his article, Ebbutt traces recent events within education that he feels have given rise to the conviction, easily demonstrable by deeper analysis, that schools traditionally have not been sufficiently called upon to report, to inform, to fulfil promises, and to show results.

The criteria by which schools are publicly judged are many and various. Criticism and indictment take many forms – banner headlines in the tabloid national press about unruly behaviour, fingers of suspicion and allegations about presumed malpractice in local schools published in local newspapers, stern admonishments by educationalists to schools when they suspect slipping of academic standards, and fewer examination passes.

Underlying the compulsory call in the 1980 Education Act for schools to publish information is the hope that a more open system of reporting to a wider public will be beneficial and enhancing to a dialogue between parents and schools. There are inherent dangers in any opening-up of a hitherto closed system. Pessimists talk of the logical extension of such openness and accessibility being that parents will demand curriculum control, and the right of intrusion into what are properly regarded as professionally sacrosanct areas.

It is said (Sockett 1976) that we have been influenced in Britain by American notions of accountability where the history and tradition of parental involvement in education is quite different from the British experience. House writes (in Finch and Scrimshaw, eds 1980)

In the American tradition any parent who is dissatisfied with the schools has the opportunity to register his complaint to the elected school board, the school administrators or the child's teacher. This intrusion is considered well within the parents' rights and school personnel are expected to make a satisfactory response to what is held to be a legitimate demand. In fact it is crucial to an understanding of the American school to appreciate its vulnerability to outside pressures (p. 363).

House's review of the accountability movement and its manifestations in America are relevant because he foresees increasing demands and forms of educational accountability as an increasing technological and expensive-to-run society becomes more cost conscious, and correspondingly demands grow for cost-effectiveness. His prediction embraces the British scene as well as other advanced societies.

Several examples lend some credibility to this view. Some have already been mentioned – notably th ; Taylor Report's recommendations and the provisions of the 1980 Education Act.

There is a growing impetus for a General Teaching Council for Britain, which according to its proponents would establish a code of conduct; elect a disciplinary committee; and raise the status of teachers by allowing them to govern their own profession as do doctors and lawyers. In other words, by drawing up criteria for professional registration and guidelines for professional practice, it would follow that the teaching profession would become more publicly accountable. The smokescreens for malpractice, inefficiency, ineffectiveness would evaporate as the professional services become more explicit and (and this is a pessimistic projection based on American evidence) constrained.

Another example, or piece of evidence for House's prediction, is the current debate as to whether schools can or should 'self-evaluate' or 'self-account' (Elliott 1979a and 1979b). Elliott defines self-evaluating as 'the school accepting responsibility for evaluating itself'

(p. 23) and he argues that a case can be made for a school self-evaluation on three grounds: those of social, economic, and professional accountability.

Two projects sponsored by the Social Science Research Council on schools' accountability have uncovered all sorts of factors pertaining to attitudes and expectations by teachers and parents, other educationalists and concerned members of the public. The Cambridge Accountability Project focused on secondary schools (Elliott *et al.* 1981). The data and insights gained from the several indepth case studies from the CAP will be valuable additional contributions to the debate on accountability, and the outcomes of the project will contribute to the evolution of a partnership between schools and parents by proposing models or styles of communication and by outlining the demarcations as well as the overlap between professional practice and responsibility and parental rights and aspirations. The other funded project was the Sussex-based Accountability (University and local education authority) in the Middle Years of Schooling, which will be reporting in book form in due course.

3. Attitudes

Recent investigations into teachers' attitudes to parents' role vis à vis schools, and parents' attitudes to teachers' and schools' functions have led to these summary points:

— teachers do have predetermined suppositions that there is a proportion of parents who are not interested in their children's schooling and educational progress (Johnson and Ransom 1981) and that this is linked in their minds with home factors (O'Sullivan 1980).
— there is no evidence that this is so, and that apparent lack of interest is probably indicative of other factors to do with domestic privation and stress (Wilson and Herbert cited earlier). There is no conclusive evidence to show that working class parents are intrinsically less concerned than their middle class counterparts.

Surveys (Cyster *et al.* 1979, Webb 1979) have indicated that *apparently* parents do not want a greater say in central policy and curricula issues in schools, they appear to be expressing preferences for increased and speedier access to teachers, and improved and more informative written communication. Seemingly contrary evidence came from a 1979 National Consumer Council poll which reported that a significantly high proportion of respondents thought that parents should have places on governing boards of schools and therefore 'should have a say in running our schools' (N.C.C. 1979).

Other research (Green 1969, Sharp and Green 1975, Wilson and Herbert 1978, Cyster *et al.* 1979, Johnson and Ransom 1981) indicates that parents are unsure and tentative about their intrusion into school life because they feel ignorant of the routines, the processes and contemporary curricula. Implicit in these parental self-perceptions is the conviction that teachers do not really want increased parent contact over and above formally-arranged open-evenings, social events or (in infant and junior schools) carefully circumscribed help with basic learning activities, *viz*, reading, painting, cooking (Bassey 1978).

But between teachers' and parents' expectations and presumptions lies unexplored territory. This pertains to what parents' responses would be if they actually had extended rights to be involved in the running of schools (and not just via the parent as governor concept) rather than it always being posed to them in hypothetical form. Neither can we know how teachers would respond once a formalised structure were erected for an enhanced dialogue with parents. When researchers present teachers with closed hypothetical issues which allow for *existing* perceptions to be expressed, it is not surprising that results which rely on confirmations of the status quo are used to make sterile projections into the future.

If a rationale for a partnership between parents and teachers is generally acceptable (see Chapters 2 and 10) then we have moved past the point where we need to sample static opinion towards a point in time when more serious issues relating to policy-into-practice should be aired, especially if an acceptable framework is now agreed to exist (within the context of post-Plowden developments).

It is not being suggested that parents are necessarily a homogeneous group, that there is a collective parental voice. This chapter has sought to demonstrate the diversity of recent professional and public thinking on home–school links and it does seem, at the beginning of the 1980's, that we do have enough evidence now of positive forging of links in some areas to use as the basis of proper policy formation. To this issue, conjoined with related issues in subsequent chapters, Chapter 10 addresses itself.

Within education, we are now in a position to consider which theoretical models for parent participation could be viable, which suggestions that have been made for increased parental involvement have potential and which forms of evaluation are applicable. Two fundamental prerequisites for the continued positive evolution of a relationship between schools and parents are that;

1) Schools have to explore, acknowledge, reconcile, accommodate to parents' and society's goals and priorities and shift position accordingly; this will mean the recasting of concepts of role, status, power.

2) Parents must with confidence expect school involvement to concern them beyond their own self-interest. As the Sussex Accountability Project draft report (see above) puts it 'unless and until parents perceive home–school relations as collectivised rather than individualised, pressure groups will be ephemeral and the position of parent representatives' will be problematic'.

References

Advisory Centre for Education (ACE), 18 Victoria Park Square, London E2 9PB.

Bacon, W. (1978) *Public Accountability and the Schooling System, a Sociology of School-board Democracy*, London, WC2: Harper and Row.

Bagnall, N. (1974) *Parent Power*, London, WC1: Routledge and Kegan Paul.

Bailey, R. (1980) 'The home school liaison teacher' Chapter 17 in Craft, M., Raynor, L., Cohen, L. (eds) *Linking Home and School*, 3rd edition, London, WC2: Harper and Row.

Bassey, M. (1978) *Nine Hundred Primary School Teachers*, NFER.

Bastiani, J. (Ed) (1978) *Written Communication between Home and School*, a report by the Community Education Working party, University of Nottingham, School of Education.

Bate, G. (1978) *A Study of the Opinion of Parents of Middleschool Children on Their Involvement and Participation in School*, unpublished M.Sc. Thesis, University of Aston in Birmingham.

Bryans, T. and Wolfendale, S. (1981) 'Changing attitudes to children – a comparative chronicle', *Early Childhood*, Vol. II No. 1., October.

Brunel University, Educational Studies Unit Dept. Government *School Governing Bodies Project 1980–1983.*

CASE, Confederation for the Advancement of State Education, 1 Windermere Avenue, Wembey, London, HA9 8DH.

Children's Committee, Mary Ward House, 5–7 Tavistock Place, London WCIH 9SS. Children's Legal Centre, 2 Malden Road, London NW5.

Cluderay, T. (ed.) (1972) 'Home and school relations', *Aspects of Education, Journal of the Institute of Education*, University of Hull, No. 15.

Concern (1980) *Secondary Schooling*, No. 36, Summer, National Children's Bureau.

Court, D. (Chairperson) (1976) *Fit for the Future*, HMSO.

Craft, M., Raynor, J. and Cohen, L. (eds) (1980) *Linking Home and School*, a new review, 3rd edition, London, WC2: Harper and Row:

Croall, J. (1978) *The Parents' Day School Book*, St Albans, Herts: Granada Publishing.

Cyster, R., Clift, P. S., and Battle, S. (1979) *Parental Involvement in Primary Schools*, NFER.

David, M. (1980) *The State, the Family and Education*, London, WC1: Routledge and Kegan Paul.

DES (1968) 'Parent Teacher Relations in Primary Schools', *Educational Survey 5*, HMSO.

DES (1977) *Education in Schools*, HMSO.

DES (1978) *Primary Education in England*, a survey by HMI, HMSO.

DES (1979) *Local Authority Arrangements for the School Curriculum*, Report on the Circular 14/77 review, HMSO.

DES (1980) *Education Act 1980: Publication of Information (Section 8)* DES August.

Douglas, J. W. B. (1967) *The Home and the School*, St Albans, Herts: Panther.

Ebbutt, D. (1980) *The Cambridge Accountability Project: Aims and Design of the Research and some initial insights*, Cambridge Institute of Education.

Elliott, J. (1979a) 'Self-accounting schools: are they possible?', *Educational Analysis*, Vol. 1, No. 1, pp. 67–71.

Elliott, J. (1979b) 'The Case for school self-evaluation', *Forum*, Vol. 22, No. 1 Autumn.

Elliott, J., Bridges, D., Ebbutt, D., Gibson, R., Nias, J. (1981) *School Accountability*, London, WC1: Grant McIntyre.

Fowler, G. (1980) 'Falling school rolls and home-school links', Chapter 2 in Craft, M. *et al.* (eds) *Linking Home and School*, 3rd edition, London WC2: Harper and Row.

Gibson, R. (1980) *Teacher–Parent Communication, one School and its Practice*, Cambridge Institute of Education, Shaftesbury Road, Cambridge, CB2 2BX.

Green, L. (1969) *An Examination of Some Teachers' Attitudes to and Experience of, Home–school Cooperation*, unpublished Child Development Thesis, London University.

Halsey, A. H., Heath, A. F., Ridge, J. H. (1980); *Origins and Destinations: Family, Class and Education in Modern Britain*, Oxford: Clarendon Press.

Home and School Council, 81 Rustlings Road, Sheffield, S11 7AB.

House, E. (1980) 'Accountability in the USA', in Finch, A. and Scrimshaw, P. *Standards, Schooling and Education*, Hodder and Stoughton (Sevenoaks, Kent) in association with the Open University Press (Milton Keynes).

Hubbard, D. and Salt, J. (1972) *Parents; Participation and Persuasion in Primary Education*, Institute of Education, Sheffield University.

ILEA (Inner London Education Authority) (1974) *Home and School*, County Hall, London, SE1 7PB.

Jackson, B. and Marsden, D. (1962) *Education and the Working Class*, Harmondsworth, Middx: Pelican.

Johnson, D. and Ransom. E. (1981) *Family and School; a Research-based Commentary on the Secondary School Years, from the Point of View of Pupils Parents*, Brunel University, unpublished.

Lynch, J. and Pimlott, J. (1976) *Parents and Teachers*, London, WC2: Macmillan.

National Consumer Council, press release May 1979.

National Confederation of Parent–Teacher Associations, 43 Stonebridge Road, Northfleet, Gravesend, Kent.

NFER Research Project *School Reports to Parents*, National Foundation for Educational Research, The Mere, Upton Park, Slough, Berkshire, SL1 2DQ.

National Home–School Liaison Association (NHSLA), c/o 69 Sand Lane, S. Milford, Leeds.

Newson, J. and Newson, E. (1977) *Perspectives on school at 7 years old*, London, WC1: George Allen and Unwin Ltd.

O'Connor, M. (1977) *Your Child's Primary School*, London SW10: Pan.

O'Sullivan, D. (1980) 'Teachers' views on the effects of the home', *Education Research*, Vol. 22, No. 2 February.

Pedley, R. (1967) *The Comprehensive School*, London, SW10: Penguin Pelican.

Pilling, D. and Pringle, M. K. (1978) *Controversial Issues in Child Development*, St Albans, Herts: Paul Elek Ltd.

Pringle, M. K. (1979) 'Children's rights and parental rights and obligations', in Doxiades, S. (Ed) *The Children in the World of Tomorrow*, Oxford: Pergamon.

Rogers, R. (7.11.1980) 'On the side of the child', *Times Educational Supplement.*

Sallis, J. (1977) *School Managers and Governors; Taylor and After*, London, W1: Ward Lock Educational.

Sallis, J. (1979) *School Governors: Partnership in Practice*, An ACE. Guide, ACE, 18 Victoria Park Square, London, E2.

Schools Council (1981) *Home/School Communications*, 160 Gt. Portland St., London, W1.

Sharpe, R. and Green, A. (1975) *Education and Social Control: a Study in Progressive Primary Education*, London, WC1: Routledge and Kegan Paul.

Sharrock, A. (1970) *Home–School Relations*, London, WC2: Macmillan.

Sockett, H. (1976) 'Teacher Accountability', *Proceedings of the Philosophy of Education Society of Great Britain*, Vol. x, July, pp. 34–55.

Stone, J. and Taylor, F. (1976) *The Parents' Schoolbook*, Harmondsworth, Middx: Pelican.

Taylor, F. (1980) *A School Prospectus Planning Kit*, ACE, 18 Victoria Park Square, London, E2.

Taylor, F. (1981) *Choosing a School*, 2nd revised edition, ACE (as above).

Taylor, T. (Chairman) (1977) *A New Partnership for our School*, HMSO.

Webb, D. (1979) 'Home and School: Parental Views', *Education* 3–13, 7, 2, pp. 24–9.

Wilson, H. and Herbert, G. (1978) *Parents and Children in the Inner City*, London, WC1: Routledge and Kegan Paul.

CHAPTER 5

Intervention in the Community – Focus on Families

The spotlight was angled onto schools in Chapter 3, within an overall community context. That wider perspective is under scrutiny in this chapter with variations on formal education systems being appraised as part of community provision. As ever, the focus is on the place of parents and their actual and potential contribution towards the development and education of their children.

1. Definitions

1.1. Family

'Family' will refer to the domestic setting in which children find themselves and are reared, in whatever combination of adults and children. It will include fostering, adoptive, 'in-care' situations as well as so-called 'natural' families. This working definition presupposes bondings and allegiances of all kinds and is supplementary to, and in distinction from, the standard dictionary definitions of the word 'family', e.g. the Oxford Dictionary (1975) 'members of household, parents, children, servants, etc. Set of parents and children or of relations, whether living together or not'. The aridity of this formal definition cannot convey the significance of a unit which is 'a haven and a source of identification and information for all children' (Kagan 1979, p. 235).

1.2. Community

The word 'community' is more difficult to pin down. Standard dictionary definitions beg further linguistic and semantic analysis.

As a working concept, 'community' is defined according to the orientation and framework of academic/professional disciplines using the term, whether it be physical space, functional relationships among institutions, communications networks, common heritage, or emotional-relational bondings. Leichter (1978) acknowledges the sheer difficulty, even undesirability of welding the diversity of definitions into one that would be all-embracing or universally applicable, but points out that 'If one is attempting to understand the character of education in a society, it is important to be able to make shifts in perspective in defining community for different purposes of enquiry, so that one does not miss important sources of education' (p. 581).

Hobbs (1978) perceives the child as central in an ecosystem (ecological system). Diagrammatic representation allows for all close and more distant systems that impinge upon a child to be plotted in relation to their significance in the child's life. Contemporary convictions that 'there is evidence of a coming together of family and work place and of family and school' (Hobbs, p. 759) could be reflected accordingly in ecosystem representation to denote where and how the child is juxtaposed in relation to school, his/her family, his/her parents' work, his/her friends, the places he/she goes to.

As far as an educational connection is concerned, Raggatt (1979) defines 'community' as 'related to the catchment area of any given school' in his general discussion on community and education. He affirms that community is a 'slippery' concept and reports that 94 definitions of the word have been established.

Taking formal–traditional definitions as a starting point, and considering the more flexible connotations employed by a number of behavioural disciplines, an amalgam of these is proposed for the purpose of this chapter. The salient characteristics of 'community' that are relevant for *this* chapter, within the overall context of the book, are as follows:

— people living in the same defined locality
— some commonality of interests – business, cultural, socio-economic, leisure pursuits
— perceived political or municipal or social unity.

1.3. Intervention

The term 'intervention' has been used on both sides of the Atlantic in association with disadvantage and compensatory education and this, with its implicitly preventive approach, has been summed up as a 'conscious and purposeful set of actions intended to change or influence the anticipated course of development' (see Wolfendale and Bryans 1979).

Thus 'intervention' has been used to denote particular and specific action designed to bring about change that would not necessarily have come about without such intervening action. The hypothesis is that in the normal course of events factors governing change towards the desired social or educational end are imperfectly understood or controlled and therefore only have chance occurrence or incidental influence. Whereas planned intervention, using goals and appropriate sequences of action designed to achieve these, is reckoned to be an effective means of bringing about desired change – to develop parents' awareness and understanding of child development and educational aims; to bring about constructive communication between home and school; to boost development and raise levels of functioning in subject and skill areas.

The US Head Start, Follow-Through and Home-Start programmes are the most comprehensive and widely-publicised of all the world-wide attempts to intervene directly in the lives of young children and to influence their parents' behaviour, attitudes and child-rearing methods on their behalf. Many other ventures have taken place in Europe, America, Canada (London Educational Review, 1974, Pauli 1975, Stukat 1976, Woodhead 1979) as well as in Third World countries, in South America, parts of Africa and elsewhere. The Bernard Van Leer Foundation (1977, 1981) has published its finding from a considerable number of endeavours from all over the world.

2. Rationale – Intentions and Outcomes

This international collective consciousness is based on twin rationales or underlying intentions. One is the 'compensatory intention' invoking the deprivation model, whereby intervention is by professionals and experts who manipulate the environment to promote learning and other experiences to offset a basically depriving environment (Anderson 1978). The other, which is linked to this 'deficit' model concentrates on optimising human potential by forms of intervention rather more than it emphasises the 'compensatory' nature of the intervention (McDill, McDill, Sprehe 1969). The compensatory model being the umbrella has been the most pervasive (Open University 1975). The rationale has been based on some of these assumptions that families in 'need' materially:

— lack opportunities to sample a wide range of human experience;
— cannot fully benefit from society's resources;
— are ill equipped to cope and develop competencies:
— are powerless in society to inform, to make and affect decisions (Bruner 1979);
— do not and cannot benefit from formal education where the codes and aspirations are disparate from theirs;
— have lowered self-esteem and feel diminished in themselves.

According to this line of argument, it follows that children in these families are 'at risk' of perpetuating the behavioural patterns (Rutter and Madge 1976) and are therefore in need of help (Evans 1979).

School-focussed compensatory intervention approaches within Headstart, and British Education Priority Area (EPA) projects have included three main components:

— 'extra' input in the way of resources, including staff, equipment and in-service;
— special curricula, language programmes, cognitively oriented approaches;
— fostering of home school links, via a contact person (home-liaison teacher) or bringing parents into school.

Where the institution of school has not been the predominant focus, effort has been directed at

1) the home – where expertise, training facilities and support have been brought into the home setting;

2) community or local centres (including clinics and units) – where parents and professionals meet in joint ventures, aimed at supporting and training children via their parents;

3) combination of 1) and 2) where the aims may be severalfold.

Advocates of early intervention have argued powerfully and cogently (Deutsch 1965, McVicker Hunt, 1969, Bruner 1971,

Bronfenbrenner 1976) about the estimated benefits to children and their parents. The hypotheses have been tested in all sorts of ways and the effectiveness of outcomes evaluated by various means on a number of criteria, which include conventional pre- and post-test measures of ability and attainment, attitude and adjustment scales and indices. Some of the thousands of studies have proved to be seminal in the thoughtfulness of their approaches, the care with which their methodologies have been designed and their apparently conclusively successful results (Karnes 1966, Gray and Klaus 1967, Heber *et al.* 1973, Shipman 1977, 1979).

It is not surprising that large-scale evaluation reports which attempted an overview of the many disparate American projects should appear equivocal. Pessimistic conclusions (see Raven 1980) as to the long-term retention of early gains ('wash-out' effect) have been counterbalanced by optimistic sounds that there is a longer-term spin-off which can be assessed according to criteria which were not necessarily anticipated or built-in (Lazar 1979, Schweinhart and Weikart 1980/81).

It certainly seems that success is better guaranteed if basic requisites at the outset of intervention projects are clearly enumerated and adhered to (Kelsall and Kelsall 1971). Evans, in introducing the framework for a 'technology of intervention' writes (1979)

intervention which is based upon a thoroughgoing evaluation of children's strengths and weaknesses and supported by a clearly perceived framework of developmental objectives is likely to have the greatest effect in the long term (p. 52).

In advocating 'ecologically valid intervention' which focusses on the mother and child as a interacting dyad, Evans says that

the key to successful intervention . . . may be based upon a thoroughgoing functional analysis and developmental task analysis set within a framework of perceived growth objectives (1979, p. 53).

One fundamental requisite that many writers agree on for programme effectiveness is for substantial parental involvement which is perceived as having advantages. Donachy (1979) lists nine main benefiting outcomes of parent participation or home in- tervention programmes which are the logical sequiturs of the invocation of a disadvantage model (also see Hom and Robinson, eds 1977). Many studies and projects, whether lasting months or several years, have regarded parental participation as the cornerstone, even *raison d'être* of the venture. The model of parent participation (Day 1980) adopted in the studies cited above, as well as others have been of varying kinds; some have focussed on curricula, with an emphasis on cognitive activity (Weikart 1976); some have made the target agent for change the home visitor (Lambie 1976); others the parent as change-agent (Gordon 1978); yet others have viewed the total home environment as the springboard for the development of the child, as long as there is structured input (Shipman 1979).

The young children (usually pre-school, up to six years or thereabouts) at whom the studies have been directed have fallen into the well-established (though not necessarily well validated) categories of disadvantage, physical and/or mental handicap, disturbed behaviour (Robinson 1980). All have made the presumption that intervention via parent training, parent support, curricular focus, home visitor as intermediary will have the effect of promoting gains in IQ, attainment, adjustment, and school readiness (Bernard Van Leer 1976, Tizard Moss and Perry 1976, Pilling and Pringle 1978). The aim of parent education has in some projects been explicit (Gordon 1978) and this particular focus, parent education, is one of the topics examined in more detail in Chapter 9.

3. Intervention for Whom – Broadening the Scope

The justification for the tremendous financial and time investment into the application of intervention programmes for young 'deprived' children and their families has been humanitarian and political/economic expediency. Many writers and those active in the field do not deny the fragility of their presuppositions and the ideological debate continues, as to whether a dichotomisation into advantaged and disadvantaged is tenable (Robinson 1976) or even a useful working conceptualisation.

The concepts might be less vulnerable to scrutiny if we were certain of the input-output equation. If we knew the precursors, requisites and parameters for effective learning (Wedell and Raybould 1976) it might be possible to design learning programmes which ensured a match between child and task, so that performance (output) could be assessed against the original learning programme specification (on which input would be based). Investigators have had to rely on easily measurable bits of behaviour, using conventional assessment procedures. There have been ingenious attempts to 'get at' the early-established roots of skill acquisition, such as the verbal learning approach of Bereiter and Engelmann (1966), the tutorial language scheme of Blank (1968), the cognitive model of Weikart (1976) the critical thinking approach built into the Peabody Language Development Kit (Dunn and Smith 1966).

The theoretical orientation has demonstrably been a skills/developmental approach (Deutsch 1965, Hunt 1969, Butler, Gotts and Quisenberry 1975) in which the patterns of development of all children are respected, skills training is a necessity and attention to potential sources of learning difficulty is an integral part (Wolfendale 1981).

Is this formulation not applicable to *all* children? According to some writers (Bernard Van Leer 1980) the aspiration should be to 'intervene' early on behalf of all children; not just to make up a shortfall between manifest performance and prevailing standards for attainment and competence on the part of disadvantaged children, but to optimise the potential of each and every child. Evidently, it is felt that schools, whose responsibility it is to do just that, are either not succeeding in the task, or they are an insufficient provider of what only the community in toto should be offering towards the fullest development and educational opportunity of every child.

Increasingly, it *is* felt that schools, as separate, even shut-off institutions, cannot contribute maximally to the overall development of children, without recourse to children's caretakers and without the incorporation of the wider community network. This theme was introduced in Chapter 2 and elaborated within a context of a fast-changing world situation which calls for the reappraisal of the curriculum to take direct account of children's need to develop critical thinking, problem-solving strategies and coping skills. Woodhead, in his review of European compensatory approaches (1979) includes a quotation '... the school must become adjusted and provide variegated education' (p. 41) and this exhortation is intended on behalf of all children.

The crux of the dilemma has been whether or not we should distinguish between children at a disadvantage for coping in childhood and later adulthood and who could benefit from intervention from intermediaries, and children who appear to be better equipped with life-coping strategies and resilience.

Finally, if societal divisiveness is acknowledged to be endemic to the human situation, even political solutions and aspirations towards an egalitarian society might defy us (Rainwater 1973). The demarcations may remain as clear-cut: copers/non-copers: succeeders/non-succeeders; those who possess/those who do not; those to whom life experiences accrue/those who are reduced by limited opportunity. An egalitarian society could turn out to be little different to one organised in a rather more ramshackle way, where *ostensibly opportunity* and support are offered to all, and additionally, life-lines to some (welfare state concept).

The intolerable and unresolvable ideological dilemma is the backcloth to everyone working with and on behalf of children. Notwithstanding the force of this debate, many child developmentalists feel that there is a genuine case for advancing our knowledge of early learning and developmental processes via research in real-life settings. Indeed, there is so much yet to explore, relating to the child in school, at home and in society. The exploration of some of these behavioural phenomena would undoubtedly have implications for those dealing with children, for example:

— the nature of adult–child verbal dialogue (Wells 1981);
— adult–child non-verbal interaction;
— overt and covert codes of communication;
— transmission of information, knowledge, codes for behaving, how these are passed on from adult to child, and translated into action by the child;
— the fullest development of critical, reasoning, analytical, cognitive, creative skills.

Of these several examples from the many areas that continue to be ripe for exploration, we know so little about *process product* links.

If intervention on behalf of all children is justifiable and tenable, then the holistic approach has much appeal. In Shipman's words (1979) there is 'the need for working with the total ecology of the child if we truly care and wish to serve our nation's children well'. Caldwell asks (1975) 'What is the optimal learning environment for the young child?' and discusses requisites that incorporate the child's total environment.

Bronfenbrenner (1976) is often referred to as being one of the seminal influences and shapers of what he has termed 'ecological intervention'. By adopting a 'whole' approach and conceptualising it along the lines of Hobbs (1978) and his ecosystem referred to at the beginning of this chapter, it becomes possible to act in terms of optimising the learning and social environments of all children, as well as meeting the needs of vulnerable children (Cantrell and Cantrell in Hogg and Mittler, ed. 1980). Conceptual mapping could show how school, in its overall community context is neither ancillary nor predominant, but complementary to the position of the child. Each child's ecosystem is unique, according to Hobbs and can change with time. In drawing up an ecosystem for an individual child, therefore, it is possible to incorporate shifts of activity, growth points, transient or enduring problems, the people who impinge upon the child and the institutions they represent – parents, siblings and relatives in the home; teachers in the school, psychologists, social workers, doctors in the support services; peers and friends in the neighbourhood, shopkeepers, churchpersons, youth leaders in the community.

Whatever the orientation, parents' role and relationship with their children remain the crux. Indeed, according to the preliminary principles outlined in the draft reports from the OECD/CERI† project *The Educational Role of the Family* (which will be referred to in Chapter 9), since it is from the parents or parent-figures that children's receptivity, responsiveness and resilience to life-events are fashioned, it is the family who should be in prime receipt of investment and support by society.

4. British Initiatives in Family Support

In Chapter 3 examples were given of EPA, post-EPA and community action initiatives in which the focus was the school setting and/or the educational process.

Other ventures have shared some of the aims and goals of these projects, but have had a predominantly community-oriented focus,

---

† Organisation for Economic Cooperation and Development Centre Educational Research and Innovation.

in which any links with education have been but one of a variety of intentions. Some of the better known, well designed, well documented and enduring of the British ventures will be briefly described. They have invoked a disadvantage, or need-meeting model, and have perceived that many families need and respond to external support, advice and guidance with the rearing of their children, coping with employment problems, marital strains and general life stresses. Some projects have explicitly aimed to develop self-help strategies and have attempted to reduce or phase out the involvement of the project workers. The wider context has been community education and the thin dividing line between teams' aspirations to offer support and their zeal to promote power-sharing amongst members of the community has been a possibly unresolvable paradox. The contradictions inherent in these sometimes politically motivated philosophies are highlighted by Lovett (1979) who describes a number of such recent British initiatives, and assesses whether or not the original aims have been achieved. He also spells out the nature and purpose of community education endeavours and within the following quotation, we can see where working with parents on behalf of them and their children fits in:

The emphasis on working in the community; identifying with local people and their problems, opening up access to resources tied up in institutions; recognising the wide range of educational needs and interests; utilising popular and working class cultures as well as making use of the best of middle class culture; using people's lives, hopes, dreams, problems as the basis for their own education: utilising the skills of local people and the resources found in local schools; assisting local people to run their own community education programme; all this does build up to a distinct community approach (p. 124).

Some of the notable projects are given brief descriptions below.

4.1. Family Service Units (See chapter references for address)

Their aims are to promote the welfare of families and communities which are seriously disadvantaged through lack of personal, social or economic resources. Each unit is responsible for assessing needs in its local community and matching its service to those needs, where possible. Amongst services offered are social work with families; group work with families; intermediate treatment aimed at children; community work, advice centres, welfare rights groups, play-schemes; day centres opened to families and children referred to the units; educational work aimed at children who find difficulties in the ordinary schools, at pre-school children and their parents, and liaison with schools and other community groups.

FSU operate in about a dozen provincial cities and in a dozen or so centres in and around London. The units also provide training and consultancy facilities.

4.2. *Leicester Home-Start Project* (Harrison 1981)

This project started in 1974. The Home Start volunteers are parents themselves. They receive an initial training before they become linked with families who, in the main, are referred by social workers or health visitors, but who also can self-refer. The Home Start Volunteers are assigned to families to give support, work through problems, offer practical advice, and perhaps introduce activities, designed to foster pre-academic and early cognitive skills, for parents to work on with their young children. Harrison describes eight basic objectives of the scheme and details ten requisites for successful intervention. The 'ethics of intrusion' are discussed fully in the initial training period. By 1979–80 there were 104 Home Start Volunteers working with 200 families; there were six day centres, and provision for evening group work.

Because the scheme is regarded as worthwhile and effective in terms of meeting families' needs (but not via the traditional child guidance or social work structure and ethos) expansion is planned for the near future, and one funded innovation will be a Home-Start consultancy, which will run for two experimental years.

4.3. *Liverpool Home-Link* (Bell and Burn, Bernard Van Leer 1979)

This is one of the best known projects. it was established in 1973 and its primary focus in its first three years was to develop a home visiting scheme using local mothers as home visitors. The provision of informal and college-linked courses on many topics concerned with rights, child development, and community resources, has been one off-shoot from the original plans. The paid workers do not see themselves as experts passing on 'knowledge' to those who lack it. The theory in which the activities and practice are rooted is that the recipients or targets of the scheme have acknowledged needs, areas for potential development, and individual strengths on which to draw. Community education and support are seen as a participant activity. The Bernard Van Leer Foundation funded the initial project and in 1978–79 an urban aid grant was made available to allow the work to continue and expand.

4.4. London Voluntary Service Council

1) Family Groups in the Community (Knight, Gibson and Grant 1979)

This EEC funded project is described as an experiment in social and community work, in which eight 'family groups' were set up in various areas in and around London. It was based on earlier work in the area of family groups, in which the aim was for the evolution of self-help, mutually-supporting groups.

The initial objectives for the project team were: to set up and monitor family groups, assess the effects of group participation in the lives of attenders, evaluate the role of non-professionals in social welfare work, chart the effects on the leaders of the groups, monitor relationships with official welfare agencies, and investigate whether or not a wider network of family groups could work in other areas. The key aspect of the scheme was the convenor and each pivot of group, that is, the family group leaders. They were non-professionals, and in fact, formal educational qualifications were disregarded as a criterion for selection. Knight *et al.* (1979) maintain that the leaders, who were warm and tolerant people had usually experienced lives similar to those of other local people; experiences which included poverty, social isolation and depression.

Group members attended on a sessional basis and activities included discussions about common problems, local issues, a practical focus such as sewing, craft-making, cooking. Evaluation of the project which lasted over a period of a couple of years is reported by Knight and his colleagues, who attempt to translate the research findings into recommendations for policy. They advocate the continuation and proliferation of these 'support networks' stressing that the potential for mutual care and support already exists in neighbourhoods, and that the 'powerless' in our communities have untapped abilities for self-fulfilment.

4.5. Special Services for families (London Voluntary Service Council, 1980, Richardson and Knight 1981)

Research workers in the London Voluntary Service Council drew up a directory of innovative schemes based around the London area which were designed to combat feelings of despair, isolation and inadequacy in adults and parents bringing up young children. Richardson and Knight distinguish the traditional service offered by statutory agencies to families with transient or lasting problems from that of services that penetrate into the community web, offering direct and relevant advice and support. Richardson and Knight review 127 schemes which could be categorised into:

1) groupwork and workshops – 29.9%;

2) family centres, including community nurseries – 23.6%;

3) intervention work, covering casework, therapy and intermediate treatment – 10.2%;

4) advice and information – 7.1%;

5) 'mixed' – 9.4%;

6) miscellaneous – 19.7%.

Amongst characteristics noted by Richardson and Knight were: use of non-professional volunteers (paid or unpaid); preponderance of mixed group membership (i.e., groups not catering just for exclusive categories *viz* handicapped); emphasis on prevention or reduction of personal and family problems; financial dependency on statutory agencies or outside trusts and foundations (see also Brinson in Field 1977). As the authors affirm, this dependency on external sources of money makes many of the schemes vulnerable and Richardson and Knight are pessimistic regarding the continued survival of a number of them, although the agreed need is acute.

4.6. Mixenden Home-Link Project and Home-Visiting scheme, (Halifax, Yorkshire)

This is a resource centre for the use of parents – planned partly on the lines of the Liverpool Home Link Scheme – to fulfil the need of all parents for reinforcement of their parental skills and the need to have an outlet for sharing these skills and their experience. It is organised under the umbrella of the Halifax Association for Parents. The centre is a meeting place and a resource for imparting advice, information and support.

The Home Visiting scheme was established in 1978 under the Urban Aid Programme and is grant-aided for five years in the first instance. Two qualified teachers are employed as home visitors and attached to two primary schools. The aims of the project are to: prepare pre-school age children for the transition from home to school; promote understanding on the part of parents of the role of the school and the contributions they can make; to increase parental involvement in and support for the work of the local infant school. The home visitors, adopting the format tried out in earlier EPA projects (described in Halsey 1972, Poulton and James 1975 and Bell 1976) visit homes, discuss language development, discuss ways in which parents can enhance general development and school readiness, and leave toys until their next visit. Initial evaluation indicates that the scheme is worthwhile in bringing about increased parental understanding of and interest in child development and the educational process and raising parental expectations. It is felt, too, that it is serving as an early means of identifying children who might experience later learning and/or emotional difficulties.

4.7. SCOPE – for parents and children   (Poulton and Poulton 1979, Poulton 1980)

SCOPE was set up in the Southampton area in 1976 to help families to help themselves. Groups of parents meet weekly in their neighbourhood and while their young children play in a crèche, mothers examine and discuss their child-rearing attitudes and techniques, sharing their experience and providing mutual support. It is hoped thereby that isolation and depression, so often features in the lives of young mothers (Brown et al. 1975) will be combatted and anticipated problems tackled or averted.

The 1979–80 report of SCOPE rests its case on the statement in the Court Report (see Chapters 1 and 9) 'we have found no better way to raise a child than to reinforce the ability of his parent(s), whether natural or substitute, to do so'. So one central aim is to reinforce the role of parents as educators of their own children. There are thirteen local groups under the overall auspices of SCOPE, and there is also a

Family Centre for whole families to make use of, to meet or stay in. The SCOPE Council consists of group representatives and professionals from service agencies. It has a full-time coordinator and finance has been forthcoming from local authority grants, outside bodies and 'self-generated efforts'. Poulton and Poulton (1979) conclude their description of SCOPE by saying

Using the collective strengths of families can produce a considerable neighbourhood resource to be matched with the resources of social agencies in an area (p. 81).

5. Community Schools and Alternative Schools

The last few years have seen a spate of publications which have reflected growing social and professional anxieties that schools fail children and society, that curricula are out of touch with and irrelevant to the demands of society and people's needs, and the conviction that, anyway, there is more for children (and their parents) to learn by direct experience and participation in local communities than through schools. Even when schools have attempted to combat the charge of irrelevancy by developing links with local industry and commerce, and innovating social service activities for pupils to engage in, they have been criticised on the grounds that these are merely cosmetic exercises.

Radical alternatives have been put forward by Illich (1973), Postman and Weingartner (1971), Goodman (1971), Reimer (1971) none of whom had the British educational system particularly in mind when they wrote their books. Little literature in this country has had the same force of impact, though there are derivatives (Chanan and Gilchrist 1974) which have addressed themselves to some of the same themes of cultural discontinuities, mismatch between curriculum and its societal context, and what solutions there could be to effect a realignment.

One development that has gained some momentum post-Plowden is the concept of community schools, though the acknowledged pioneering ventures of Henry Morris with the Cambridgeshire Village Colleges pre-dated the Second World war. The community school 'attempts to relate fluently and productively with the ethos, character and values of the community it serves' (Midwinter p. 22). The school described in Chapter 3 Belfield in Rochdale, Lancashire, is one exponent of the approach whereby parents and other locally-dwelling adults are welcomed into the school by day or by evening, to engage in self-chosen pursuits with or without the schoolchildren. In turn, the community school adopts a central policy that it exists to serve the neighbourhood and locality. Well-known examples include the Sutton Centre School Nottinghamshire, the Sidney Stringer School in Coventry, Minsthorpe High School and Community College, Yorkshire and those in Walsall, West Midlands.

This necessarily brief reference to the concept of community schools must not obscure the very real issues to do with social divisiveness, elusiveness in pinning down what common interests and aspirations there are between disparate groups, and the sheer impossibility of schools, as a local focus, successfully being all things to all persons. The OECD/CERI report (CERI 1980) provides a wide-ranging review of policy and practice in this area in Europe and North America and addresses itself to a number of these ideological and political issues, in the form of posing eleven searching questions for discussion, and then proposing a 'model for coordination'.

One of the avowed goals of community schools has been to bring together children and their parents in a two-way allegedly beneficial process and there would be a variety of ways in which the postulated advantages could be examined. The most obvious are by attitude sampling and gauging changes or gains in attainment that could be attributed to these means of intervention (using the term broadly as defined at the beginning of this chapter). Less obvious ways would involve the adoption of and adherence to a strong and articulated theory and a taxonomy of objectives, so that over a period of several years, the validity of the venture could be assessed.

Similar measures would apply to the concept of Alternative Schools, or 'schools without "walls"', in that community institutions and agencies become the classroom settings where teaching takes place and/or people from the community become teachers of what skills and knowledge they have to offer' (CERI 1980, p. 28). They are 'alternative' to but exist within the regular school system.

In the case of Barrowfield School (Field 1977) parents were the impetus behind its creation and students at the school help to determine their own curriculum. The same volume edited by Field gives a brief description of the Danish Lille School system whereby any group can start a school and provided it meets certain criteria the government will contribute 80% of the costs. By the end of the 1970's there were about 40 Lille (little) schools in Denmark, each with between 50 and 150 pupils. Also described by Field (1977) is the White Lion Free School in Islington North London, at which meetings are open to children, parents and school workers, to plan expenditure, discuss curriculum content and policy issues. In 1982 the Free School became part of the 'off site' provision of the Inner London Education Authority.

Toronto Alternative School System

The Alternative Schools system in the City of Toronto, Ontario, Canada, has been well documented by Durno (1980). There are approximately 16 of these 'schools' in metropolitan Toronto, and since the scheme is well established, it is worth highlighting some of its features. The sources are Durno and the Toronto Alternative Schools Annual Report of 1979.

Definitions

Alternative School 'the students, teachers, catalysts and parents who are collectively, the school since teaching and learning very often happen in the community and not in one building. The schools range from 'free schools' where students organise their time to 'structured schools' where teachers and administrators devise the timetable'.
Catalyst resource person donating time, effort and skills to the facility.
Contract Learning individual learning, the evaluation of which is based on the fulfilment of a contract between student and teacher.
Experiential Learning 'learning by doing' in the community.

Alternative schooling in Toronto originated in the late 1960's and its philosophy is rooted in part, in the writings of educational theorists cited earlier (Illich, Goodman and others). The existence of these within the orbit of public education is summed up as 'public boards supportive of alternatives have come to realise they must serve a plurality of interests'. Durno discusses the pros and cons of the system in which parental participation is central. Parents are involved in curriculum planning, expenditure, and other educational decision-making processes. Although the purpose and function of the Toronto Alternative School system has changed since its inception (? a requisite feature of a viable system perhaps) it is a firmly-established part of the Toronto education scene, and appears to co-exist with regular school board provision.

The projects and systems described in this chapter, irrespective of model or rationale, are examples of *community education* in its widest sense (Midwinter 1972, Midwinter in Craft *et al.* 1980), that is, education intended to benefit children, parents and other adults – by promoting incentive to learn, and the fullest participation in learning activities and other self-developing, self-enhancing activities; and by putting some element of choice and decision-making into the hands of the people who consume the basic services in any one locality. It is complementary and part of the growth in latter years of civil rights movements (womens' liberation, homosexual liberation, social benefit claimants, race relations, self-help organisations) and as was shown in Chapter 4, there has been a determined move to ensure the granting of some, albeit limited, rights to parents within mainstream education.

Fundamental questions are raised in community education such as 'Who is a learner?', 'Does structured learning need to cease when children leave school or further/higher education?'. If learning (information and skill acquisition, self-discovery processes) *is* a corporate and continuing activity (Ireland 1981) then the integrative approach posed in a recent Bernard Van Leer Foundation report (1979) would constitute a viable model. In this, parents are not unquestioning client–recipients of services meted out, but fully participant partners on their own behalf and that of their children, during the transitory period of childhood and the longer-lasting span of adult citizenhood.

It would mean that parents have an acknowledged part to play in the development and education of children. Their contribution would not be a 'hit or miss'· affair, but one which explicitly takes account of what they can constructively do to promote their children's learning, competence and personal fulfilment, as well as maintain their own. These remarks could be translated from the realm of empty rhetoric into workable technologies of intervention. The hopeful outcomes of the small-scale projects tried out in a number of countries attest to this.

References

(† denotes projects referred to)

Anderson, S. (1978) 'Educational compensation and evaluation – a Critique', Chapter 8 in Stanley, J (ed.) *Compensatory Education for Children Ages 2–8*, Johns Hopkins London, W1: University Press.

† Bell, S. and Burn, C. (1976) *A Kind of Challenge, the Story of Liverpool Home-Link*, 54 Brittarge Brow, Liverpool 27.

Bereiter, C. and Engelmann, S. (1966) *Teaching Disadvantaged Children in the Pre-school*, Hemel Hempstend, Herts: Prentice Hall.

Bernard Van Leer Foundation (1976) *Parent Involvement in Early Childhood Education, Selected Titles*, Koninginnegracht 52, P.O. Box 85905, 2508 CP, The Hague, Holland.

Bernard Van Leer Foundation (1977) *Evaluation Studies on Early Childhood Education Programmes, Selected Titles*, as above.

Bernard Van Leer Foundation (1979) *Newsletter 26*, Spring, as above.

Bernard Van Leer Foundation (1979) *Parent and Community Involvement in Early Childhood Education*, as above.

Bernard Van Leer Foundation (1980) *Newsletter 30*, Winter, as above.

Bernard Van Leer Foundation (1981) *Integrated and Early Childhood Education: Preparation for Social Development*, Summary report, abstracted version, as above.

Blank, M. (1968) 'A tutorial language programme to develop abstract thinking in socially disadvantaged children', *Child Development*, 39, 379–89.

Brinson, P. (1977) 'Foundations and the urban crisis – a personal view', in Field, F (ed.) *Educational and the Urban Crisis*, London, WC1: Routledge and Kegan Paul.

Bronfenbrenner, U. (1976) 'Is early intervention effective? Facts, and principles of early intervention: a summary', Chapter 14 in Clarke, A.D.E., and Clarke, A. (eds) *Early Experience, Myth and Evidence*, Shepton Mallet, Somerset: Open Books.

Brown, G. Bhrolchain, M. and Harris, T. (1975) 'Social class and psychiatric disturbance among women in an urban population', *Sociology* 9, 225–54.

Bruner, J. (1971) *The Relevance of Education*, London, SW10: Penguin Education.

Butler, A. Gotts, E. and Quisenberry, N. (1975) *Early Childhood Programmes*, Wembley, Middx: Charles E. Merrill.

Caldwell, B. (1975) 'What is the optimal learning environment for the young child?', Chapter 11 in Sants, J and Butcher, H. J. (eds) *Developmental Psychology*, Harmondsworth, Middx: Penguin.

Cantrell, R. and Cantrell, M. (1980) 'Ecological problem-solving: a decision-making neuristic for prevention-intervention education strategies' in Hogg, J. and Mittler, P. (eds) *Advances in Mental Handicap Research Ud. I*. Chichester, Sussex: John Wiley & Sons.

CERI (1980) *School and Community*, Vol. II, CECD, Paris.

Chanan, G. and Gilchrist, L. (1974) *What School is for*, London, EC4: Methuen.

Day, B. (1980) 'Contemporary early child education programs', Chapter 2 in Range, D. and Layton, J. and Roubinek, D. (eds) *Aspects of Early Childhood Education: Theory to Research to Practice*, London, NW1: Academic Press.

D

Deutsch, M. (1965) 'The role of social class in language development and cognition', *Am. J. Orthopsychiatry*, 35.

†Donachy, W. (1979) 'Parent participation in pre-school education', Section III in Clark, M. M. and Cheyne, W. (eds) *Studies in pre-school education*, Sevenoaks, Kent: Hodder and Stoughton.

Dunn, L. and Smith, J. (1966) *Peabody Language Development Kit*, American Guidance Service.

Durno, E. (1980) *Public Alternative Schools in Metro Toronto*, Toronto: Learnxs Press.

Evans, R. (1979) 'Identification and Intervention', in Gains, C. and McNicholas, J. (eds) *Remedial Education: Guidelines for the Future*, Harlow, Essex: Longman and NARE.

†Family Service Units, 207 Old Marylebone Road, London, NW1 5QP.

Field, F. (1977) *Education and the Urban Crisis*, London, WC1: Routledge and Kegan Paul.

Goodman, P. (1971) *Compulsory Miseducation*, London SW10: Penguin Education Special.

Gordon, I. (1978) 'The Application of infant research; policy-making at the local level', in Scott, M. and Grimmett, S. (eds) *Current Issues in Child Development*, National Association for the Education of Young Children.

Gray, S. and Klaus, R. Miller, J., Forrester, B. (1967) *Before First Grade, the Early Training Project for Culturally Disadvantaged Children*, Teachers College Press.

Halsey A. H. (ed.) (1972) 'Educational Priority', *EPA Problems and Policies* Vol. 1, HMSO.

†Harrison, M. (1981) 'Home start', *Early Childhood*, Vol. I, No. 5, February.

Heber, R. *et al.* (1973) *Rehabilitation of Families at Risk for Mental Retardation*, Progress Report, University of Wisconsin.

Hobbs, N. (1978) 'Families, schools, and communities; an ecosystem for children', in *Teachers College Record*, Vol. 79, No. 4, May.

Hom, H. and Robinson, P. (eds) (1977) *Psychological Processes in Early Education*, London, NW1: Academic Press.

Hunt, J. McVicker (1969) *The Challenge of Incompetence and Poverty – Papers on the Role of Early Education*, University of Illinois Press.

Illich, I. (1973) *Deschooling Society*, Harmondsworth, Middx: Penguin Education Special.

Ireland, T. (1981) *Gelpi's View of Lifelong Education*, Vols. I and II, University of Manchester.

Kagan, J. (1979) *The Growth of the Child*, London, EC4: Methuen.

Karnes, M. (1973) 'Evaluation and Implications of Research with young handicapped and low-income children', in Stanley, J. C. (ed.) *Compensatory Education for Children Ages 2–8*, London, W1: Johns Hopkins University Press.

Kelsall, R. and Kelsall, H. (1971) *Social Disadvantage and Educational Opportunity*, Holt, Eastbourne, East Sussex: Rinehard and Winston.

†Knight, B. and Gibson, M. Grant, S. (1979) *Family groups in the community*, London Voluntary Service Council, 68 Chalton Street, London, NW1–1JR.

Lambie, D. (1976) *Parents and Educators: Experts and Equals*, High/Scope Report 1975–1976, High/Scope Educational Research Foundation, Ypsilanti, Michigan.

Lazar, I. (Ed) 1979) *Lasting Effects After the School*, Washington, US Printing Office.

Leichter, M. (1978) 'Families and communities as educators – some concepts of relationship', *Teachers College Record*, Vol. 79, No. 4, May pp. 567–658.

London Educational Review (1974) *Compensatory Education*, Vol. 3, No. 3 Autumn, University of London Institute of Education.

† London Voluntary Service Council (1980) *Special Services for Families*, London 1978–79, 68 Charlton St, London NW1 1JR.

Lovett, T. (1979) 'Community education in action', Chapter 6 in Bloomer, M. and Shaw, K. (eds) *The Challenge of Educational Change: Limitations and Potentialities*, Oxford: Pergamon Press.

McDill, E. McDill, M. Sprehe, J. (1969) *Strategies for Success in Compensatory Education: an Appraisal of Evaluation Research*, London, W1: Johns Hopkins Press.

Midwinter, E. (1972) *Priority Education*, Harmondsworth, Middx: Penguin Education Special.

Midwinter, E. (1980) 'Community education', Chapter 13 in Craft, M. Raynor, J. Cohen, L. (eds) *Linking Home and School*, 3rd edition, London, WC2: Harper and Row.

† Mixenden Home-Visiting Scheme, 47 Stanningley Road, Mixenden, Halifax, HX2 8BJ.

Open University (1975) *Deprivation and Disadvantage*, Milton Keynes: Open University Press.

Pauli, L. (1975) 'Disadvantage and compensatory education', Chapter 3 in *Developments in Early Childhood Education*, OECD/CERI.

Pilling, D. and Pringle, M. K. (1978) *Controversial Issues in Child Development*, St. Albans, Herts: Paul Elek.

Postman, N. and Weingartner, C. (1971) *Teaching as a Subversive Activity*, Harmondsworth, Middx: Penguin Education Special.

Poulton, G. (1980) 'The educational home visitor', Chapter 18 in Craft, M. Raynor, J. Cohen, L. (eds) *Linking Home and School*, 3rd edition, London, WC2: Harper and Row.

Poulton, G. and Jane, T. (1975) *Pre-school learning in the community*, London, WC1: Routledge and Kegan Paul.

† Poulton, L. and Poulton, G. (1979) 'Neighbourhood support for young families', *Early Child Development and Care*, Vol. 6, Nos 1/2.

Raggatt, P. (1979) 'Community and education', Chapter 5 in Bloomer, M. and Shaw, K. *The Challenge of Educational Change: Limitations and Potentialities*, Oxford, Pergammon Press.

Rainwater, L. (1973) in *Deprivation and Disadvantage* (p. 25), Milton Keynes: Open University Press.

Raven, J. (1980) *Parents, Teachers and Children*, Sevenoaks, Kent: Hodder and Stoughton.

Reimer, E. (1971) *School is Dead*, London, SW10: Penguin Education Special.

† Richardson, M. and Knight, B. (1981) 'Experimental Family Services', *Early Child Development and Care*, Vol. 7, No. 2, August.

Robinson, P. (1976) *Education and Poverty*, London EC4: Methuen.

Robinson, P. (1980) 'Research and the child: the family', Chapter 5 in Range, D. Layton, J. and Roubinek, D. (Eds) *Aspects of Early Childhood Education: Theory to Research to Practice*', London, NW1: Academic Press.

Rutter, M. and Madge, N. (1976) *Cycles of disadvantage*, London, WC1 : Heinemann.

Schweinhart, L. and Weikart, D. P. (1980/1981) *Young Children Grow Up : the Effects of the Perry Preschool Program on Youths through Age 15*, High/Scope. Monograph, London, WC1 : Grant McIntyre.

Shipman, V. (1977) 'Research findings as related to educational programming' in Scott, M. and Grimmett, S. (eds) *Current issues in Child Development*, National Association for the Education of Young Children.

Shipman, V. (1979) *Maintaining and Enhancing Early Intervention Gains*, Educational Testing Service, Princeton, New Jersey.

Stukàt, K. (1976) *Current Trends in European Pre-school Research*, NFER.

Tizard, J. Moss, P. and Perry, J. (1976) *All Our Children*, London, WC1 : Temple Smith.

Wedell, K. and Raybould, E. (eds) (1976) 'The early identification of educationally "at risk" children', *Educational Review*, Occasional Publications No. 6, University of Birmingham.

Weikart, D. (1976) *Alternative Assessment and National Follow-Through* in High/Scope Report 1975–76, High/Scope Educational Research Foundation.

Wells, G. (ed.) (1981) 'Learning through interaction', Vol. I of series, *Language at Home and at School*, Cambridge: Cambridge University Press.

Wolfendale, S. and Bryans, T. (1979) *Identification of Learning Difficulties – a Model for Intervention*, National Association for Remedial Education, 2 Lichfield Road, Stafford.

Wolfendale, S. (1981) 'Early identification and intervention', paper in *Proceedings of the Fourth International Symposium on Learning Problems*, June 1979, Ontario Institute for Studies in Education, Toronto, Canada.

Woodhead, M. (1972) *Pre-school Education in Western Europe : Issues, Policies and Trends*, for Council of Europe, Harlow, Essex: Longman.

CHAPTER 6

Parents in the Pre-School

So far in this report, particular age-groups of children have not been singled out in discussions on parental involvement. The bird's-eye view has been a sweep across some of the issues within mainstream education relevant to this study and an appraisal of recent work which has concentrated on *groups* of children, some of which have been typecast by a perceived problem or area of need, rather than by age. Chapter 7 will continue this pattern by dealing with children with acknowledged special educational needs or identifiable handicaps, across the age-range.

Much of this work has been aimed at pre-school children. It is because the age-range of children, up to six years, but especially three to five years, has received so much recent attention in Britain and elsewhere that it is felt justified to include a chapter which addresses itself to some of the issues in the pre-school area and which could have direct bearing on and relevance to the evolution of a policy for parental participation right through the school system and age-range.

Much pre-school investigatory and innovative work has had as central aspirations, long-term integrated child development, adjustment to school, learning effectiveness, social competence. So the demarcation between the pre- and post-five-year-olds is bound to be blurred, and has had significance only because our system at present provides minimal state and some voluntary provision for children below the age of five years on a part or full-time basis, then requires compulsory full-time schooling after that age.

The recommendations in the Court Report of 1976 and the Warnock Report of 1978 (see Chapter 7) which seem to apply to the pre-school sector are intended to have bearing too on later provision of services for parents and their children. Thus the issue of continuity is one which bridges the gap between pre-school and school.

Many of the pre-school projects – some of which are referred to in other chapters – constitute models of parent involvement and participation that might be applicable to older age-groups, describe ways in which parents, teachers and sometimes co-professionals collaborate, and present outcomes that could provide invaluable guidelines for replication and further experimentation. In the previous chapter some scrutiny was given to concepts of community and the juxtaposition of formal institutions like schools to and within the wider neighbourhood/locality network. A number of collaborative pre-school ventures demonstrate how the 'mix' of formal and informal provision can work productively and beneficially on a number of criteria. On the whole, accounts report these positive outcomes, even when practical difficulties and methodological stumbling-blocks are aired.

This chapter aims to be a selective foray into the pre-school arena, singling out the involvement of parents, particularly mothers, in their children's pre-school experience within various forms of provision. The specific involvement of parents in and contribution to children's early development overall is looked at in Chapter 9.

1. Pre-School Provision

The diversity of provision for children in Britain below the statutory school starting age of five years is amazing, by comparison with the pre-Second World War dearth of such educational or play facilities for young children. On the face of it, it seems that opportunities for young children's access to some form of adult-planned, structured pre-school experience have increased dramatically.

Several books and reports chronicle the array of pre-school facilities (Parry and Archer 1974, Advisory Centre for Education 1976, Tizard, Moss and Perry 1976, Department of Health and Social Security/Department of Education and Science (DHSS/DES) 1975, Trades Union Congress working party 1977, Eyken 1977, Hughes *et al.* 1980). These include private and state-run nursery schools, nursery classes attached to infant schools, opportunity groups for handicapped children, nurseries in the workplace, childminding, community nurseries, combined nursery centres, family day centres, mother and toddler groups, and crèches.

Two recent surveys give the percentages for attendance in various forms of pre-school provision at two or three periods between one and five years of age. The proportion of children receiving some form of day care is at its highest between the ages of four and five years. The percentage in both surveys is around 70–72% in the samples studied (Bone in D.H.S.S./D.E.S. 1976, Butler in Voluntary Organisations Liaison Council for Under Fives (1977). Both surveys reveal that the most commonly used form of day care within the private sector is the playgroup, and within the public sector, educational nurseries (school and classes). The figures given by Butler pertain to the ongoing Child Health and Education Study based at Bristol University. More recent statistics from this survey are given by Osborn (1981) who concludes 'there was a steady though small, annual growth of nursery school and nursery class places throughout the decade' (of the 1970's) and 'the declining birthrate has done more to increase the *proportion* of 3–4 year-olds in maintained schools than either expansion in provision or increased part-time attendance' (p. 102).

Issues such as regional disparity of provision, parents' preferences for day care as against what is actually provided in their localities, are discussed in some of the texts and reports referred to above (and Osborn 1979). Other matters of especial concern have been the suitability and relevance of nursery curricula (Tizard 1974) aims, roles and practice in nursery education (Clift *et al.* 1980, Wood *et al.* 1980, Garland and White 1980), actual and desired curriculum objectives in pre-school activities (Sylva *et al.* 1980).

One kind of provision in particular – childminding – continues to be of academic and social concern (Mayall and Petrie 1977, Bryant *et al.* 1980, Newton 1981). The fact that working mothers in particular make use of this provision (Raven and Robb 1981) reflects on the unsatisfactory, piece-meal nature of pre-school provision in Britain today, and directs our attention on the agreed unsatisfactory nature of childminding as it is practised at present, as a 'solution' to the care, welfare and education of thousands of toddlers and pre-schoolers. It has been recommended (Jackson in DHSS/DES 1976, Coulter 1981, Edridge 1981) that the status, pay and standards of training should be raised, but the problems within this sphere of pre-school are likely to be exacerbated in a time of economic recession, as public services like nurseries and crèches are axed.

2. Innovation – a Recapitulation

Despite (or, in fact, because of) the inadequacy of pre-school provision in Britain, the lack of state investment in a pre-school policy, the absence of a coordinated through-system (pre-and post-five) for care and education, there have been a considerable number of research studies and innovative enterprises which have focussed in the pre-school years and which have involved parents. The rationale on which these have been based has been described in previous chapters. The main examples fall into several categories, and a brief reminder to the reader is given, with the chapter in which the pre-school project is described given in brackets:

Parents into school (group activities, participating in programmes) Donachy (3), Froebel (3), Rathbone (3), Wandsworth (3)

School to home (home liaison, educational home visitor) Sandwell (3), Coventry (3), Cleveland (3) Newham (3)

Community focus (mothers' self-help groups, classes, mothers and children's groups, home-link) Family Service Units (5), Leicester Home-Start (5), Liverpool Home–Link (5), Mixenden Home–Link (5), London Voluntary Service Council (5), SCOPE (5).

General or more extensive accounts of EPA and Urban Aid projects which explicitly focussed on young children and their parents are contained in books which have already been referred to – Bell, Halsey, Poulton and James, Craft *et al.*, – also Smith (ed. 1975), and Armstrong and Brown (1979).

It was emphasised in previous chapters that outcome evaluation differed from project to project and at present it is not possible to make generalisations. These remarks are not intended to be critical of the innovators for failing on any count; rather they reflect an unavoidable phenomenon within scientific endeavours, and certainly those in the behavioural sciences, namely the time-lags between theory formulation, hypothesis development, hypothesis testing and take-up.

In this area of recent pre-school initiatives, one current piece of research is a timely arrival on the scene. It is the Pre-School Evaluation project based at Bristol University, funded by the Social Science Research Council, and directed by Sonia Jackson. Aiming to report during 1981 or 1982, its brief was to:

— prepare a feasibility study of innovation and good practice in the pre-school field;

— to categorise the schemes into pre-school education and play provision for three to five year-olds; day care; support schemes for mothers and families with very young children (up to three years); projects designed to involve parents in their children's learning;

— to identify these as breaking new ground or providing examples of especially good practice;

— to select ten schemes from the seventy up and down the country to be case studies for close evaluation.

The research style chosen was illuminative. Jackson (1978) draws a parallel between earlier US intervention studies and these British projects in terms of their rationales and aspirations for manifest short or longer term gains by children and their parents. She and her team perceived differences between the US and British work regarding organisation, focus and content. Indeed Jackson, in her initial report of 1978, drew attention to the dearth of curriculum-focussed initiatives that, in many US studies, were their *raison d'être*, that is, the main vehicle by which cognitive/affective development were to be achieved. It may be worth noting at this juncture that Parry and Archer in their Schools Council-sponsored review of pre-school education in Britain (1974) described several US curriculum in-tervention models, and Wolfendale and Bryans (1979) consider the lack of take-up in this country, concluding

there is an evident need for similar examination of nursery school curricular practices in this country and ... how these dovetail into the overall aims and objectives of the education system (p. 258).

Some of the US models exemplified in practice the tie-up between cognitive development and parental involvement or participation.

3. Other Forms of Innovation

In this section several ventures will be briefly described that are characterised by these two features:

1) they constitute 'new' pre-school provision for children and their families, i.e., they do not take place established settings;

2) their perpetrators are clear that the specific function is to offer a particular type of service to families in the community.

Thus these projects or service provisions are in contra-distinction to several pieces of action-research, which will be mentioned later in this chapter and that took place in well-established pre-school centres although the central aims are common to them all – to involve parents in the early development and learning of their children.

3.1. *Under Five Info-Phone* (Eyken 1980)

The aim of the Islington (North London) pre-school Info-Phone, started in 1978, was to provide a direct link between families, to acquaint parents with local community provision, to offer support, and 'to play a role in coordinating services and thus facilitating a greater multi-disciplinary approach to child care' (p. 160).

This experimental scheme formed part of a pre-school expansion programme in the borough. Three staff supervisors, appointed under specific terms of reference, worked three shifts of five hours each (9–2 pm; 1–6 pm; 5.0–10.0 pm). The pattern, frequency and nature of calls was closely monitored over a period of several months. Eyken's account gives a detailed breakdown of all the factors, and while it is described as 'initial evaluation' the scheme was clearly regarded locally as a beneficial, maybe vital part of pre-school and community services to young parents. It could be regarded as an alternative or complementary resource to the family support systems described in Chapter 5.

3.2. *Gloucestershire Family Centres* (Bullough 1980)

These evolved from the fact that nursery units (schools and classes) has been planned for Gloucestershire but expansion was halted due to financial constraints. However, the premises had already been built and local teachers needed to be redeployed so Family Centres were conceived, initially modelled on the playgroup idea with 'its essential parental involvement' and based on the three already designated nursery sites.

Each of the three centres serves different functions, according to its community setting and perceived areas of need. Each has a teacher in charge (Coordinator of Activities) who also has a brief for home/pre-school links. Among activities offered at the Centres that service children, mothers and fathers are supervised playgroups, discussion sessions, relief/emergency groups for mothers under stress or in crisis, antenatal and mothercraft classes, contact with statutory agencies, crafts, a drop-in centre for childminders. The Local Education Authority pays the salaries of the teachers in charge and the heating, lighting and cleaning bills. Each centre is self-supporting in other respects, so fund-raising forms a part of the activities.

3.3. Community Nurseries   (Eyken 1979, Hughes *et al.* 1980)

Rather than directing attention to any particular nursery that falls into the category of 'community nursery' this segment of this section on innovation will describe features in general, some of which can be applied to the Gloucestershire Family Centres described above. The terminology denotes the usage and function – in Australia such places are called 'neighbourhood centres'. In England, as Eyken points out (p. 72), some community nurseries do have this wider neighbourhood oriented mandate, whereas others, while involving parents by definition, concentrate on the child care provision itself.

Both Eyken and Hughes *et al.*, in surveying the scene, confirm that there are few community nurseries in England, with most of them based in London. Decisions about running the nursery are taken jointly by staff and parents, though representatives from the locality and agencies may sit on committees. All staff work as educators and care-givers in trying to meet children's needs as they arise.

The idea of community nurseries in Britain is at such an early stage of development that there are many unexplored and unresolved issues to do with ideals and ideologies, management, the rightful limits of parental responsibility, and curriculum balance. As Eyken and Hughes *et al.* make clear, the impetus for community nurseries has been not only parents' and professionals' dissatisfaction with in-adequate pre-school, day care facilities (and perhaps particularly for working mothers) but an expressed collective preference for parents to be actively involved where possible in much of their children's daily pre-school experience.

3.4. The Nova Scotia Experience in Day Care (See Wolfendale 1979)

Until recently the private pre-school day care centres in the province of Nova Scotia, Canada were run mostly by mothers who had not received any particular training in preschool or nursery work.

Ruth Bakewell and Jane Norman, from the Teachers' College, Truro, Nova Scotia, have instituted a comprehensive training course for pre-school Day Care Centre staff, who can be slotted into the course at a point commensurate with their own educational background and level of awareness and current expertise. Receiving in-service training in their own localities and at periodic study sessions held at the Teachers' College, these pre-school personnel work through highly detailed, carefully worked out sequences of instruction and learning, based on the notion of competencies – that is, they gradually attain a broad-based, theoretical and practical set of skills to apply to their work with pre-school children. Area leaders, who have themselves worked through the training schedules, act as tutors and course co-ordinators. The training is acknowledged at the end by certification. The course content and structure emphasise the interrelatedness of developmental processes and early learning, and draws attention to developmental delays, problem areas.

The scheme is attracting the attention of the Canadian Federal Government and it is being backed by provincial and federal funds. The system is called Child Development Services, and Bakewell and Norman are directors. They have extended their scheme to provide at the Teachers' College a two-year full-time training course for students intending to work with pre-school children.

The visit by the author and her colleague, Trevor Bryans, to Nova Scotia during 1979, and discussions held with the directors and personnel, led to the observation that the growing skills of the day care staff enhanced in tandem their professional role and their contribution to their own children's development and learning. As with the community nursery ideal, the distinction between care and education are abolished – a child's primary and secondary needs (Pringle 1975) are conceived of as inter-connecting.

3.5. Combined Nursery Centres (Hughes *et al.* 1980, Makins 1980, Ferri *et al.* 1981)

These combine day nurseries (run since 1970 by social services) and educational nurseries within one centre, so that, as with community

nurseries and the Nova Scotia concept, the care/education demarcation is blurred. The pioneer combined centre is usually
acknowledged to be Hillfield in Coventry (ACE 1976); others which
followed suit are in Salford, Nottinghamshire, and London. There
are now at least thirty.

Makins and Hughes *et al.* contend that as long as there are two
separate employers, differing staff training, salary structure and
conditions of working, then the ideal of meeting children's and
parents' needs by offering high-quality physical care, welfare facilities
and an early childhood educational programme under one roof
cannot be achieved.

The controversy persists. An evaluative study of four combined
nursery centres, published during 1981 (Ferri *et al.*) highlights some of
the difficulties but in a 'trailer' to the book Ferri (1981) remarks

an important conclusion of the research was that the problems encountered in the setting up
and running of combined centres were not inherent in the concept of joint provision but in the
anomalies and discrepancies created by the separate development of day care and nursery
education provision (p. 8).

One observation germane to this study is that 'there was no
characteristic approach to parental involvement in the combined
centres which would distinguish them from other types of nursery'
(p. 8). One or two Institutes of Higher Education have just begun to
offer diploma-level courses for personnel in the pre-school field which
take an interdisciplinary, integrated approach.

3.6. The Lothian Region (Scotland) Educational Home Visiting Scheme
(Raven 1980)

Each of six Home Visitors visited about ten families per week. Five
visitors were trained teachers. Their brief was to work with two to
three year-old children in their home and in their parents' presence
for about an hour a week. The objective of the weekly visits was to
encourage mothers to play a more active role in promoting the
educational development of their children. Two experimental years
were allotted to the project and recording and evaluation were in-
built.

The account given by Raven is factual but also speculative
regarding the probable effects on the children in the sample. In
keeping with the illuminative research approach, Raven's conjec-

tures are illuminating, because he fits them to reported experience from the American Head Start programmes, and as we now know (see Chapter 5) enough time has elapsed to assess retrospectively and contemporaneously, the longer-term outcomes.

The value of Raven's report is that he takes a very broad sweep indeed. Such a prospective view is justified on the grounds that all such intervention is intended to be pervasive in its effects. His endorsement of the theory-into-practice principles of educational home-visiting are evident in that he suggests further areas for action research arising from the Lothian study.

4. Action Research Within Existing Provision

The three examples in this section are given because in an area characterised by a dearth of focussed action research, each is a unique contribution to the body of knowledge about parents' involvement or participation in their children's experience within established pre-school settings.

4.1. Parental Involvement in Pre-School Centres (Laishley and Lindon 1980)

A course for day nursery staff to develop skills in helping parents with personal or family problems was run by the authors. They distinguish six identifiable approaches to parental involvement (see later in this chapter), one of which is the receipt by parents of help and support offered by sensitive, skilled staff. To this end, the course drew upon the work of notable theorists in the fields of counselling and therapy, the approach being to view the progress of a helping relationship in terms of three stages.

The authors feel that any parental involvement programme should be accompanied by commensurate staff training in therapeutic and social skills, and conclude

the indications are that developments in other areas of parental involvement need equal attention to planning, some agreement on objectives and some specific training (p. 19).

4.2. Parents and Pre-School   (Smith 1980)

This account is of a detailed enquiry using observation and interview techniques, into the extent and type of parental involvement and participation in various pre-school settings, exploring attitudes of staff and parents, and delineating areas for further development. The study formed part of the Oxford Pre-school Research Project, directed by Jerome Bruner, and is number six in a series of six concurrently published books, all of which have emanated from that project.

The first 'trawling exercise' (p. 52) of the research team was to consult with headteachers and supervisors in about 100 nursery classes, schools, playgroups, private nursery schools, day nurseries and crèches throughout Oxfordshire. This elicited certain preliminary information regarding parental involvement – that there was a substantial amount of practical help given by mothers; that involvement is not defined or viewed uniformly by all pre-school personnel; that pre-school centres differed in their reasons for involving parents.

As a result of this first exercise, Smith and her colleagues formulated the design for the subsequent stages, namely to explore in greater depth the extent and type of parental involvement in fifteen selected settings; to make observations; to interview staff and then parents. They were concerned, above all, to examine *process* in styles and type of parental involvement rather than to address themselves to outcomes, for they feel that many studies (Headstart, EPA, etc.) have dealt more with the effects of pre-school intervention, and have paid less attention to the experience as it was taking place.

The Oxfordshire study brought to light the fact that there are indeed various types of parental involvement, and that staff views and expectations varied widely from seeing parents as clearers-away, an extra pair of hands (the majority view) to participant agents in their children's learning experiences. Involvement in management featured far less than the parental activity which has now come to be accepted in nursery and infant schools, that is engaging in teacher-directed classroom chores, including hearing children read.

While acknowledging the difficulties in the way of implementing a policy with a radically different ideological slant, Smith unequivocally calls for a 'more participative approach', in which everyone concerned should 'experiment far more boldly' with the possible ways of effecting that partnership.

4.3. Involving Parents in Nursery and Infant School (Tizard, Mortimore, Burchell 1981).

While being in the same broad topic area as the Oxfordshire study described by Smith, this was an intervention project. It was designed to effect some change, and to measure those effects, in part by an analysis of the planned antecedent events, mainly via the exploration of teachers' and parents' views at the outset, during and one year after the project team had withdrawn.

It took place in seven pre-school nursery settings (classes, schools, and one nursery class in a primary school) in and around London, and represented a range of socio-economic and ethnic backgrounds. For two years the research team helped the schools to develop and carry through parent-involvement programmes.

Again, as with the Smith enquiry, it is confirmed that staff and parents do not have one-dimensional, simplistic views on the value of parents being directly involved at several levels in nursery experience. The sheer variety of views (even if there are trends, as is apparent in the Smith study) could be said to be an encouraging basis for the further development of participant activities, that is, no aspect of actual or potential involvement is represented by an unshakeable concensus of opinion.

The research team developed, with the teachers of the classes, parent-involvement programmes which included the provision of additional resources, mostly in the way of equipment. The book by the team (Tizard et al., 1981) describes the components of the programmes, and documents those elements that met with 'success' (as deemed by staff and/or parents), and those that appeared to falter, fade away, have little impact or take-up. A brief description cannot do justice to the minute detail presented which relies on being interpreted within its individual context.

The study highlights the areas of difference in perception, values, aims between staff and parents; also the areas of parental involvement which were thought to be effective and worthwile, and which persisted over the whole period of three years. Mention is also made of the activities which were rated as unpopular and were dropped.

Tizard *et al.* pay attention to some of the underlying difficulties and areas needing conceptual clarification, such as the distinction between cooperation and involvement, lack of appropriate resources, lack of knowledge as to effective procedures by which to achieve closer home–school links, communication difficulties between staff and parents with differing ethnic, social and educational backgrounds.

Notwithstanding the conceptual, ideological and practical obstacles, the research team came up with positive suggestions for closer collaboration with postulated two or three-way benefits (child, parents and teachers) in the form of policy recommendations, which are elaborated in Part II of the book. The envisaged programme incorporates home contact initiated by the school before the child enters, various forms of communication and ways of working with parents. Many nursery and infant schools have already instigated a good many of these approaches. The contribution of Tizard *et al.*, however, is to assemble all the actual and possible elements into a parent involvement programme with clearly set out aims for each activity, and a checklist of types of evaluation.

5. Coordination and Cooperation in Pre-School Services

Evidence exists, from a survey of current pre-school provision in Britain, from current figures for attendance at various age-groups (Woodhead 1981) and from the number of reported innovative projects that parental involvement varies tremendously, in extent and type. The fullest example of maternal participation in the organisation and daily minutiae of children's early play and learning experiences in groups is of course the playgroup movement, started in the 1960s in Britain as a determinedly constructive attempt to provide voluntarily, for mothers of pre-school children, adequate nursery services the state was patently failing to offer.

A discussion on the potential for increased collaboration within formal provision has to take into account current thinking on the universality of pre-school opportunities and tie-up among providing institutions. The authors describing the current availability of pre-school resources who were referred to at the beginning of this chapter all remark on the ad hoc, piecemeal nature and deplore the absence of a policy coordinated by and common to the major services–education, health and social services.

For example, Wolfendale and Bryans (1979 p. 256) examined the recommendations of the Court Report, incorporated the later recommendations of the Warnock Report, both of which endorse the idea of pre-school multidisciplinary assessment, and interdisciplinary service coordination for treatment and placement of children with special needs, and suggest an encompassing approach which would include:

— parents, the community and provisions of the social services;
— expansion of pre-school educational provision and home-school links;
— methods of educational health identification, and surveillance for early-appearing handicaps and developmental/learning difficulties.

In this model, the variety of forms of parental involvement is fully compatible with the statutory provision of services. Tizard *et al.* (1976) outline guidelines which could be used as the foundations of a nursery service, and again, within this envisaged structure, parent participation is an integral component.

In these and other models for a nursery service parents are viewed as one contributory element in a blueprint of services to come, as well as – bringing the debate back to reality – in the fragmented services we have now.

Recently, there have been calls for personnel to get together to work productively on behalf of linking services. Community nurseries and combined centres exemplify the trend (also Watt 1977, Chazan 1979). The DES and DHSS urged local authorities and area health authorities to find ways of coordinating practice (Circular Letters March 1976, January 1978) and there are certainly examples now, at local level, of endeavours to do just that, together with the many enterprises described by the author throughout this report involving pre-school children and their parents. Moon and Reid (1979) in a discussion on the DHSS/DES initiatives, reinforce their support for coordination and cooperation by reference to the needs of ethnic minority parents and underfive children. 'Home-school bridging schemes and methods of easing the child's entry to nursery need especially sensitive interpretation for many children whose origins lie overseas (p. 58). Dicks (1981), too, puts in a powerful plea for coordination and cooperation, particularly as she foresees that 'If basic expectations for underfives are to be maintained while the shift to family concerns develops, we shall need all the means at our disposal' (p. 19).

The Centre for Information and Advice on Educational Disadvantage (CED) had collected over a period of time examples of cooperative practice in the pre-school and school-based spheres (see journals of the CED) and one of its last acts before its demise during 1980 was to publish an Under Fives Directory, listing many organisations and associations concerned with underfives (CED 1980). A considerable number of these are voluntary bodies, and the Children's Committee (1981) while deploring the piecemeal nature of pre-school services, acknowledges that services for families have to be coordinated offerings from statutory and voluntary agencies. Within such a policy of planned cooperation, parents are 'recognised to be central people in the life of the child and treated as such' (Children's Committee, 1981, p. 15) and requisites are spelled out in the Committee's report on the needs of the underfives in the family for the effective translation of a 'parents as partners' policy into practice across the board – health, education, social services, voluntary sector. Some of this thinking is amplified in Pringle (ed. 1980).

6. Parents in Pre-School Settings

There is overwhelming evidence that measures that do not involve parents achieve only short-term gains (Court Report 1976).

In fact, the evidence to back up this assertion is still growing – many of the projects described in this and other chapters are all contributing to the accumulating body of knowledge concerning actual and desired forms of parental participation, the attitudes and values brought to the enterprise by teachers, pre-school workers and parents, as well as, in some instances, information about rates of short and longer term change, benefits, and so on.

There is certainly no disagreement with the contention that parents' involvement in the development and education of their young children is positive. But in this country professionals and academics are still groping towards typologies, descriptive frameworks, classification systems.

Smith (1980) and her team invoke Gordon's five-point scale of parental involvement:

— parents as supporters;
— parents as learners;
— parents as teachers of their children;
— parents as teacher aides and classroom volunteers;
— parents as policymakers and partners.

She offers five categories of parental involvement in pre-school groups:

1) working with the children on education activities;

2) working in the groups doing chores;

3) servicing the group – making and mending;

4) ongoing contact and surveillance (author's summary words for Smith's description);

5) involvement in management.

Laishley and Lindon (1980) distinguish six identifiable approaches to parental involvement or participation, which are:

1) parents as organisers or fund raisers;

2) parents on management committes;

3) parents as helpers;

4) social contact for parents;

5) information and knowledge for parents;

6) offering help to parents with their problems.

These categorisations can be compared and contrasted with Osborn's listing (1979) of types of maternal help in nursery classes and playgroups of the Child Health and Educational Study (CHES) sample. These were:

— working with staff and directly involved with children (by far the most popular from of involvement);
— on management/advisory committees;
— general administrative and routine activities;

— working parties/groups set up for specific purpose, *viz*, fund raising;
— helping at special occasions, *viz* 'one-off' involvement (least prevalent activity).

Tizard *et al.* (1981) on the basis of their exercises (see earlier in this chapter) detail types of parental involvement as well as the range of collaborative activities, that are possible.

From all this information a full specification of a pre-school parent-participation policy becomes possible, even within the existing framework. The growing emphasis is on parents being partners rather than clients and the difficulties that writers have frankly addressed themselves to (Tizard *et al.* as one example) are not seen as deterrents in the pursuance of community services for all pre-school children and their families (Woodhead 1981), irrespective of alleged category of need (Moon and Reid 1979, Chazan 1979).

At the beginning of this chapter it was posed that it might be possible to apply the models or some of the constituents within models of pre-school parental involvement to a home–school policy across other age-ranges. It is the author's contention, that recent developments in pre-school and particularly those which have been described in this chapter, would have some relevance to primary and even secondary schools. The typologies and classification systems could be tested empirically for 'goodness of fit' in schools, and if parents could have the opportunity to be involved rather more intimately with the educational process, advocates as well as opponents (or doubters) of a parent-participation policy would be in a stronger position to argue their case.

References

(† denotes project or study referred to in the chapter)

ACE (1976) *The Best of Where on Preschooling*, 18 Victoria Park Square, E2.
Armstrong, G. and Brown, F. (1979) *Five Years On: a follow up study of the long-term effects on parents and children of an early learning programme in the home*, Social Evaluation Unit, Dept. of Social and Administrative Studies, University of Oxford.
Bryant, B. Harris, M. and Newton, D. (1980) *Children and Minders*, London, WC1: Grant McIntyre.
Bullough, A. (1980) 'Family Centres', *Early Childhood*, Vol. I, No. 2, November CED. (1980) *Under Fives Directory*, DES for further information.

Chazan, M. (1979) 'Towards a comprehensive strategy for disadvantaged pre-school children', *Early Child Development and Care*, Vol. 6, No. 5 1/2.

Children's Committee (1980) *The Needs of the Underfives in the Family*, Mary Ward House, 5–7 Tavistock Place, London, WC1H 9SS.

Clift, P. Cleave, S. Griffin, M. (1980) *The Aims, Role and Deployment of Staff in the Nursery*, NFER.

Coulter, A. (1981) *Who Minds About the Minders?*, Low Pay Unit, 9 Poland St. London W1.

Court, D. (Chairperson) (1976) *Fit for the Future?* Norwich: HMSO.

DHSS/DES (1976) *Low Cost Day Provision for the Underfives*, conference paper, Norwich HMSO.

DHSS/DES (1976 + 1978) *Coordination of Local Authority Services* for Children Under 5, Circular Letters 1) March 1976 2) January 1978, Norwich: HMSO.

Dicks, E. (1980) 'What has been happening to our underfives?', *Early Childhood*, Issue No. 1, October.

Edridge, S (1981) Editorial, *Early Childhood*, Vol. 1, No. 9, June.

Eyken, W. van der (1977) *The Preschool Years*, 4th edition, London, SW1: Penguin.

Eyken, W. van der (1979) 'Community nurseries', *Early Child Development and Care*, Vol. 6, Nos 1/2.

† Eyken, W. van der (1980) 'Under fives Info-Phone', *Early Child Development and Care*, Vol. 6, Nos 3/4.

Ferri, E. (1981) *Combined Nursery Centres*, description of research in Handbook published by the under fives Research Dissemination Group, April, DES.

Ferri, E. Birchall, D. Gingell, V. and Gipps, C. (1981) *Combined Nursery Centres*, London, WC2: Macmillan.

Garland, C. and White, S. (1980) *Children and Day Nurseries*, London, WC1: Grant McIntyre.

Hughes, M. Mayall, B. Moss, P., Perry, J. Petrie, P. Pinkerton, G. (1980) *Nurseries Now, a Fair Deal for Parents and Children*, London, SW10: Penguin.

Jackson, S. (1978) *Pre-School Evaluation Project*, SSRC/School of Applied Social Studies, University of Bristol.

† Laishley, J. and Lindon, L. (1980) 'Schemes of parental involvement in pre-school centres', *Early Childhood*, Vol. 1, No. 2., November.

Makins, V. (1980) 'Can the centres hold?', *Times Educational Supplement*, 3rd October, p. 16.

Mayall, B. and Petrie, P. (1977) *Minders, Mother and Child*, University of London Institute of Education.

Moon, J. and Reid, D. (1979) 'Some considerations in social policy for the underfives in a multi-racial Britain', *Early Child Development and Care*, Vol. 6, Nos. 1/2.

Newton, D. (1981) 'Childminding from the outside: what is it really like', *Early Childhood*, Vol. no. 9, June.

Osborn, A. (1979) 'Sources of variation in uptake of preschool provision', *Child Health and Education Study*, Department of Child Health, University of Bristol, un-published paper, to form part of the CHES report (forthcoming).

Osborn, A. (1981) 'Underfives in England and Wales', *Educational Research* Vol. 23, No. 2, February.

Parry, M. and Archer, H. (1974) *Preschool Education*, London, WC2: Macmillan.

Pringle, M. K. (1975) *The Needs of Children*, London, W1: Hutchinson.

Pringle, M. K. (ed.) (1980) *A Fairer Future for Children*, London, WC2: Macmillan.

† Raven, J. (1980) *Parents, Teachers and Children*, Sevenoaks, Kent: Hodder and Stoughton.

Raven, M. and Robb, B. (1981) On childminders, *Early Childhood*, Vol. 1, No. 6, March.

Smith, G (ed.) (1975) *Educational Priority; Vol. 4, The West Riding EPA*, HMSO.

† Smith, T. (1980) *Parents and Preschool*, London, WC1: Grant McIntyre.

Sylva, K. Roy, C. Painter, M. (1980) *Childwatching at Playgroup and Nursery School*, London, WC1: Grant McIntyre.

Tizard, B. (1974) *Early Childhood Education, a review* N.F.E.R. London, WC1: Grant McIntyre.

† Tizard, B. Mortimore, J. and Burchell, B. (1981) 'Involving parents in nursery and infant schools', Grant McIntyre.

Tizard, J. Moss, P. Perry, J. (1976) *All Our Children*, Temple Smith/New Society.

TUC (1977) *The Underfives*, working party report, Trades Union Congress.

VOLCUF (1977) *0–5: a Changing Population*, Voluntary organisations liaison council for underfives.

Watt, J. (1977) *Cooperation in Preschool Education*, SSRC.

† Wolfendale, S. (1979) 'Visit to Nova Scotia – Child Development Services project', in *OMEP Newsletter* (World Organisation for Early Childhood Education).

Wolfendale, S. and Bryans, T. (1979) *Identification of Learning Difficulties – a Model for Intervention*, N.A.R.E. (National Association for Remedial Education) 2 Lichfield Rd, Stafford.

Wood, D. McMahon, L. and Cranstoun, Y. (1980) *Working with Underfives*, London WC1: Grant McIntyre.

Woodhead, M. (1981) 'Cooperation in early education – what does it mean? Why does it matter?', *Early Childhood Development at Care*, August.

CHAPTER 7

Special Educational Needs and the Place of Parents

The concern of this chapter will be to define the concept of children's special needs and to appraise these within educational contexts. Identified areas of need and concern will be linked with the scope and boundaries of parental involvement with assessment, intervention and educational programming.

This book takes the developmental and learning needs of *all* children as its proper context. Acknowledging first that each child is special, and is certainly so in the eyes of his/her parents and caretakers, attention can then turn to those children and those groups of children whose problems, and hence needs, may be enduring, severe, mild or transient.

In espousing a policy for parental involvement and participation in the development and education of children, it has to be emphasised that this must be universally applicable. The particular needs of some children and the part that their parents can play in reducing or coping with their problems can then be appraised within this framework. The provision of special education or special educational treatment, whether in normal or special schools and classes, in terms of parental cooperation and direct participation, is therefore compatible with mainstream provision, because the same philosophy is shared and embraced throughout.

From time immemorial, humans have sorted, grouped and categorised. Minorities in any society along any dimension of social and intellectual behaviour and appearance are always vulnerable to discriminative, dismissive, perjorative labelling (Thomas 1978) and continue to be at risk in educational and social settings when their deviancy on any conventionally accepted set of norms is visible, apparent and long-lasting. They are at the mercy of unpredictable responses from the rest of the community, and what is acceptable/rejectable handicap varies at different periods of any society's history (Shearer 1981).

Inadvertently, perhaps, traditions within British special education over the last hundred years or so have aggravated and perpetuated a divisive approach (normal versus abnormal, deviant, etc.) by the creation and maintenance of separate institutions – mainstream education, and separate special education for children with a range of handicaps.

The effects of labelling are now acknowledged to be rather more negatively and pervasively stigmatising than they are a positive aid in educational planning by teachers who deal with handicapping conditions and problem behaviour (Pilling 1973, Cave and Maddison 1978, Wolfendale 1980).

1. Needs and Special Needs

The Warnock Report (1978) was established to 'review educational provision for children and young people handicapped by disabilities of body or mind ... and to make recommendations'. It considered that the continued existence and use of the eleven statutory categories of handicap† could not be justified on humanitarian, social or educational grounds.

The Report outlines its philosophy and its reasons for proposing a new system and a broader view of special educational provision. Warnock's continuum of special educational need has had, even in the short time since the publication of the report, a profound effect on educational thinking.

Basically what was proposed was a reconceptualisation of existing problem areas and handicapping conditions which was designed to:

— avoid the ill effects of labelling;
— enable teachers and educationalists to adopt flexible approaches within schools, acknowledging the impermanence of some problems, developmental delays;

---

†The Handicapped Pupils and School Health Services Regulations 1945 defined eleven categories of pupils: blind, partially sighted, deaf, partially deaf, delicate, diabetic, educationally subnormal, epileptic, maladjusted, physically handicapped, with speech defects.

— abolish the rigid demarcation between special (separatist) and mainstream education;
— ensure that a child's *overall* educational, social, personal needs could be met, via a reorganisation of the assessment procedures and provision.

What special educational needs was to mean in practice was outlined by the Warnock Committee. At this point it may be relevant to examine the concept of *needs*.

Kellmer Pringle (1975) spelled out the primary needs of all humans for food, water, heat, shelter and secondary needs which are as crucial to human survival and which can be listed as: the need for love and security; the need for new experiences; the need for praise and recognition; the need for responsibility (Ch. 2).

The equation can be made that if certain of these needs are not met, the likelihood of problems in personal/cognitive/social behaviours is increased, in children and in adults. Wolfendale and Bryans (1979) in re-assessing the viability of the concept of needs and the consequences of unmet needs, propose the need for interest and affection, the need for continuing stimulation, the need for endorsement of self, the need for training in empathy and compassion, as being equally valid dimensions. These authors take a broad developmental spectrum and attempt to assess some of the basic early requisites or preconditions for later development in areas of language and communication, social and cognitive behaviour.

Needs are both universal and culture-specific. Two examples from other countries demonstrate how the needs of children can be conceptualised and classified within cultural frameworks. An enquiry into the needs of the child was undertaken in Japan as a contribution to the International Year of the Child in 1979. This was a pragmatic attempt to chronicle in minute detail a child's day, his/her routines and activities, family interactions and so on, and thereby to effect a match between perceived need and the likelihood of it being met (International Federation for Parent Education, IFPE). In Finland, the Mannerheim League for Child Welfare has produced a chart which sets out a child's basic needs (security, attachment, respect); how adults can respond appropriately to the child; what educational aims will effect the need-meeting; what general and specific skills and competences the child is being assisted to work towards (source, IFPE).

While there is always the inherent danger of oversimplification in classification systems, the merit of charting children's needs, matched with commensurate strategies to meet these and the specified objectives, can be justified as a positive exercise.

In the light of the above discussion on the acceptance and use of 'needs' concepts in child development, we can return to the usage of special educational needs as set out by the Warnock Committee. Its members acknowledged that 'for the sake of convenience descriptive terms will be needed for particular groups of children who require special educational provision' (p. 43, para. 3.26). These covered children with physical or sensory disabilities (physical handicap), children with learning difficulties, mild, moderate, severe (to replace educationally subnormal) and maladjusted children, about which the Committee had reservations, but endorsed retention of the label on the grounds that it 'remains a serviceable form of description' (p. 44, para. 3.27).

Mittler (1979) has encapsulated the distinctions between the universal needs of all children and the extra, specific or special needs of 'problem' or handicapped child in these words

we cannot know what a child's needs are merely on the basis of experience and intuition, nor can we provide a learning environment which is geared to his specific needs until we have assessed those needs and planned systematically how to meet them (p. 67).

The view that society has a duty to ensure that children's special needs, which they cannot articulate for themselves, are 'identified and cogently represented' (from the Court Report 1976) is expressed by Brimblecombe (in Pringle, ed. 1979). He deplores the erstwhile absence of a commitment by successive British governments to coherent policies for children. However the present government, in its White Paper response to the Warnock Report, (Special Needs in Education August 1980), accepted and endorsed the principle and the continuum of special educational needs and consequently the abolishment of the statutory handicaps. This commitment to the 'broader concept of special education' is now enshrined in the Education Act 1981 which amends the law relating to special education and which became law 1 April 1983. There will be discussion later in this chapter on those aspects of the Act that directly affect and involve parents.

2. Definitions and Incidence

Wedell (1981) avers that the term special educational needs 'refers to the gap between a child's level of behaviour or achievement and what is required of him. This raises all the familiar questions about what these requirements or expectations may be and on what assumption they are based'. He goes on to present a variety of explanatory and descriptive models which are invoked by differing groups of professionals working with children.

The use of such a variety of models reflects in part the difficulty, recognised and readily admitted by professionals working in areas of handicap and problems in childhood, of separating cause from effect, and of defining the parameters of each 'condition' or presenting problem. Hoghughi (1981) has referred to a problem being 'an unacceptable condition', so that once adults perceive child behaviours as being beyond their levels of tolerance or coping ability, a problem area is defined and given the resources now available, must be dealt with.

Longitudinal and epidemiological surveys of the last few years into incidence and prevalence rates of handicap and behaviour and learning difficulties in children (Rutter *et al.* 1970, Shepherd *et al.* 1971, Davie *et al.* 1972, Cave and Maddison 1978, Clark and Cheyne, Eds 1979, Chazan *et al.* 1980, Weale and Bradshaw 1980) have not made it easier for people working with children and their parents to unequivocally define and intervene with a variety of these problems.

Even the figures obtained by large-scale studies can only be approximate and blunt (Wall 1973 and 1979) reflecting as they do cultural contexts and regional differences, and the fact that there are finally no absolute yardsticks by which to gauge the infinite variations and complexities of human behaviour and interaction. Furthermore, as Cave and Maddison have remarked, there are methodological problems inherent in information-gathering of the incidence of handicapping conditions and problem behaviour.

The Warnock Report scrutinised data from major surveys, pertaining to the incidence of special educational needs, bore in mind the qualifications and limitations of such statistics-gathering exercises, and concluded '. . . the figure of one in six represents what we believe to be a reasonable judgement on the evidence' (p. 40, para. 3.16). Translating these figures for purpose of educational planning, the key recommendation of the Report is

that the planning of services for children and young people should be based on the assumption that about one in six children at any time and up to one in five children at some time during their school career will require some form of special educational provision (p. 41, para. 3.17).

3. Parents and Special Educational Needs

3.1. The Education Act 1981 and the Place of Parents

One of the fundamental shifts of social and educational philosophy in recent years has been the recognition that parents should have rights in principle which are exercised in practice in matters of school selection, appeal, access to information, and some involvement in the education process (see Chapter 4). This thinking pervades the Court and Warnock Reports, which called for a partnership with parents in assessment and educational programming. Professionals and parents are already engaged upon collaborative work of this kind.

For example, the Court Report on Child Health Services had suggested the adoption of systems of developmental surveillance and early identification of developmental delays, handicap and early-appearing difficulties in language, sensori-motor skills, emotional-social development (Wolfendale 1979). The Warnock Report advocated that parents should play a part in the assessment procedures which are used by local education authorities. Cave and Maddison (1978) identify the increasing involvement of parents in these processes as a trend in Britain; in many parts of America and Canada these parent–professional exercises are well established.

The philosophy and spirit behind the Education Act 1981 was introduced earlier in this chapter (Welton, Wedell, Vorhaus 1982). It places an obligation on local educational authorities to ensure that adequate provision is made for all children with special educational needs and lays down specific procedures for the assessment of such children. The involvement of parents is seen as essential: the assessment procedures are seen as partnership ventures between the teacher, other professionals and the child's parents. Explicitly, parents are to be involved at each stage of the process, from assessment to making statements on a child's special educational needs, to recording and reviewing progress. Parents' rights are enumerated as follows:

1) account has to be taken of the views of the parent in the provision of special education (Section 2(3));

2) the local educational authority shall serve notice on the parent informing him/her as to the proposed assessment and pointing out the parent's right to make 'representations' (Section 5(3)). The parents will be able to complete a form outlining their views which will comprise part of the assessment:

3) where special educational provision is being proposed for a child after assessment the local education authority has to 'serve on the parent of the child concerned a copy of the proposed statement.

4) The parent has the right to appeal against the special educational provision specified (Section 8);

5) the parent of a child has the right to request an assessment of his/her child's educational needs (Section 9).

Critics of the Act's provisions assert that while the place of parents in the procedures is now assured, nevertheless there is no legal machinery by which parents can become true partners in the provision of special educational services, whether in special or ordinary schools.

British legislation can be compared and contrasted with recent US legislation on special education, which spells out the full extent of parental rights in no uncertain terms. This is the Education for all Handicapped Children Act (Public Laws 94–142) of 1975 (fully in force from September 1980). Basically, it states that a free and appropriate public education must be extended to every handicapped child in the USA and that states and schools have to follow prescribed administrative procedures to ensure that basic rights are extended to handicapped children and their parents.

Part of this process calls for each local educational agency to develop an individualised educational programme (IEP) in respect of each handicapped child. This is regarded as a form of contract between the school, the child and his/her parents or guardians, and parents have to sign acceptance of and agreement with the plan, once they agree, after due discussion and consultation between teachers, parents and other professional workers.

The IEP must include an evaluation of the child's present level of performance, annual goals and short range objectives, services the school will provide to ensure that those goals and objectives are met, and evaluation procedures which are to be used. The IEP must also include specific dates, timelines, and at least an annual evaluation schedule (Semmel and Heinmiller 1977, p. 4).

The parents are involved at all stages.

The Public Law 94–142 also outlines the 'due process procedures' that must be followed in order for each state to receive federal funds and which incorporates the notion of rights. Some of the main points of the due process procedures that apply to parents are presented below.

1) that parents or guardians have the right to examine all relevant records of the child as well as the right to obtain an independent educational evaluation of the child;

2) that parents or guardians must be given written prior notice in their native language whenever the school proposes to initiate a change or refuses to initiate a change in regards to the identification, evaluation, or educational placement of the child;

3) that parents or guardians have the right to present complaints with respect to the identification, evaluation, or educational placement of their child;

4) that upon presentation of a complaint, the parents or guardians shall have an opportunity for an impartial due process hearing. In the hearing they are to be given the right to be accompanied and advised by counsel. Parents are also to be granted the right to a written or electronic verbatim record of such hearings and the right to written findings of fact and decisions;

5) that any party aggrieved by the decision has the right to appeal to the State educational agency and ultimately the right to bring a civil action. (Source: Chiba and Semmel 1977.)

It is still too early to assess the full impact of Public Law 94–142, but certainly up to now one effect has been to generate a spate of textbooks for professionals and parents, outlining many ways in which they can work productively together on behalf of the children they have in common (Kozloff 1979, Osman 1979).

The considerable number of British parent–professional partnership ventures in the spheres of special education and programmes for young handicapped children (see later in this chapter) will doubtless continue to increase apace, but developments will continue to be based on professional and parental convictions and enthusiasm, rather than be spurred on by any legal requirements.

3.2. Parental Access to Information and Support

Parents' reactions and attitudes to having handicapped babies are now well documented, in studies and first-hand parents' accounts (Thomas 1978, Hannam 1980, Mittler 1980, Boston 1981, Murray and Cornell 1981, Purser 1981). Accounts of problems experienced by parents of handicapped children include those of McMichael (1971), Hewett (1970), Spain and Wigley (1975), Butler et al. (1978), Laing (ed. 1979). These reports and descriptions chronicle parents' despair, doubt, confusion, guilt, ambivalent emotional reactions and highlight, time and again, the dearth of adequate procedures for professional support and guidance, not only at the crucial post-natal time, but during the many child-rearing years that lie ahead. Until very recent times it was a bleak and lonely scene for parents of handicapped children.

Growing recognition of parents' acute need for information on handicap, sources of material help and emotional support, and practical ways in which they could assist in their handicapped children's welfare and development, have led to a clutch of published information. The Advisory Centre for Education has produced guides on the Warnock Report, integration, parents' rights under the Education Act 1981. MIND (see references for address) publishes parents' booklets, as does the Voluntary Council for Handicapped Children, and during 1981 three national associations (ACE, MIND, and the Children's Legal Centre) combined to produce a leaflet *Education to 19 – the right of ALL mentally handicapped people.*

There is an accumulating stock of books written for parents of children with handicaps, learning and behaviour problems, offering information and support (Richardson, Brutter and Mangol 1973, Perske 1973, Stott 1974, Hayes 1975, White 1978, Rosner 1979, Lansdown 1980), outlining programmes for behaviour management (Becker 1971, Patterson 1976, Westmacott and Cameron 1981), and basic skills training for severely mentally handicapped children (Carr 1980). The *Human Horizons* series (Souvenir Press) produces many books for parents and teachers of handicapped children.

These developments indicate clearly how parents of children with special needs are being increasingly recognised in the public eye, as not only having the right to information and support, but as a source and resource in the development, education and welfare of their children.

4. Special Needs: Towards a Partnership with Parents

Parallel to – and indeed ideologically linked to – the growing participation by parents of pre-school and allegedly disadvantaged children (see previous chapters) is an equally burgeoning area of collaboration between professionals and parents of young, handicapped children. Parents are taking a more active part now than in the past in assessment, diagnosis and intervention.

Elizabeth Newson (1976) offers a valuable distillation of the advantages of using parents as a resource in diagnosis and assessment which maximises their skills as observers of their own children, as the key informants, and as contributors to the overall appraisal of their children's development and problem areas. The disadvantages of possible unreliability (of parents as informants) and latent bias and distortion of perception regarding the problem, are felt to be outweighed by the advantages.

Basically, this view summarises the rationale on which parent–professional cooperation rests. The overwhelming current concensus by workers and writers (Riley 1978, Russell 1979, Mittler 1980, Newson and Hipgrave 1982) is that such cooperation is beneficial. At best it enhances parent–child relationships, facilitates professional–child–parent relationships, and can promote demonstr-

E

able progress in skill-acquisition, and positive behaviour change in the child (depending on the objectives of the intervention).

Whittaker (1979) surveying the parental participation scene in areas of assessment and treatment mainly in residental settings concludes 'success in treatment depends substantially on our ability to involve parents or parenting persons as full and equal partners in the helping process' (p. 137). The keynote is partnership. In most of the joint enterprises reported in journals and local reports, parents are not playing the client role (Chapter 2). This is increasingly being abandoned and seen as divisive, unethical and unproductive.

Along with the evident enthusiasm of professionals and parents working on joint programmes is a realistic acknowledgment that there are many dimensions and problem areas in collaborative work that have to be explored and resolved (Kiernan, undated). One account by a psychologist (Harris 1978) of a parents' group (of pre- and school-age mentally handicapped children) run on behaviour modification lines examines the difficulties encountered over several years and offers constructive suggestions for the alleviation of these practical and methodological issues.

A good number of the intervention programmes with handicapped children and children with a range of special educational needs are home-based and Chazan (in Laing, ed. 1979) lists nine reasons which have been advanced for the introduction and adoption of these. He endorses the general principles yet adds cautionary remarks mainly centring on how little we do know about learning that takes place at home, and the proper role delineation of those involved. Honig (1980) provides an overview of the field and gives a ten point summary list of skills parents can be helped to acquire when involved in intervention programmes for their handicapped children. The main elements of this list are given to convey the 'flavour' of thinking in this area:

1) parents need flexibility;
2) parents need observation skills;
3) parents need to challenge the child;
4) parents need to meet the match in teaching new behaviour;
5) a parent needs to nurture;
6) parents need to teach and reward imitation;

7)   manual guidance can help;

8)   parents need to use strong stimulation when necessary;

9)   parents need to discipline wisely;

10)   parents need supports.

5. Intervention Work with Parents of Children with Special Needs

The Warnock Committee endorsed the parents-as-partners principle, and in part based its thinking on examination of collaborative work (group work, support groups, child training programmes) mainly with mentally handicapped children and their parents, which began to be reported in Britain in the early 1970s and onwards (Parfitt 1971, Pugh and Russell 1977, Laing, Ed, 1979, Cave and Maddison 1978, Mittler 1980, Pugh 1981).

Some of the work is original, imaginative and complex in its design and execution, some is of a more routine nature but still a radical departure from traditional approaches whereby professionals (psychologists, paediatricians, therapists, teachers) and parents kept their distance from each other. A number of projects have been fully documented in journals and books, whereas others may be described in duplicated form for local purposes, and yet others go unrecorded. As with the ventures described in previous chapters, the format and procedure of the projects in this area of special needs could constitute models for try-out and adoption in similar or parallel environments. Most of the accounts give positive outcomes and measurable gains (in quantitative or qualitative terms) and some provide sophisticated analyses.

One function of this chapter is to offer an overview of this contemporary work, in a form that enables the reader to note the type of project or service offered, and track the source.

Although interrelated in theoretical orientation and overall purpose (training and support of parents who have children with special needs) it is possible to distinguish two main target populations in a fairly blunt fashion, of children who have been in receipt of parent-focussed services

PARENT–PROFESSIONAL COLLABORATION IN SPECIAL NEEDS

Area of Special Need	PRESCHOOL SCHOOL AGE (Alphabetical order)	Setting for Training	Home-based dev/skill pro- gramme	Training workshop group support	Approach + format	Professional focus
PHYSICALLY HANDICAPPED CHILDREN	Attwood 1978/79	School		✓	developmental + skills training	psychologist multidisciplinary
	Bevington et al 1978	School		✓	behavioural/ skills	psychologist
	Burton et al 1981	Centre		✓	Skills training	,,
	Cowan and Brenton 1975	Centre	✓		developmental training	paediatric/ health vistor
	Cummings 1975	School		✓	developmental + skills training	psychologist
	Firth and Newton 1979	Hospital			observation + skills training	psychologist + community liaison officer
	H.A.R.C. Home Visiting	Home	✓		developmental + skills training	psychologist + health vistor
	H.A.R.C. Workshop	Centre and School		✓	,,	psychologist +teachers
	Haringey Home Intervention	Home	✓		,,	psychologist + social worker

MENTALLY AND/OR

Study		Location		Intervention	Professional
Harris 1979	✓	Centre	✓	skills/behavioural	psychologist
Hattersley + Tennant		School	✓	management advice, inf. and support	psychologist + co-professionals
Honeylands Home Visiting	✓	Home	✓	developmental therapy	multidisci-plinary
McCall & Thacker		School	✓	skill training	psychologist
Moore et al 1981	✓	Centre	✓	developmental behavioural	,,
Pollock & Stewart 1979	✓		✓	developmental + skills training	psychologist + co-professionals
PORTAGE: Wales + Wessex	✓	Home	✓	developmental + skills training	multi-disciplinary
Robinson 1979		School	✓	management training + learning	teacher
Sandow + Clarke 1978	✓	Home	✓	developmental skill training	psychologist
Southend Group Therapy		Centre	✓	therapy/disciplinary	multidisciplinery therapy

A) severe mental handicap (*synonymous labels*: subnormality, educationally subnormal-severe, severe learning difficulties) physical handicap (sensori-motor disabilities, cerebral palsy, etc.) and multiple-handicapped (combinations/variations of mental and physical handicaps)

B) emotional and behaviour difficulties, maladjustment, neurotic behaviours, conduct problems, management problems at home.

Category A

Recent British work in category A is presented above in chart form, entitled parent–professional collaboration in special needs, and the exact references are given at the end of this chapter in List B. The examples given in the chart are representative and typical of current approaches, but not intended to be exhaustive, for as has already been pointed out, some of the work forms a routine part of local service provision. For instance, a recent (1979) survey of involvement by educational psychologists in parent workshop activity revealed that one-third of the local education authorities which replied to a questionnaire were carrying out such work – and this is an expanding area.

The Portage Project in Britain, the model of which originated in Wisconsin, USA (see references) began in two places, Wales and Wessex, and is now being replicated in an increasing number of local authorities (see Daly 1980, Cameron 1982). Some local initiatives have drawn on the pioneering work of the Hester Adrian Research Centre, which is based at Manchester University and which, in addition to parent-focussed research, carries out theoretical and empirical studies into the functioning of mentally handicapped children.

There are other interesting lines of development which do not neatly fall into the confines of the chart presented here, and which in Britain constitute isolated examples of an ideological approach which has a longer history in the USA and Canada, that is, initiative for parents of children with handicaps, which are community based and *parent run* with professional backing (Magnus 1974, Kleisinger undated, Timm and Rule 1981). A British example is Kith and Kids Two-to-One Project (in Pugh 1981) which incorporates parental assessment of children, skills training and mutual support. An example of a community based support and advisory service for handicapped children and their families is the Family Centre in Sheffield. It serves as a multidisciplinary meeting place, resource centre, clearing house and focal point for research projects. One of the services the Sheffield Family Centre offers is a Toy Library, which is another way in which professionals have been working in the last few years with families who have young handicapped children (Head 1976, and 1978, Freeman 1979, Laing, ed. 1979, Pollock and Stewart 1979).

An especially useful description and discussion of theoretical and practical issues is the chapter by Bricker *et al.* in Hogg and Mittler (1980) on early intervention with young mentally handicapped children. They go into the minute learning sequences essential to delineate at any level of skill-acquisition from the earliest stages of development, setting this within overall curricular frameworks. On the basis of their considerable experience at their Institute, the authors outline the model and the case for parental inclusion into educational programming for handicapped children, and the necessity of obtaining direct feedback from the parents at all stages of the intervention process.

Category B

Intervention and work with parents of children presenting behaviour and management problems who may include mentally and physically handicapped children, has a well-established tradition in the USA and, by now, a fairly solid body of empirical work in Britain. Mostly, it has been educational and clinical psychologists who have instituted behavioural approaches with parents, teaching them the principles of applied behaviour analysis and guiding them in the application of behaviour modification programmes at home. The aims are usually to reduce or eliminate persistently irritating, disruptive, negative, undesired behaviours and to develop and incorporate desired behaviours into a generally accepted and acceptable behavioural repertoire.

An article on the many US studies which is regarded as seminal is that of Johnson and Katz (1973). These authors are quoted by Yule

(1975) whose article is also a critical review of the field. He concludes that 'parent training can be very effective', and that the evident problems 'can be regarded as technical and soluble' (p. 14). Gordon and Davidson (in Gurman and Kniskern, Eds 1981) endorse the focus in behavioural parent training on the parents' behaviour rather than on the child as patient (the medical model) and assert that 'parents possess an extraordinary potential for generating behavioural change due to the fact that they are often the ones with control over the significant elements in the child's natural environment' (p. 518). They examine hundreds of American studies and note that the outcomes are invariably reported as positive and successful. In Britain, reports of this kind of collaborative work with parents are contained in professional journals, for example, the work of Presland (1975, 1976).

In conclusion, mention can be made of an annotation by Gath (1979) which consists of a short but comprehensive review of the main forms of parent–professional collaborative work in the area of special needs. The generally encouraging results noted by Gath are sufficient justification to continue to explore constructive ways of bringing about behaviour change, skill-acquisition on the part of the children, lightening parents' burdens, and equipping them with effective techniques to achieve change and promote the welfare and well-being of the family (also Russell 1981).

6. Special Needs and Parent Partnership: Towards a School-Based Policy?

Work with parents and children with special educational needs has concentrated on the acute and severe clusters of handicap and severe learning difficulties (Mittler and Mittler 1982). These have been perceived as the priority areas; the settings in which the work has taken place include clinics, centres, homes and to a lesser extent, special schools.

However, there is little evidence yet of joint endeavours taking place in ordinary schools. In these, children with a variety of learning and behaviour difficulties, who would be placed at the less severe end of Warnock's continuum of special educational need, have usually been designated as 'remedial', and have received remedial provision. This has usually taken the form of full-time, small class attendance, or time-tabled withdrawal from regular classes into remedial/'opportunity' groups. In Chapter 3, some examples were given of home collaboration between teachers and parents of children who had reading difficulties, but there is a paucity of exploratory work in this whole field.

As the demarcation lines between remedial and special education become increasingly blurred and less tenable and as the principle of integration of children with special needs into normal schools[†] written into the Education Act 1981, becomes increasingly accepted and implemented by local education authorities, so a greater number of teachers in ordinary schools will encounter a greater number of children with learning and behaviour difficulties (DES 1976, Beresford and Tuckwell 1978, City of Bradford 1979, Galloway and Goodwin 1979, Special Education 1980, Booth 1981, Brennan 1982). Could their task of meeting the needs of children with perceived problems be facilitated and their professional practice enhanced by increased contact with parents? Chazan et al. (1980) advocate an explicit home–school policy on behalf of children with handicaps and presenting problems who are in ordinary schools.

It is proposed that the elements which would combine to form a policy into practice approach could include:

— parental involvement in initial observation, diagnosis, and assessment;
— parental participation in school-based learning (including remedial) and behaviour management programmes;
— home-based learning activities with educational home visitor liaison as well as link with class teacher/remedial teacher;
— in-service training and workshops for teachers and parents on shared learning and behaviour programmes;
— support groups involving school representatives, parents, and other representative professionals from other agencies;
— mutual (school and home) use of supporting services;
— parental contribution to case conferences, progress reviews, and

---

[†] excepting those children with disabilities and handicaps so severe and enduring that they require specialised treatment, care and education, sometimes in residential settings.

decision-making concerning the child: this would include report-writing and forms of home–school communication;
— parental representation (possibly via parent/governor) regarding the school's policy and provision for special needs.

Some of the innovative work reported earlier in the chapter paves the way for further experimentation and adoption of these elements into a coordinated school–home policy for the substantial number of children with special educational needs. Such a policy could be applicable to special schools.

A modest, small-scale but illuminating enquiry into the curricular aspirations of teachers, governors and parents of children with severe learning difficulties (de Souza and Bailey 1981) revealed a match between parents' and professionals' curricular aims for the children. These were broadly grouped into self-help skills, communication, socialisation. There is surely scope here to delve further into parents' educational aspirations for their children in order to effect the two-way beneficial dialogue.

7. Accountability

There was mention in Chapter 4 of recent work into the concept of accountability in education and a move towards the introduction of 'tightening up procedures' whereby teachers and schools give an account of their work and their results to parents and the public.

In this chapter we have seen that the principle of accountability is explicitly built into the provisions of the American Public Law 94–142 Education for all Handicapped Children Act. Doubtless there are educators in this country who are horrified at the explicit parental right to be fully involved in the assessment and IEP procedures, and dismayed that teachers in the US seem so publicly vulnerable, under professional threat and so at risk of litigation for failing in their duties. Perhaps we in Britain do not want to take US legislation on special needs as a model for our own practice (see Mittler 1979 on accountability). Yet, as Ainscow and Tweddle (1979) point out, for children with special needs in ordinary schools (and their argument would not preclude special schools) a voluntary system of accountability within an overall approach to school-based assessment and educational programming should be part of the special educational needs philosophy. They cite three conditions which must pertain for accountability to become a reality:

1) there must be a programme of objectives, defined in behavioural terms and including details of performance levels;

2) the programme must be understood, as far as possible, by everybody concerned;

3) it must be clear to everybody concerned what everybody else is 'contracted' to do in terms of producing and operating the programme (i.e., role specification) (p. 142).

In the accountability procedure, all the persons involved with the special educational needs of any one child at any one time, including the parents, formally or informally contracts to play their part. Ainscow and Tweddle provide a case study illustration of how this could work in practice for a child presenting learning and reading problems in a junior school. The procedure would be a compatible element within the teacher–parent partnership programme suggested above.

Within the wider educational and societal context Bryans and Wolfendale (1979) have asserted that on behalf of children in ordinary schools with special educational needs, schools, with or without the assistance of the supporting services will have to demonstrate that:

1) the curricula and special programmes that they devise work, i.e., that children make demonstrable progress;

2) that alternative teaching strategies are employed if progress is not manifest;

3) that account is taken of differential rates of learning and production;

4) that the deficit/failure model is not invoked to explain lack of progress;

5) parents' rights to be fully acquainted with the educational programmes provided for their children are exercised.

The premise is that if a concept of special needs in education is postulated, and accepted, then the onus is on the service-providing institutions to meet the needs.

References

List A

Ainscow, M. and Tweddle, D. (1979) *Preventing Classroom Failure*, Chichester, Sussex: John Wiley and Sons.

Becker, W. (1971) *Parents are teachers, a Child Management Program*, Research Press.

Beresford, P. and Tuckwell, P. (1978) *Schools for All – Education for Severely Mentally Handicapped Children*, National Association for Mental Health and Campaign for the Mentally handicapped, March.

Booth, T. (1981) 'Educating children with Down's Syndrome in an ordinary school', *Early Child Development and Care*, Vol. 7, Nos. 2.

Boston, S. (1981) *Will my Son*, London NW1: Pluto Press.

Bricker, D., Seibert, J. and Casuso, V. (1980) 'Early intervention' in Hogg, J. and Mittler, P. (eds) *Advances in Mental Handicap Research*, Vol. I, Chichester, Sussex: John Wiley and Sons.

Brennan, W. (1982) *Special Education in Mainstream Schools*, National Council for Special Education, 1 Wood Street, Stratford-upon-Avon, CV37 6JE.

Bryans, T. and Wolfendale, S. (1979) 'Educational screening and special education in ordinary schools', *Proceedings of the DECP Annual Course*, University of Nottingham.

Butler, N., Gill, R., Pomeroy, D., Fewtrell, D. (1978) *Handicapped Children, Their Homes and Life Styles*, Department of Child Health, University of Bristol.

Carr, J. (1980) *Helping Your Handicapped Child*, London, SW10: Penguin.

Cave, C. and Maddison, P. (1978) *A Survey of Recent Research in Special Education*, NFER.

Chazan, M., Laing, A., Shackleton-Bailey, M., Jones, G. (1980) *Some of Our Children, the Early Education of Children with Special Needs*, Shepton Mallet, Somerset: Open Books.

Chazan, M. (1979) 'Home-based projects', in Laing, A. (ed.) *Young Children with Special Needs*, Department of Education, University College, Swansea.

Chiba, C. and Semmel, M. (1977) 'Due Process and least restrictive alternatives: new emphasis on parental participation', in *Viewpoints, Bulletin of the School of Education*, Indiana University, Vol. 53, No. 2, March, pp. 17–31.

City of Bradford (1979) *The Education of Handicapped Children in Ordinary Schools*, Education Services Directorate.

Clark, M. and Cheyne, W. (eds) (1979) *Studies in Preschool Education*, Sevenoaks, Kent: Hodder and Stoughton.

Davie, R., Butler, N. and Goldstein, H. (1972) *From Birth to Seven*, Harlow, Essex: Longman.

DES (1976) *Integrating Handicapped Children*, DES, Elizabeth House, York Rd, London, SE1 7PH.

Galloway, D. and Goodwin, C. (1979) *Educating Slow-learning and Maladjusted Children: Integration or Segregation?*, Harlow, Essex: Longman.

Hannam, C. (1980) *Parents and Mentally Handicapped Children*, London, SW10: Penguin Handbook.

Hayes, M. (1975) *Oh Dear, Somebody said Learning Disabilities, a Book for Teachers and Parents*, Academic Therapy.

Hewett, S. (1970) *The Family and the Handicapped Child*, London, WC1: Allen and Unwin.

Hoghughi, M. (1981) *What's So Special About Special Education*, lecture given at Homerton College Cambridge.

Honig, A. (1980) 'Parent involvement and the development of children with special needs', *Early Child Development and Care*, Vol. 6, Nos 3/4.

IFPE *The Needs of the Child-a Reply from Japan*, International Federation for Parent Education, Sèvres, France.

Kiernan, C. (undated) *Problems Arising from Research*, Thomas Coram Research Unit, University of London Institute of Education.

Kozloff, M. (1979) *A Program for Families of Children with Learning and Behaviour Problems*, Chichester, Sussex: John Wiley and Sons.

Laing, A. (ed.) (1979) *Young Children with Special Needs*, Department of Education, University College, Swansea.

Lansdown, R. (1980) *More than Sympathy*, London, EC4: Tavistock Publications.

McMichael, J. (1971) *Handicap, a Study of Physically Handicapped Children and their Families*, St Albans, Herts: Staples Press.

MIND Bookshop, 155/157 Woodhouse Lane, Leeds, LS2 3EF.

Mittler, P. (1980) *People not Patients*, London, EC4: Methuen.

Mittler, P. and Mittler, H. (1982) *Partnership with Parents*, National Council for Special Education, 1 Wood Street, Stratford upon Avon, Warwickshire.

Murray, J. and Cornell, C. (1981) 'Parentalplegia', *Psychology in Our Schools*, 18, 201–207.

Newson, E. (1976) 'Parents as a resource in diagnosis and assessment', in Oppe, T. and Woodford, F. (eds) *Early Management of Handicapping Disorders*, IRMMH Reviews of Research and Practice, Associated Scientific Publishers.

Newson, E. and Hipgrave, T. (1982) *Getting Through to your Handicapped Child*, Cambridge: Cambridge University Press.

Osman, B. (1979) *Learning Disabilities: a Family Affair*, New York NY: Random House.

Parfitt, J. (1971) *Group Work with Parents in Special Circumstances*, National Children Bureau.

Patterson, G. (1976) *Living with Children, New Methods for Parents and Teachers*, Champaigne, ILL: Research Press.

Perske, R. (1973) *New Directions for Parents of Persons who are Retarded*, Nashville, TN: (Harlow, Essex) Abingdon Press.

Pilling, D. (1973) *The Handicapped Child; Research Review III*, Longman in association with the National Childrens Bureau.

Pringle, M. K. (1975) *The Needs of Children*, London, W1: Hutchinson.

Pringle, M. K. (ed.) (1980) *A Fairer future for children*, London, WC2: Macmillan.

Purser, A. (1981) *You and Your Handicapped Child*, London, WC1: Allen and Unwin.

Pugh, G. and Russell, P. (1977) *Shared Care, Support Services for Families with Handicapped Children*, National Childrens Bureau.

Pugh, G. (1981) *Parents as Partners, Intervention Schemes and Group Work with Parents of Handicapped Children*, National Childrens Bureau.

Richardson, S., Brutter, M., Mangol, C. (1973) *Something wrong with my child: a parents book about learning disabilities*, London, NW1: Harcourt.

Riley, M. (1978) 'LATON: a parenting project to foster understanding of handicapped children', *International Journal of Early Childhood*, Vol. 10, No. 1, 30–32.

Rosner, J. (1979) *Helping Children Overcome Learning Difficulties – a Step-by-Step Guide for Parents and Teachers*, New York NY: Walker and Co.

Russell, P. (1979) 'The young handicapped child in the community', *Early Child Development and Care*, Vol. 6, Nos. 172.

Russell, P. (1981) 'Towards an equal partnership', *Concern*, No. 38, National Childrens Bureau.

Rutter, M., Tizard, J. and Whitmore, K. (1970) *Education, Health and Behaviour*, Harlow, Essex: Longman.

Semmel, M. and Heinmiller, J. (eds) (1977) 'The education for all handicapped children Act of 1975, national perspective and long range implications, *Viewpoints*, Bulletin of the School of Education, Indiana University, Vol. 53, No. 2, March, 1–17.

Shearer, A. (1981) *Disability: Whose Handicap?*, Oxford: Basil Blackwell.

Shepherd, M., Oppenheim, B. and Mitchell, S. (1971) *Childhood Behaviour and Mental Health*, University of London Press.

Spain, B. and Wigley, G. (1975) *Right from the Start, a Service for Families with a Young Handicapped Child*, NSMHC.

Special Education (1980) 'Issue theme: meeting special needs in ordinary schools', Special Education, *British Journal of Special Education*, Vol. 7, No. 1, March.

'Special needs in education' (1980) *Command* 7996, August, HMSO.

Souza, D. de and Bailey, T. (1981) 'What do parents, governors and professionals consider to be the most important aims for children with severe learning difficulties?', Appex, B. *Inst. Mental Handicap*, Vol. 8, No. 4, 130–131.

Stott, D. (1974) *The Parent as Teacher: a Guide for Parents for Children with Learning Difficulties*, University of London Press.

Thomas, D. (1978) *The Social Psychology of Childhood Disability*, London, EC4: Methuen.

Voluntary Council for Handicapped Children, 8 Wakley Street, ECIV 7QE.

Wall, W. D. (1973) 'The problem child in schools', *London Educational Review*, Vol. 2, No. 2 Summer.

Wall, W. D. (1979) *Constructive Education for Special Groups: Handicapped and Deviant Children*, UNESCO/Harrap, (London).

Warnock, M. (Chairperson) (1978) *Special Educational Needs*, DES/HMSO, (Norwich).

Weale, J. and Bradshaw, J. (1980) 'Prevalence and characteristics of disabled children: findings from the 1974 General Household Survey', *Journal of Epidemiology and Community Health*, 34, 111–118.

Wedell, K. (1981) 'Concepts of special educational needs', *Journal of the College of Preceptors*, April.

Welton, J., Wedell, K. and Vorhaus, G. (1982) "Meeting Special educational needs", Bedford Way Papers 12, The Windmill Press, Kingswood, Tadworth, Surrey, KTZ 6TG.

Westmacott, S. and Cameron, S. (1981) *Behaviour Can Change*, Basingstoke, Hants: Macmillan.

White, R. (1978) *The Special Child, a Parents' Guide to Mental Disabilities*, Boston, MA Little, Brown and Co.

Whittaker, J. (1979) *Caring for Troubled Children*, San Francisco: Jossey Bass.

Wolfendale, S. (1979) 'Interdisciplinary approaches to preschool developmental surveillance', *Remedial Education (Journal of the National Association for Remedial Education)*, Vol. 14, No. 4, November.

Wolfendale, S. and Bryans, T. (1979) *Identification of Learning Difficulties – a Model for Intervention*, National Association for Remedial Education.

Wolfendale, S. (1980) 'Learning difficulties: a re-appraisal' (editorial), *Remedial Education (Journal of the National Association for Remedial Education)* Vol. 15, No. 3, August.

References

List B

Studies, Projects, Treatment and Training Programmes referred to in the chapter-see 5. Intervention Work with Parents of Children with Special Needs, Category (A) and Category (B)

Attwood, T. (1978) 'The Croydon workshops for parents of pre-school mentally handicapped children', *Child: Care, Health and Development*, 4, 2, 79–97.

Attwood, T. (1979) 'The Croydon workshop for the parents of severely handicapped school-age children', *Child: Care, Health and Development*, 5, 3, 177–188.

Bevington, P., Gardner, J. and Cocks, R. (1978) 'An approach to the planning and evaluation of a parental involvement course', *Child: Care, Health and Development*, 4, 217–227.

Burton, A., Miller, A., Willis, B. (1981) 'A workshop for parents of pre-school children with delayed development: an SPS Project', *Journal of the Association of Educational Psychologists*, Vol. 5, No. 5, March.

Cowan, M. and Brenton, A. (1975) 'Developmental training by parents of the very young child with potential handicap', *Child: Care, Health and Development*, 1, 239–250.

Cummings, P. (1975) *You and Your Handicapped Child*, Psychological Services, Birmingham Education Department.

Firth, H. and Newton, K. (1979) 'Parent workshops as part of the service', *Parents' Voice*, 29, 1.

Freeman, A. (1979) 'A survey of toy libraries', *Journal of the Association of Educational Psychologists*, Vol. 5, No. 1, Summer.

Gath, A. (1979) 'Parents as therapists of mentally handicapped children', annotation in *Journal of Child Psychology and Psychiatry*, Vol. 20, No. 2, April.

Gordon, S. and Davidson, N. (1981) 'Behavioural parent training', in German, A and Kniskern, S. (eds) *Handbook of Family Therapy*, Brunner Mazel.

Haringey Home Intervention Scheme, Chapter 6 in Pugh, G. (1981) *Parents as Partners*, National Children's Bureau.

Harris, J. (1978) 'Working with parents of mentally handicapped children on a long-term basis', *Child: Care, Health and Development*, Vol. 4, No. 2, March/April, 121–131.

Hester Adrian Research Centre

Health Visitor Home Visiting Project, Chapter 7 in Pugh, G. (1981) 'Parents as Partners', National Children's Bureau.

Cunningham, C. (1979) 'Early stimulation of the mentally handicapped child' and 'Parent Counselling', both in Craft, M. (ed.) *Tredgold's Mental Retardation*, 12th Edition, Balliere Tindale.

Cunningham, C. *Parents as Therapists and Educators*, HARC, University of Manchester.

McConkey, R. (1978) 'Parental involvement in language development', in *Special for Life, Proc. of the Annual conference of the National Council for Special Education, July 1977*.

McConkey, R. (1979) 'Reinstating parental involvement in the development of communication skills', *Child: Care, Health and Development*, 5, 17–27.

Parental Involvement Project, HARC, University of Manchester.

Hattersley, J. and Tennant, L. (1981) 'Parent Workshops in Worcestershire', Chapter 9 in Pugh, G. (1981) *Parents as Partners*, National Childrens Bureau.

Head, J. (1976) 'Research Centering on a Toy Library Service', in Oppé, T and Woodford, F. (eds) *Early Management of Handicapping Disorders*, IRMMH. Reviews of Research and Practice, Amsterdam: Ass. Scientific Publishers.

Head, J. (1978) *Toy Libraries: a Resource for Parental Partnership*, Division of Educational and Child Psychology, British Psychological Society, Occasional Papers, Vol. II, No. 1.

Honeylands

Honeylands Home Visiting Project, Chapter 2 in Pugh, G. (1981) *Parents as Partners*, National Childrens Bureau.

Burden, R. L. (1978) 'An approach to the evaluation of early intervention projects with mothers of severely handicapped children: the attitude dimension', *Child: Care, Health and Development*, 4.

Burden, R. L. (1979) 'Intervention programmes with families of handicapped children', *Bulletin of the British Psychological Society*, 32, April, 137–141.

Burden, R. L. (1980) 'Measuring the effects of stress on the mothers of handicapped infants: must depression always follow?' *Child: Care, Health and Development*, 6, 111–135.

Burden, R. L. (1981) 'Evaluating early intervention projects: one possible way forward', *Early Child Development and Care*, August.

Judson, S. and Burden, R. L. (1980) 'Towards a tailored measure of parental attitudes: an approach to the evaluation of one aspect of intervention projects with parents of handicapped children', *Child: Care, Health and Development*, 6, 47–55.

Key, J., Hooper, J. and Ballard, M. (1979) 'A parental perspective on the Honeylands home visiting project for severely handicapped infants provided by three mothers of older handicapped children', *Child: Care, Health and Development*, 5, 2, 103–109.

Rayner, J. (1978) 'The Exeter home-visiting project: the psychologist as one of several therapists', *Child: Care, Health and Development*, 4, 1, 1–7.

Johnson, C. and Katz, R. (1973) 'Using parents as change-agents for their children: a review', *Journal of Child Psychology and Psychiatry*, Vol. 14, No. 3, 181–200.

Kleisinger, G. (undated) 'The value of a parent-operated preschool center to personnel in the preventive health field', *Canadian Journal of Public Health*.

Kith and Kids Two-to-One Project, Chapter 10 in Pugh, G. (1981) *Parents as Partners*, National Childrens Bureau.

Magnus, R. (1974) 'Teaching parent to parent: parent involvement in residential treatment programs' *Children Today*, 3, 25–27.

McCall, C. and Thacker, J. (1977) 'A parent workshop in the school', *Special Education*, 4, 20–22.

Moore, S., Nikolski, I. and Presland, J. (1981) 'A workshop for parents of young handicapped children', *Journal of the Association of Educational Psychologists*, Vol. 5, No. 5, March.

Pollock, G. and Stewart, J. (1979) 'Development of provisions for preschool children with special needs within the framework of a School Psychological Service', *Journal of the Association of Educational Psychologists*, Vol. 5, No. 1, Summer.

Portage Project

Cameron, S. (1979) 'A lot can happen at home too', *Remedial Education*, 14, 4, 173–178.

Cameron, R. J. (ed.) (1982) Working with Portage in the UK, NFER, Walton-on-Thames, Surrey: Nelson.

Clements, J. C. *et al.* (1980) 'A home advisory service for preschool children with developmental delays', *Child: Care, Health and Development*, 6, 1, 25–33.

Daly, B. (1980) *Evaluation of Portage Home Teaching Pilot Project*, Barking and Dagenham School Psychological Service.

The Portage Project in South Glamorgan, Chapter 4 in Pugh, G. *Parents as Partners*, National Childern Bureau.

The Wessex Portage Project, Chapter 5 in Pugh, G. (1981) *Parents as Partners*, National Childrens Bureau.

Revill, S. and Blunden, R. (1979) 'A home training service for pre-school developmentally handicapped children', *Behaviour Research and Therapy*, 17, 207–214.

Revill, S. and Blunden, R. (1980) '*A Manual for Implementing a Portage Home Training Service for Developmentally Handicapped Preschool Children*', National Foundation for Educational Research.

Shearer, D. (ed) *Portage Project Readings*, CESA 12, Portage, Wisconsin.

Shearer, M. and Shearer, D. (1972) 'The Portage Project: a model for early Childhood education', *Exceptional Children*, 39, 3, 210–217.

Presland, J. (1975) *Success and Failure with Token Reinforcement at Home*, Occasional Papers of the DECP., 8, 370–379.

Presland, J. (1976) 'Token reinforcement by parents–a guide for action', *Journal of the Association of Educational Psychologists*, Vol. 4, No. 3, Xmas.

Robinson, W. (1979) 'How can we involve the parents?', *Special Education*, Vol. 6, No. 2.

Sandow, S. and Clarke, A. D. B. (1978) 'Home Intervention with parents of severely subnormal preschool children: an interim report', *Child: Care, Health and Development*, 4, 29–39.

Sheffield Family Centre, Union Road, Sheffield, 11.

Southend on Sea Group Therapy Scheme, Chapter 11 in Pugh, G. (1981) *Parents as Partners*, National Children Bureau.

Timm, M. and Rule, S. (1981) 'RIP (Regional Intervention Program): a cost-effective parent-implemented program for young handicapped children', *Early Child Development and Care*, Vol. 7, Nos. 2 and 3.

Yule, W. (1975) 'Training parents in child management', *Journal of the Association of Educational Psychologists* Vol. 3, No. 10, Autumn.

CHAPTER 8

Schools, Support Services and the Place of Parents

Changes in ideology, focus and intent are discernible in recent years in the vast area of supporting services and welfare networks the concern of which are children, their parents and families. Whether or not the changes are seen to be marginal or radical, 'flash in the pan' or long-lasting in their effects, they beg questions about the precise relationships between the 'vast armies' of personnel trained to work with or on behalf of children and may only serve to perpetuate the dilemma as to how we gauge the need for and the effectiveness of intervention.

Birley (in Craft *et al.* 1980) in the context of Liverpool – but which he says could be anywhere – paints a graphic picture of the seething proliferation of agencies existing to cater for the problems and needs of children

'each with its own traditions and techniques. Some owed administrative allegiance to education, some to other services, some were statutory, some voluntary. Most had been set up in earlier days to meet specific needs as they had emerged. Their paths crossed frequently, but more by accident or impromptu effort than design' (p. 305).

To the unitiated, the scene (and it is not unique to Britain) is a confusing array of what appears at worst to be a duplication of services. Within each of the major statutory services there are core, centrally placed personnel and a host of ancillary, field-based and para professionals. Several writers provide diagrammatic descriptions or representations of services (Milner 1974, Bolger 1975) which illustrate the complexity of the network.

The scope of this chapter is to provide an overview of some current developments in so far as they are designed as services for children and their families, and to examine the extent to which parents and child caretakers are client recipients, or partners in enterprises that purport to be interventions on their and their children's behalf.

1. Welfare and Support Services for Children

1.1 Issues Concerning Definition

A scan through sections on child services on library shelves would confirm the maze of provision and would highlight the underlying *raison d'être* of many services which is the presupposition and expectation of 'problems'.

Every practitioner receives a training which is oriented to particular conceptual frameworks and working definitions of problem-areas. Proper concentration on the chosen subject-area cannot but preclude indepth consideration of alternative theoretical formulations of what constitutes a problem in childhood and what other, equally viable treatment/intervention strategies there might be.

Any practitioner in any one area of working therefore has the advantage of being able to bring highly-developed sets of skills and a range of solutions or supports to the resolution of a child's difficulties, but is at a disadvantage in not having access to theory and practice in related areas. As far as parents of referred children are concerned, it is now part of the folklore among them and professionals that they find it very hard to distinguish the purpose and function of one agency from another. Often the generic word 'welfare' is used by parents as a counter to the bafflement of knowing exactly what any service has on offer for an individual child.

In an historical analysis over the last hundred years or so of society's responsiveness to children's needs, Heywood (in Stroud 1975) traces the roots of social concern and the growth of provision. She contrasts factors pertaining to former times and the factors governing child services that operate today – among others they are

'... our body of psychological knowledge about the development of children which has recognised their nature and emotional rights, and so individualised them, enfranchising them from categorisation' (p. 13).

Despite Heywood's hopeful view, the stumbling-block of problem definition appears insurmountable. Chapter 5 examined the categorisation of children into 'disadvantaged' and 'advantaged'. Chapter 7 drew attention to the eleven statutory handicaps and described the Warnock proposition of a special educational needs continuum, accepted now as a working conceptualisation. But the need to assess children, to diagnose a problem, to record a statement of their needs, to match these to the appropriate provision may only perpetuate the unavoidable use of labelling. There have been research-based attempts to classify and provide taxonomies of behaviour disturbance and allied 'conditions' (see Wolfendale and Bryans 1979 for a distillation of these). But to what extent there formulations are an aid to practice and inter-professional communication is not established.

2. The Scope of Intervention

Kelman and Warwick (quoted by Marshall in Craft *et al.* 1980) highlight the dilemmas facing personnel from social and caring agencies when

'in an effort to get on with practical action, the values underlying both the definition of the problem and the terminal state are treated as obvious or are glossed over as matters of science' (p. 291 in Craft).

The ethical issues in the intervention of social work are perceived by these authors as the choice of goals, the definition of the target, the choice of means and the assessment of consequences. Murgatroyd in an examination of 'issues facing helpers' (1980) raises several issues to be considered at the outset of any intervention.

Because we do not, and may never have, foolproof systems of identification of incipient social, educational, behavioural problems and latent handicapping conditions (Wedell and Raybould, eds 1976), and because we do not have at present sophisticated 'technologies of intervention' (Evans 1979, and see Chapter 5) current intervention approaches are intended primarily to ensure that problems, situations, and relationships do not deteriorate further beyond the point of referral. Thus approaches are not preventive – but they can be constructive steps towards alleviation and resolution of problems.

Intervention on behalf of children and their families takes various forms. The list below sets out the range of support service help which is available in Britain. Each category of professional intervention is given with the assistance giving agencies in brackets.

1) *Practical intervention*: obtaining information on behalf of the referred child, parents and schools; assistance with claiming rights to

benefit; access to financial assistance (social services, education welfare service).

2) *Statutory intervention*: children taken into care; parents and children before courts; residential placement (social services, education welfare service as mediators).

3) *Therapeutic/supportive intervention*: variety of therapeutic techniques, from general case-work to structured approaches within theoretical frameworks and along prescribed lines (education welfare service, social services, child guidance clinic, psychological services, psychotherapy).

4) *Educational intervention*:

(a) *School-based*: diagnosis, assessment of children; advice and support with curricular approaches and behaviour management (psychological service, remedial advisory service), residential placement (psychological service).

(b) *Unit/centre based*: further assessment; provision for behaviour and learning difficulties (psychological services, remedial advisory services).

5) *Treatment/Intervention outside school*: (centres, clinics)

(a) *Specialist assessment* (psychological service, child guidance, paediatric units, health and medical services).

(b) *Treatment and help with specific problems and handicap* (*viz* speech therapy, hearing difficulties).

Given the extensive and advanced nature of prior training and the specificity of role, it is easy to see how the client concept (see Chapter 2 for definition and discussion) arose and became an endemic part of professional practice. Clients, mostly parents, became 'dependents' and 'customers' of services offered by experts in child development, child rearing, psychopathology, and procedure.

Midwinter (1977) in tracing the evolution of the caring agencies, points out, in a searing indictment, how separated the professionals within them now are from the people and the community they were designed to serve.

They have become bureaucratised, defensive about manning and function, haunted by false fears of 'dilution', jittery about evaluation and open accountability, jargon-plagued, status conscious, and sheltering in a pother of insecurity, behind a barricade of mystiques (p. 106).

The ultimate criterion by which service provision can be justified is of course the perceived effectiveness of their interventions and the extent to which expertise can bring about alleviation or resolution of the defined problem.

A number of professionals working with children have been dissatisfied with the piecemeal service they offer within an expert-client ethos. Within and between agencies, new and different ways of working with children and their families and schools are being tried out. Basically, these initiatives are designed to:

— facilitate links between services;
— improve the quality of service delivery;
— demonstrate greater community relevance, irrespective of service setting;
— reduce role demarcations, including that of parent as passive recipient of services.

2. Tradition versus Trends

These recent developments can be distinguished from core duties that continue to be carried out by individual professional workers. As with innovation in any sphere, some novel and imaginative departures from established practice, once proven, become part of the overall provision, and this phenomenon is evident within contemporary child care services.

2.1 Cooperative Care

The main characteristic that emerges from a survey of recent endeavours to offer improved care and treatment services to children and their parents is the multidisciplinary emphasis. The descriptive term Cooperative Care was used by the Centre for Information and Advice on Educational Disadvantage (CED) when it set out to gather examples of 'good practice' within and across the boundaries of separate agencies. The Centre assembled sets of profiles from all over Britain showing how, in varying combinations, school staff (class-teachers, year heads, pastoral teachers, home liaison teachers), social workers, and education welfare officers have set up projects aimed variously at:

— developing preventive social work based in schools (Coventry, Ellesmere Port, Gateshead, Haringey, Manchester, Sheffield).
— promoting home–school links (Halton, Cleveland, Coventry);
— establishing interdisciplinary working parties and committees to form general working links (Hertfordshire, Penge in Bromley) or to focus on one target group of children, *viz*, disruptive children (Staffordshire);
— effective school-agency communication on behalf of 'vulnerable' children (Bicester, Halifax), and handicapped school leavers (Northumberland).[†]

These joint ventures have not always involved parents. They are forward-looking in that the people involved have demonstrated that it is possible to break down some communication barriers, to cut through established procedure (for example, the 'correct' route by which an adolescent suspended from school might be referred to the appropriate agency), and effect cooperative means of working in schools and with children. The preventive element in some social services and education collaborations relates to early warning systems, whereby emerging emotional behaviour problems can be identified and the communication network can ensure prompt action.

Examples of interdisciplinary cooperation have been presented in previous chapters of this report. Chapters 3 and 5 examined projects and studies which were designed for the needs of allegedly socio-economically disadvantaged children. In these the interface of community and schools has been paramount, irrespective of the project's siting. Workers in these contexts have come from education (home liaison, educational home visitors) social services (community social workers) and voluntary agencies (community workers). In Chapter 7 a summary chart shows that the multidisciplinary focus is

---

Project descriptions appear in Centre for Educational Disadvantage (CED) journals covering the period from mid to end 1970's, in separate profiles published by CED, and the main CED compendium Cooperative Care 1977. The CED is now defunct. An interested reader could pursue enquiries from the Department of Education and Science which funded the CED.

rather different. In the projects which have been designed to meet the special educational needs of handicapped children, the representatives from education are mostly educational psychologists and teachers, the representatives from health services are paediatricians, child health community medicine specialists, health visitors, clinical medical officers, clinical psychologists. There has been less input in this sphere from social services and voluntary agencies. In some of the projects there has been university or research centre input. All of these have espoused the parents-as-partners principle.

Despite discernible and quite legitimate differences in philosophy, intention and method, one trend emerges clearly and that is the acknowledgment by professionals that the quality of service they offer to families can be improved if expertise and experience are shared.

2.2 Changing Directions within Services

Each of the main statutory services employs personnel who have an explicit brief to work with families. The main agencies are:

— social work (social services);
— psychological services (in education, and social services);
— education welfare (education service);
— child psychiatrists (health service).

Comprehensive descriptions of each service, core duties and scope of each job are contained in Bolger (1975) and Fitzherbert (1977).

Each agency has evolved, over the years since its inception, styles of working with children and their parents that reflect the main mandate of each, as well as prior training within each discipline. The list presented earlier in this chapter portrays the various kinds of intervention offered by agencies to children and families. While some basic duties remain unaltered, within each agency there are developments, over and above the collaborative exercises referred to earlier, which are indicative of changing philosophies and professional aspirations. Mainly these reflect a greater commitment to considering child and family 'problems' within community settings, a rejection of some underlying assumptions regarding pathologies, and a diffusion of the expert-client dichotomy.

These different ways of working are documented in professional journals and texts. The purpose of the following section is to illuminate these major redirections, *vis à vis* direct work with or on behalf of families. Key references are given to further reading in each area.

2.3 Child Guidance and Therapeutic Orientations

Petrie and McConachie (1975) describe the functions and mode of working of psychiatrists, social workers and play therapists which could be said to be typical of many British child guidance clinics until very recently. Critiques of the medical model employed by psychiatrists in 'diagnosing' 'pathologies', of the alleged remoteness of child guidance from schools and wider public have included Shepherd *et al.* (1974), Rehin (1974) and Wolfendale and Bryans (1979). Tizard (1975) criticised child guidance for being 'ineffective in treatment, insensitive to the needs of the community they are meant to serve...' (p. 22).

The traditional treatment model has been hierarchical, involving the expert (psychiatric social worker/psychiatrist) versus the client, who is in a subordinate, dependent position. Increasing dissatisfaction with this divisive and largely ineffective approach (in terms of bringing about lasting positive change on the part of the 'patient', adult or child) has partly accounted for the adoption of family therapy by staff in child guidance clinics. Support and guidance can be effected by dealing with the family as a whole using family therapy techniques (Skynner 1976, Walrond-Skinner 1976). Whilst the clinician is still the expert who aims to impart and develop skills of self-understanding, insight, self-control, and coping strategies, the professional–client dialogue is rather more democratic. Family therapy sessions are a learning experience for the family members and the clinician, who will then utilise events and the accounts in discussion with the family to effect the desired changes.

Behaviour modification represents another current approach, whereby psychologists, and sometimes social workers and psychiatrists help parents to develop appropriate management and child-rearing techniques. Several references to applied behavioural analysis and behaviour modification work with parents were given in Chapter 7 (also see McAuley and McAuley 1977). The aim is for

parents, who initially seek help with home-based behaviour problems, to become independent of the need for expert support by
developing understanding and self-generating skills. The therapist is
a catalyst rather than a crutch.

Herbert (1975) and Rutter (1975) give extensive accounts of
traditional and 'newer' therapies and treatment approaches.

2.4. Social Work Within Education

1. Education welfare officers

The history of the education welfare service is described and
summarised by Bolger (1975), Fitzherbert (1977) and MacMillan
(1977). The major functional areas in which education welfare
officers are involved are: school attendance; handicapped children;
court proceedings; transport; clothing, child employment; free
meals; maintenance; placement of children; child neglect, extra-
district pupils. In the widest context their brief is to be a link and the
agent of communication between home and school.

The main area of change is that now the profession wants to
incorporate a more explicit social-work function with families
(casework and preventive social work) in addition to core and
statutory duties. Increasingly the job title is that of education social
worker, and most local authorities have opted to retain the service
within education rather than transfer it to social service departments.
Robinson (1976) says graphically that if the education welfare officer
is to play this part (of education social worker) he 'must die to be born
again as a school social worker' (p. 109). This is one way of expressing
just how radical a shift to professional focus it would be for education
welfare officers to move unequivocally in this direction. The role
demarcation between education social workers and social workers
within social services is blurred in practice, and there remain
unresolved intra-professional issues (MacMillan, in Craft *et al.* 1980).

2. Social workers in schools

As can be seen from referring to the CED profiles on Cooperative
Care, one development during the 1970s was the introduction of
social workers based in schools, working preventively, liaising with

teachers and following through casework with children and their parents (Marshall in Craft *et al.* 1980). The rationale for this siting of social-work intervention is the facilitation of home–school links via the pairing of education and counselling services (see below) as well as improving school service links.

3. School-based liaison and counselling roles

Mention of home liaison teachers and educational home visitors has cropped up in earlier chapters (Bailey and Poulton, in Craft *et al.* 1980). These education-employed personnel, usually trained teachers, would seem to be the ideal link between school and home. Yet their existence could absolve schools from implementing a thorough-going policy for parent participation, because the brief of home contact staff can be confined to that of a school-based social worker. Parents do not necessarily gain increased access to schools or greater knowledge of educational processes and routines. The same potential constraints apply to the provision in some schools of teacher–counsellors, whose frame of reference is to offer counselling and support to adolescents going through 'normal' developmental crises as well as rather more intractable personal/social problems. With the role, counsellors promote and maintain links with other services, and may or may not instigate contact with parents. However, there is not much scope for parent–counsellor cooperation within the role of school-based counsellors as it has been practised up to now in the hundred or so, invariably secondary, schools in England and Wales fortunate enough to employ counsellors. Daws (in Craft *et al.* 1980) forsees that during the 1980s counselling services will spread to primary schools 'in which counselling is offered to anxious parents rather than to pupils' (p. 255).

The danger of continuing to prevent parents from having a greater presence in schools could be averted by an extension of the educational home visitor concept along lines suggested in Chapter 10.

2.5. Child Psychological Services

1. Educational Psychologists

Accounts of the work of psychologists employed in education are given by Chazan *et al.* (1974), Bolger (1975), Fitzherbert (1977),

Gillham, ed. (1978) and Wolfendale (1981). For years, educational psychologists who are also trained teachers, have had a wide-ranging brief to be involved in depth with children and teachers in schools and to be the main link between schools and parents. This calls for a multi-facetted role on the part of educational psychologists, which includes assessment, diagnosis and special education planning for children with special educational needs, in-service work with teachers, and extensive casework with parents. In latter years, as the chart in Chapter 7 confirms, a number of educational psychologists have used behaviour modification techniques in working with children and their parents, and school-based family counselling to a lesser extent (Taylor 1977).

The move away from family-focussed casework by educational psychologists in favour of systems and curriculum-focussed approaches (Gillham, ed. 1978), Ainscow and Tweddle 1979, McPherson and Sutton, eds 1981) is deplored by Knapman (1976) who carried out a localised enquiry to verify this 'trend'. He makes out a case for the continued investment by educational psychologists in work with parents. In fact the 'move away' may represent a redirection of *some* aspects of the educational psychologist's job.

A survey into the in-service teacher training activities (INSET) of local education authority educational psychologists (Wolfendale 1980) confirmed that the core feature of the work continues to be involvement with children, and with teachers on behalf of individual children. Even if a proportion of educational psychologists want to relinquish the home contact part of their work—and there is insufficient documented evidence at present to suggest that a significant number of them do want to—the chief decision-making responsibility in the special education procedure has been theirs. In the Education Act 1981 (which seeks to amend the law on special education – Chapter 7) educational psychologists continue to have that paramount duty towards educational decision-making, and their advisory and supportive relationship to parents will continue to be crucial.

It was seen in Chapter 7 that an increasing number of educational psychologists are collaborating with co-professionals and parents in the setting up and running of learning programmes for handicapped children and others with special educational needs. This is likely to be a growth area, and indeed there is scope for fruitful partnerships involving schools, parents and educational psychologists in which teachers and psychologists design learning packages for children and parents to work on at home (see Chapter 3).

2. *Psychology in the Community*

Some educational psychologists argue that the proper domain for their practice is within the community, and that includes schools as one community resource for children and their parents (Reeve 1979). Some examples of community-based work for children with special needs and their families which involved psychologists were described in Chapter 7. Loxley (in Gillham, ed. 1978) indicts the psychological practice which does not take into account wider social forces and which fails to critically examine social institutions like schools. He mentions several community-based projects in his locality with which educational psychologists are involved. These include the education of gypsy children, community rights and advice centres, and community toy libraries.

As Brown (in McPherson and Sutton, eds 1981) points out, educational or clinical psychologists employed by social services departments are beginning to work in ways other than the traditional psychometric assessment role ascribed to them. These include social skills training programmes and job preparation schemes for delinquents, social learning approaches, in-service training of child care and residential social workers, and involvement in management and institutional decision-making.

Psychologists can work within the community network without necessarily owing allegiance, as paid employees, to the statutory services (Shackleton–Bailey 1979) and in these circumstances the psychologists can be more properly client-centred and can concentrate on service delivery, unhampered by bureaucratic constraints. Thus psychological services to children and their parents can be direct, accessible and accountable.

3. The Relation Between Schools and Agencies and the Siting of Help

Teachers in schools and personnel in the statutory agencies have long expressed ambivalent attitudes and views about each other which are benevolent or discordant depending on the frequency and type of contacts they have enjoyed. Informal consumer research carried out by practitioners (Fitzherbert 1977) as well as more formally conducted pieces of research (Johnson *et al.* 1980) bear this out. In a continuing enquiry carried out into home-school links and the work of the support services (Welton), a preliminary questionnaire to secondary schools revealed the degree of satisfaction expressed by them with the contribution of the various agencies. The researchers comment.

Services to which schools give low scores indicating a less satisfactory working relationship appear to be penalised for lack of accessibility, lower degree of regular contact, and failure to give feedback of information to schools.

It is the author's experience, acquired from working in schools and running in-service courses, that teachers always welcome information about each of the services and the ways in which they function, and need to know what the criteria for referral are to each service and how to distinguish between the contributions of each. The author and an Open University Post-Experience course team devised a format to assist teachers with their decision-making over referrals (Wolfendale 1979). There is also evidence (see CED profiles referred to earlier) that schools welcome the opportunity to work cooperatively with members of other teams. Whether or not the permanent siting of some agency workers in or adjacent to schools would be successful is queried by Robinson (1978) when she examines the suggestions put forward by Rose and Marshall for school social service centres.

Within the context of parental participation in the development and education of children, the question has to be asked as to whether home–school links are enhanced by the presence in schools of co-professionals from other services, bearing in mind that at any one time around 20% of a school population has special needs that justify or warrant service intervention (Warnock 1978).

Craft (in Craft *et al.* 1980) puts forward a model for school welfare provision, in which there are three essential components:

1) there should be an internal coordinator or convenor within each school;

2) there should be the elements of a team in each school;

3) there should be the establishment of a clear channel out of the school to neighbourhood welfare services.

Craft explains how the basic model could apply in various ways and with differing emphases in schools, taking into account differential school size, location, existing structure and organisation. Johnson *et al.* (1980) put forward models of school-based, pastoral care. In Model Two the school counsellor is seen as the link person with agencies. It may not need research confirmation to presuppose that clear and explicit channels of intra-service communication cannot but benefit school–home relationships and provide parents with accessible means of help and support for their children.

Fitzherbert (in Craft *et al.* 1980) describes a research project, which could also be a viable model for interdisciplinary cooperation centred in schools. In three junior schools, one whole year group of children was screened by a team comprising representatives of the major services.

Any child who is identified by his teachers or another member as giving rise to concern is discussed at an interdisciplinary meeting and each member contributes what he can to understanding the problem and perhaps to its solution (p. 362).

An extension of this model could be to involve parents of children evincing early signs of learning and/or behaviour difficulties. Perhaps they should have the right to be involved with early-warning systems of this type.

4. Interdisciplinary/Multidisciplinary Cooperation

There is little dissent from the view, expressed with particular conviction in the Court and Warnock Reports, that cooperation among the main services is beneficial for the recipients of those services.

Recommendations were for joint consultative committees and joint care planning teams at local and regional level, and district handicap teams (Court Report). These were endorsed in the Warnock Report, which also proposed, within its envisaged several-stage assessment procedure, multi-professional assessment at local level. At regional level this would take place at the multi-professional centres suggested by Court. As in the area of pre-school provision, coordination of services for children with special educational needs was urged by the Warnock Committee, which also put forward a far-sighted proposal that there should be joint, initial training courses leading to a dual qualification, and post-qualification courses of inter-professional training. Examples of various combinations of specialist areas were given in the Report.

These proposals add up to a far more rigorous conception of what inter- and multi-professional cooperation should be, as a replacement of the ad hoc, impromptu holding of case conferences and use of the telephone to exchange information and treatment plans. Galloway (1976) and Murgatroyd (ed. 1980) give case study examples which show how professionals can work together on individual problems, but they do not discuss these within the overall machinery of an accepted policy for joint working.

A project was mounted as a joint enterprise between the education and personal social services in one area of Wales (Department of Health and Social Security 1977). It was designed to explore 'the interface of concern and responsibility' between these services for the whole range of children with special educational needs. It was hoped that one outcome would be that those responsible for practical delivery of services to children and their families should help evolve new approaches from their own experience. Some outcomes of the project are being implemented in local practice. Quite intentionally one of the aims 'was to evolve a model of working liaison between social and educational services which could be used by other local authorities'.

These moves are hopeful and the benefits to children and their parents seem evident though in reality would be difficult to measure precisely. The advantages of joint planning and modes of working would appear to be facilitation of communication, sharing of professional perceptions, information exchange, learning the methods of co-workers, evolution of joint problem-solving techniques, and opportunities for coordinated community service.

Set alongside the postulated benefits are the snags and pitfalls, amongst which number the following:

— duplication of resource; difficulties in communication; clash of professional perception; discrepant ideologies and theoretical frameworks; genuinely different spheres of knowledge; allegiances to own employing institutions; different aims and aspirations regarding intervention; disputes over role; demarcation; problems of hierarchy and status; time constraints.

F

5. Parents as Partners in Service Delivery

Despite the formidable nature of the disadvantages and obstacles precluding easy cooperation (Pringle, ed. 1980), continued take-up in local authorities of Court and Warnock recommendations, is advocated alongside the pursuance of policies for joint services for children.

However, what has been notably absent from research and discussions on home–school links and support services has been the place and contribution of parents themselves in processes of referral and intervention. Most blueprints for school—agency coopera-tion, for intra- and multi-disciplinary coordination and assessment, and for joint planning teams have not included the presence of parents as full, contributing team members when their own children are the focus of concern. Recommendations for and examples of parental involvement have tended to be incidental or tangential to a whole referral, diagnosis and intervention process.

Irrespective of one theoretical view that parents 'cause' and contribute to child pathologies and that children are interlocked into destructive patterns of familial interaction, it may not be too sweeping to assert that parents and child caretakers have undeniable citizen's rights to be involved in the policy and planning of child services. We have seen how the principle of parents as partners in specific areas of handicap and special need is replacing the outmoded client-model view that parents of 'problem' children are ineffective in child management, and need the 'topping up' of professional expertise in order to function and do their parental duty.

The same principles surely then apply to the statutory services that purport to exist on behalf of children and their parents, in whom all responsibility for their welfare is finally vested. It should not be forgotten, too, that requests for help and referral come, on many occasions directly from parents themselves, so a willingness to cooperate as a basic requisite is there from the outset in many cases.

Radical alternatives in which parents are participant members of an integrated child service and regarded as equal agents of change, are being pursued in parts of Canada and the USA. King (1978) describes a multi-disciplinary early childhood service in which 'participation by many parents is a mandatory part of the pro-gramme although the kind of involvement may vary considerably' (p. 26). And Weissman (1978) outlines the working of a community-based, client-involved agency created in New York City in 1972. It integrated all the services, reduced family stress, and helped to prevent family break up in many cases. A central feature was the family service contract. Thus accountability on all sides was in-built.

Kellmer Pringle (Pringle, ed. 1980) outlines some components for a committed parent–professional partnership. She envisages that the provision of services will be within an overall conception of community in its widest sense, incorporating professional services, self-help movement and voluntary bodies.

6. An Integrated Service for Children

A model of accountable service delivery where parents would play an equal part within an integrated service for children could adopt a procedure which would apply equally to all participants. The chart below shows how this could be organised. The involvement of parents is seen to be as integral as that of the professional workers. The full team comprises representatives from main agencies and co-opted ancillary workers where appropriate.

6.1 Integrated Service for Children

PROCEDURE	PARTICIPANTS (Professionals and parents)
problem identification and definition	⟶ full team
problem agreement	⟶ full team
further assessment	⟶ sub team
contractual basis for intervention	⟶ sub team
INTERVENTION	⟶ sub team (with channel of information back to full team)
points of review and re-assessment	⟶ sub team and/or full team
contract-end or renegotiation	⟶ full team

6.2. Description of Each Stage

1) *Problem identification and definition*: at the point of referral, the behaviour and the situation is discussed and analysed by the full team comprising agency representatives and parent(s).

2) *Problem agreement*: if there is a concensus that there is a problem that could be alleviated or resolved, the team members agree a course of action.

3) *Further assessment*: agreement regarding the professional province in which the problem falls and, consequently, which team members have the responsibility for further assessment and diagnosis.

4) *Contractual basis for intervention*: if further assessment and diagnosis lead to recommendations for intervention, the involved parties agree on the form and the length of the intervention, and proposed systems or review and reassessment.

5) *Intervention*: school, home, clinic, centre-based. Parent participation as and when agreed is appropriate (*viz* in therapy, home-based learning).

6) *Points of review and re-assessment*: all the team may or may not combine at this stage. It may only be necessary for the team members involved in the intervention to meet at review and reassessment points.

7) *Contract-end or renegotiation*: full team reappraisal of the effects of intervention and evaluation. Renegotiation of the contract if further intervention is warranted and agreed.

The involvement of the whole team at various stages of the entire process is proposed as a precaution and safety-measure to allow for possible inter-professional, parent–professional disputes or grievances to be aired with all the team members. Those not directly involved with the intervention would be in a better position to arbitrate and act as conciliators.

One immediate charge against the efficacy of this blueprint would be that present levels of manpower and existing organisational structures preclude such an ambitious scheme. What we do not know is whether or not a redistribution of present resources, in terms of staff and locations, a reappraisal of staff allocations, a review of administrative procedures, might not intentionally create the climate in which integrated parent–professional community services for children could operate.

References

Ainscow, M. and Tweddle, D. (1979) *Preventing Classroom Failure, an Objectives Approach*, Chichester, Sussex: John Wiley and Sons.

Bolger, A. W. (1975) *Child Study and Guidance in Schools*, London, WC2: Constable.

Brown, B. (1981) 'Constructing psychological services in social service departments', Chapter 5 in McPherson, I. and Sutton, A. (eds) *Reconstructing Psychological Practice*, London SW11: Croom Helm.

CED Centre for Information and Advice on Educational Disadvantage, 11 Anson Road, Manchester (until 1980 – enquiries now to DES).

Chazan, M., Moore, T., Williams, P., Wright, J. (1974) *The Practice of Educational Psychology*, Harlow, Essex: Longman.

Court, D. (Chairperson) (1976) *Fit for the Future*, Norwich: HMSO.

Craft, M., Raynor, J., Cohen, L. (eds) (1980) *Linking Home and School*, a new review, third edition, London, WC2: Harper and Row.

in Craft *et al.* as above:

Bailey, R., Chapter 17 'The home–school liaison teacher',

Birley, D., Chapter 20 'The social education team',

Craft, M., Chapter 22 'School welfare roles and networks',

Daws, P., Chapter 16 'The school counsellor',

Fitzherbert, K., Chapter 23 'Strategies for prevention',

Marshall, T. Chapter 19 'Ethical and political aspects of counselling and social work',

Poulton, G., Chapter 18 'The educational home visitor'.

Macmillan, K., Chapter 14 'The educational welfare officer: past, present and future'.

DHSS Welsh Office (1977) *Working Together For Children and Their Families*', Norwich: HMSO.

Evans, R. (1979) 'Identification and intervention', in Gains, C. and McNicholas, J. (eds) *Remedial Education: Guidelines for the Future*, Harlow, Essex: Longman.

Fitzherbert, K. (1977) *Child Care Services and the Teacher*, London, WC1: Temple Smith.

Galloway, D. (1976) *Case Studies in Classroom Management*, Harlow, Essex: Longman.

Gillham, W. (ed.) (1978) *Reconstructing Educational Psychology*, London, SW11: Croom Helm.

Gillham, W. (ed.) (1981) *Problem Behaviour in the Secondary School*, London SW11: Croom Helm

Herbert, M. (1975) *Problems of Childhood*, Pan.

Heywood, J. (1975) 'Changing responses 1870–1970', Chapter One in Stroud, J. (ed.) *Services for Children and Their Families*, Oxford: Pergammon Press.

Johnson, D., Ransom, E., Packwood, T., Bowden, K., Kogan, M. (1980) *Secondary School and the Welfare Network*, Old Working, Surrey: Gresham.

King, E. (1978) 'Early childhood services: a service for coordinating the educational, health and social services for young children and their families', *International Journal of Early Childhood*, vol. 10, no. 1.

Knapman, D. (1976) 'The role of parents in school psychological work', *Journal of the Association of Educational Psychologists*, Vol. 4, No. 1, Summer.

Loxley, D. (1974) *Beyond Child Guidance*, Psychological Service, Sheffield.

Loxley, D. (1978) 'Community Psychology', Chapter Seven, in Gillham, W. (ed.) *Reconstructing Educational Psychology*, London, SW11: Croom Helm.

MacMillan, K. (1977) *Educational Welfare: Strategy and Structure*, Harlow, Essex: Longman.

McAuley, R. and McAuley, P. (1977) *Child Behaviour Problems: an Empirical Approach to Management*, London, WC2: MacMillan.

McPherson, I. and Sutton, A. (eds) (1981) *Reconstructing Psychological Practice*, London, SW11: Croom Helm.

Midwinter, E. (1977) 'The Professional-Lay Relationship: a Victorian Legacy', *Journal of Child Psychology and Child Psychiatry*, vol. 18, No. 2, pp. 101–113, April.

Milner, P. (1974) *Counselling in Education*, London W1: Dent.

Murgatroyd, S. (ed.) (1980) *Helping the Troubled Child, Interprofessional Case Studies*, London, WC2: Harper and Row.

Petrie, C. and McConochie, D. (1975) *Child Guidance*, London, WC2: Macmillan.

Pringle, M. K. (ed.) (1980) *A Fairer Future for Children*, London, WC2: Macmillan.

Reeve, C. (1979) 'Responses to the community', *Remedial Education*, Vol. 14, No. 4, November.

Rehin, G. (1974) 'Child guidance at the end of the road', *Journal of the Association of Educational Psychologists*, Vol. 3, No. 2, Autumn.

Robinson, M. (1978) *Schools and Social Work*, London, WC1: Routledge and Kegan Paul.

Robinson, P. (1976) *Education and Poverty*, London, EC4: Methuen.

Rutter, M. (1975) *Helping Troubled Children*, Harmondsworth, Middx: Penguin.

Shackleton-Bailey, M. (1979) *Psychology and the Personal Social Services*, unpublished paper, Hampshire Social Services.

Shepherd, M., Oppenheim, B., Mitchell, S. (1974) *Childhood Behaviour and Mental Health*, University of London Press.

Skynner, R. (1976) *One Flesh – Separate Persons*, London, WC2: Constable.

Taylor, H. (1977) 'The development of family counselling in schools', *Journal of the Association of Educational Psychologists*, Vol. 4, No. 4, Spring.

Tizard, J. (1975) 'Maladjusted children and the child guidance service', *London Educational Review*, Vol. 2, No. 2, Summer.

Walrond-Skinner, S. (1976) *Family Therapy*, London, WC1: Routledge and Kegan Paul.

Warnock, M. (Chairperson) (1978) *Special Educational Needs*, Norwich: HMSO.

Weissman, H. (1978) *Integrating Services for Troubled Families*, San Francisco: Jossey Bass.

Welton, J. *Home-School Links Project*, Institute of Education, London University.

Wolfendale, S. (1979) 'Identifying children with special problems', *Reading and Individual Development Action-Research Project*, p. 334, Milton. Keynes: Open University.

Wolfendale, S. and Bryans, T. (1979) *Identification of Learning Difficulties – a Model for Intervention*, National Association for Remedial Education, Lichfield Road, Stafford.

Wolfendale, S. (1980) 'The educational psychologists' Contribution to INSET: a survey of trends', *Journal of the Association of Educational Psychologists*, Vol. 5, No. 3, Spring.

Wolfendale, S. (1981) 'Educational Psychologists and their contribution to the community', *Early Childhood*, Vol. 1, No. 9, June.

CHAPTER 9

The Place of Parents in Child Development

The outcomes of hundreds of US Head Start programmes point to an overwhelming conclusion that, in the words of Grotberg (1979) who undertook a review of many of these, 'parents in fact have been discovered as critical to the education and development of their children' (p. 217).

It is not that children have not been growing up, exploring, testing the environment, learning to socially and emotionally attach from time immemorial. Nor is it to assert that parents have failed on any set of criteria in the duties which societies delegate to them in rearing their young. There are no comparative yardsticks by which to measure the present in relation to the past. Attempts to draw comparisons between childrearing practices of yesteryear and today (Aries 1962, de Mause 1976) rely on documentation and contemporary (of the day) accounts, but cannot hope to distil the 'flavour' of the times, cannot give a frame by frame analysis, of adult–child interaction. What child development and family-focussed researchers and practitioners internationally regard as a key issue is that now, in the latter half of the twentieth century, we are equipped with the means to set up and control the circumstances in which children are reared and to analyse in minute sequential detail the factors and influences that have bearing on any one situation.

Implications emerging from the projects and programmes on disadvantaged children and their families (Chapters 3 and 5) and handicapped and 'problem' children and their families (Chapters 7 and 8) seem to cluster around two main messages for society. The first is that there can be intervention in 'disadvantaging' environments that can counter, even reduce, their alleged ill-effects on children. It seems to be possible to promote and capitalise upon the inherently positive features within even 'depriving' families and settings.

A second message is that where children have handicaps, developmental delays and problems amenable to change, their parents or care-givers can be utilised as resources of strength and power within the change process.

Grotberg is of the opinion that these implications 'are not readily picked up by many services and professionals' (1979, p. 217, and see Chapter 8). She echoes a key theme of this book in asserting that the implications apply to the development and education of *all* children, not just to those with special educational needs or presenting problems. Irrespective of socioeconomic background or conceptualised area of concern, the parent(s) of any child is in a position to optimise and enhance the functioning and well-being of that child.

Recent research into early developmental processes will be referred to during this chapter to lend support to the view that as we uncover and reveal the precursors and sequiturs of features and processes (Wolfendale and Bryans 1979) of child development and learning so children, their families and society can correspondingly benefit. Some of the research outcomes can be heralded at this stage by mention of a piece of action-research entitled *Teaching parents a strategy for enhancing infant development* (Metzl 1980). The intention was to focus on first-born infants of two-parent, self-supporting, 'middle-class' families of mixed ethnic background, but predominantly white. Thus the study was avowedly directed towards advantaged children, said usually not to be in need of extra training or stimulation. Metzl's conclusions, were that her study 'demonstrates the potential for intervention achievement in a middle-class environment', and 'it can be hypothesised that change is possible even in a socioeconomic population that has traditionally been presumed to be providing maximum stimulation'. (p. 585).

Thus the perspective on intervention with children and their families broadens to encompass all children.

1. Universal Contexts

In a number of countries children are still deprived of the wherewithal for survival, exploited and forced to work in dangerous and unhealthy conditions by society and their own downtrodden parents

(Challis and Elliman 1979), denied opportunities to enjoy a child-hood and to benefit from education and training. In these circumstances, talk of meeting psychological needs, of providing via legislation for the meeting of children's and parents' rights, consideration of how parents might be constructively involved in their children's development, becomes an obsolete and sterile intellectual exercise (Newsons in Richards ed. 1974). These truly deprived children have been excluded regretfully from the following discussion, which is concerned with making general points.

A major theme of the international Athens symposium (Doxiades, ed. 1979) which was convened to consider the situation and needs of the child 'in the world of tomorrow' was that progress in society can only be guaranteed if all forms of social planning explicitly take account of children. The message is to paediatricians, architects, town planners, engineers, economists, sociologists, politicians, as well as to educationalists, child care services – and parents.

One of the Athens Symposium participants, Kellmer Pringle, has asserted elswhere (Pringle 1975) that in an increased number of societies, children are now guaranteed physical survival and basic health care, and thus the next major challenge is to create opportunities that allow them to develop their learning potential. Even drawing upon the limited reservoirs of available information from past eras, it seems possible to tentatively compare changing attitudes to children over the centuries (Bryans and Wolfendale 1981). The present century has been called 'the century of the child' (Kennedy 1971) in advanced societies because of the amount of legislation and the number of government reports designed to improve the quality of children's lives and protect their rights.

Margaret Mead (1970) perceived all children in all cultures as *learners* who acquire universal skills like walking, eating, talking and who learn particular and unique skills provided that they have the opportunities to do so. In these terms, the responsibility of adults is to provide the circumstances in which the learning can take place.

Humanity ... is a matter ... of our capacity to accumulate and build upon the inventions and experience of previous generations (Mead 1970).

At any one time in their histories, societies represent a dynamic cross-flow of the forces of preservation against the forces of change and evolution. Thus a major task for parents is to equip children to be adaptable to their own developmental forces as well as to societal changes and in this way 'the universals of childhood become transformed by social conditions' (Tucker 1977, p. 14).

It is a difficult exercise to make valid cross-cultural comparisons of child-rearing practices, as Blurton-Jones *et al.* have pointed out (in Shaffer and Dunn, eds 1979). However, there is every sign from available information we have of child-rearing techniques in advanced and non-advanced societies (using material and technological criteria) that parents and adult care-givers take their responsibilities for the care, welfare and development of their children most seriously. It also seems that child-rearing methods, evolved over thousands of years, are complex and intensely purposive, and parents of many cultures are able to articulate the logic on which these are founded (UNESCO 1980).

It is on these observations that the premise rests that parents have a hitherto underestimated contribution to make in their children's development.

2. The Craft of Parenting

Dictionaries define 'craft' by synonymous reference to other words, *viz*, 'dexterity', 'art', 'skilled trade', 'occupation'. Implicit in the use of these nouns is a seeming contradiction, namely the training function necessary for skill-acquisition versus connotations of a job done efficiently and competently but lacking or never needing prior training.

Parenting (used in this chapter to denote care-taking and care-giving functions carried out by any combination of adults centrally involved in and taking responsibility for child-rearing) is a full-time 'occupation' but not a 'skilled trade' in the sense that society demands and provides for the requisite prior training. Reference is made in this chapter to the fact that training and parent preparation opportunities in this country have until very recently grown slowly, haphazardly and without central coordination. On the whole, a significant number of adults take on the status and duties of parents ignorant of many aspects of child development, early learning processes, the rigours and routines of baby and child care, and the procedures by which to obtain information and support for their new role (if indeed those resources exist in widespread and accessible form).

The status and role of parents is ignored by society until or unless parents bring themselves or are brought to public, official attention by virtue of perceived and apparent problems with the child-rearing process. Negative judgements may at this stage be invoked by officials and professionals and a glib polarisation into 'good' and 'bad' parents has been a tempting base on which to predicate the client concept of 'inadequate' recipients of much-needed expert services (see Chapters 2 and 8).

It should be possible to compile a pragmatic 'check list' of parenting functions without failing into the trap of exhortation resorted to by many publications aimed as a mass market. Without claiming to be exhaustive in respect of minutiae, a table is presented below which sets out in list form the provision offered to a greater or lesser extent of frequency, intensity, intentionality, and competence by most parents. A perusal of these functions and provisions confirms resoundingly that irrespective of whatever outside intervention into children's and family lives intends or aims to effect, the reality is that parents play the central part in their children's development (positively or otherwise) and correspondingly, are their children's main educators.

3. List of Parenting Functions

1) provide means of survival (meet 'primary' needs);

2) provide emotional support and endorsement (meet 'secondary' needs);

3) provide the setting in which personal development takes place;

4) provide an environment in which exploration and hypothesis-testing take place;

5) provide a frame of reference against and in which exploration outside the home can take place;

6) provide a protective environment for their young;

7) provide opportunities and direction for the growth of independent functioning and self-organisation;

8) act as models (of language, social/emotional behaviour, etc.);

9) train and guide their young towards understanding of and adherence to social norms (controls and restraints);

10) act as possessors and transmitters of knowledge and information about the world;

11) act as decision-makers and arbiters of decisions, minute by minute and in the long term.

Schaffer and Crook (1978) group mothering activity into four rough categories: physical care activity; stimulation; interlocution; a set of attitudes. These can be subsumed into the list presented above which is intended to embrace the role and function of mother and father figures.

Resulting from extensive research work, Burton White and his colleagues (1979) perceive three primary functions for caretakers of infants: designer, consultant and authority. The 'more effective' caretakers (mothers) in the research sample handled these functions competently:

1) *Design*: involved creating safe environments where resources for child play and child use are accessible and safe.

2) *Consulting*: the mothers made themselves constantly available to their children, as sources of comfort, imparters of information, resolvers of issues and answerers of queries.

3) *Authority*: the mothers within loving and supporting environments, set clear limits for acceptable/unacceptable behaviour.

In whatever way the maternal/paternal functions are conceptualised into viable theoretical frameworks, it remains evident, even axiomatic that those who rear their children influence and affect the course and the pattern of development. What has not yet been adequately established are the relations between parental intention (whether articulated or implicit), child-rearing methods in the home and their 'effects' in terms of patterns of growth, ways in which young children make contact with and perceive other humans, ways in which they use their homes as springboards from which to explore their world, respond to routines and learn to evolve their own.

In short, are there targets for researchers, policy-makers and politicians to aim at on behalf of all parents, *if* it is generally accepted as a policy base-line that:

1) the parental contribution to child-rearing is a hitherto unappreciated and untapped resource, and;

2) the educational role of parents within the family is seen as so crucial that school-based formal learning cannot effectively proceed unless parents are aided and supported to realise and maximise their own educative role?

4. Targets in Child-Rearing – Private and Public

Parents' own views on their approaches to child rearing, child management, their aspirations for their children, their perceptions of their success or failure at their task, have largely gone unexplored and unrecorded, except for isolated pieces of research. Of these, the most seminal in Britain has been the longitudinal survey into several hundred Nottingham families carried out by John and Elizabeth Newson and their research associates at the Child Development Research Unit, University of Nottingham. Their enquiries have elicited invaluable data on parents' intentions, anxieties, methods, attitudes and attempts to prepare their children for independent lives as mature citizens able to cope in contemporary society.

In the main, however, in setting up parent-focussed information and support services, officialdom has made assumptions about parents' needs without sufficient consumer research. In order to fully optimise professionals' contribution to supporting parents in their child-rearing task and educative roles, perhaps a match should be effected between public, official intentions and targets and parents' own targets and aspirations, which often remain private and unexpressed outside the home.

Whatever the criteria are for 'successful' child-rearing, presumably countless parent-figures over the years have been or have felt successful. By the same token, innumerable parents must have felt during their offsprings' childhood and later adulthood that they had failed – that resulting behaviour and emotional settledness, life situation, occupational status and material circumstances had turned out differently from what had been initially aspired to by those parents for their children.

The vulnerability and apprehension felt by parents from the first moments of their new-found role, and the mystiques associated with being a 'good' parent makes them prey to the exhortations often to be found in 'baby' books and child-care manuals. Whilst it would be invidious to single out any particular text, one can point in general terms to publications which set out the norms of child develop- ment in a simplistic format, thereby running the risk of incul- cating misery and guilt on parents' part if their babies and toddlers' development does not appear to conform to the chronology and sequence of these postulated stages. Another charge against many of these writers is that they often cannot resist the temptation to be exhortatory to parents about the 'right' attitude and method to adopt in coping with both predictable events and unexpected contingencies in daily life. If the methods do not work, if the outcomes are unsuccessful, parents who heed the remote, impersonal advice offered in print, feel guilt, failure, powerlessness, resourceless, and bewildered. The final accusation against these well-intentioned textbooks and pamphlets is that they purport to offer a blue-print for successful rearing and effective parental involvement.

As yet we do not know enough to offer pragmatically useful guidelines and information to parents attested and affirmed by sound research evidence in terms of:

— the inevitability and immutability of stages and sequences of child development;
— continuity and discontinuity in child development;
— features of early learning and early experience that influence and promote later learning, skill acquisition, etc;
— the long-term effectiveness of any one management and training approach over another.

Consequently, self-appointed experts who present their knowledge and assertions in print risk charges by parent-consumers (who may be better equipped than are many experts) of being irrelevent and misleading. At best, texts can only offer blunt guidelines and glib panaceas.

An interesting side-thought to these arguments is that there is very little information as yet about the extent to which these books, pamphlets, newspaper articles, television and radio programmes penetrate, impinge upon and influence parents' child-rearing practices.

5. Child Development Research and Implications for Child-Rearing Practice

The pioneering pre-war infant and child observation and recording techniques by Gesell and his colleagues in the USA marked the beginnings of what is now, internationally, an active and elaborate research scene characterised by imaginative and innovative methods of probing into the earliest moments of infant life. Research workers have availed themselves of and cooperated in the development of the hardware which has enabled them to focus and record second-by-second accounts of development and human interactions.

A piece of longitudinal research currently being conducted at the Child Study Unit, Psychology Department at the North East London Polytechnic (Woollett, White and Lyon 1980) epitomises the combined use of various techniques in a series of studies designed to investigate the social learning experiences of children under five years of age. Videotype is used to record and then analyse parent–child and peer social, emotional and language interaction from birth, in a sample of more than 40 families. One of the early interactive aspects of maternal and paternal contact is that of parental baby-holding preferences and from the analysis of videotype records, the researchers were able to identify five basic hold positions.

In the last fifty years or so, then, a strong tradition of empirical research into child development has evolved. Whereas formerly there had to be reliance on society's collective stock of myth and received wisdom about family interactions and rearing strategies, there is now an accumulating knowledge-base and permanently available 'objective' records and analyses of these features and processes. For example, the considerable work into the manifestations of 'attachment' behaviour since the concept was first delineated has called for a radical reappraisal and acknowledgment that the infant–mother bond and factors surrounding separation of even a few minutes are nothing like as unidimensional or simplistic as was once supposed

(Bowlby 1969, Schaffer 1971, Rutter 1972, Corter 1974, Bernal 1974).

The linked research into reciprocity and dyadic interaction has confirmed that very far from the baby being a passive recipient of and responder to adult-initiated behaviours, he/she equally and powerfully instigates contact, elicits responses, and regulates the course of interactions with the adult caretaker (Ainsworth *et al.* 1974, Trevarthen 1974, Macfarlane 1977, Stern 1977, Dunn 1979, Schaffer 1979).

Work is reported (Ryan, 1974, Wells 1975, P. and J. de Villiers 1979) into the earliest signs and manifestations of verbal and communicative behaviour of infants. Many of these studies are casting light on the context and events in the home situation that largely determine the nature and frequency of a child's verbal behaviours. For example Wells and his colleagues report that it seems that children are the main initiators of conversation with adults in the home.   Investigations by Schaffer (1971) and Bower (1977) amongst others, have established strong perceptual components in the socialisation process from birth, and just to confirm this interrelatedness of developmental processes, Schaffer reminds the reader that

cognition and social behaviours are not separate categories.. to study social development without reference to cognitive capacity would impose an arbitrary division that has no counterpart in nature (Schaffer 1971, p. 31).

Macfarlane (1977) has described the concept of 'state' in the newborn. There seem to be manifest differences in the length of time individual babies spend in any one state, and therefore, observable differences in the extent to which they remain alert, attentive and reactive to features of the environment. These may be amongst the earliest determinants in the later development of learning competencies such as attention-control, sustained exploration and concentration. Many researchers (Bruner 1974, Bower 1977, Stern 1977) have observed the rapid rate of information-processing which takes place in the infant in the first few months of life across the range of sensory modalities. The competencies which Bruner (1974) outlines into six main areas are perceived to be the precursors to later learning. These are feeding, perceiving, attending interacting with other humans, manipulating, locomoting and gaining control over own actions.

Other current or recently reported research activity is directing attention on the children's perception of others (in McGurk, ed. 1978), sibling interaction (Dunn), the home experiences of young children (Davie *et al.*). Much of the British work of the 1970s was reported by Tizard (1974) and a wider context is given in Pilling and Pringle (1978). A source of research interest and professional concern is the relation of early learning processes and the home settings in which they occur to the different kind of learning activity that takes place in pre-school or infant school settings. Several studies are exploring the parameters and ramifications associated with these relationships: amongst them are the NFER continuity and transition studies, and the cognitive and linguistic operations in the home and school context (Walkerdine). Research and theory into concepts of developmental continuities, discontinuities and effects of early experience are described in Shaffer and Dunn (eds 1979).

This necessarily selective review of recent, mostly British, research, hopefully conveys the richness and variety of the subject matter under scrutiny as well as demonstrate how, under rigorous research conditions, the process of development in the formative years can be observed and recorded as it occurs. The strength of much of this research activity is its objectivity, the avoidance of prior assumptions and value judgments during the research operation. The interest and involvement of participating parents is evident in many research reports.

Can interpreting facts amassed by researchers and child development theorists be used as a basis for illuminating directions which parental child-rearing practices could take, improving the quality and relevance of professional services to parents, and implementing intervention technologies? Jarman (1980) thinks so, but Stern (1977) is cautious: 'restraint is called for in face of the zeal created by our new knowledge' (p. 144). He feels that we have some way to go in knowing 'our own cultural range of normal infant caregiver interactive patterns' and that we cannot always distinguish between 'potential pathological patterns and simply 'the way things are' in any given family' (p. 144). However, Stern concludes that the caregiver's functions, performed largely unselfconsciously with an intuitive trust can be enhanced by knowing more and more 'about the process and finding it easier to create and perform in and enjoy it more thereby' (p. 146).

The view that as we discover more and more about fundamentals and uncover the principles underlying developmental processes, so society has a duty to apply the accumulating knowledge and intervene positively on children's behalf is endorsed by Caldwell (1975) and Bruner (1974). Indeed, this view comprises a major element of the rationale behind Head Start and compensatory education (Chapter 5).

One lesson to be learned is that if courses, books, articles and programmes are to continue to be provided for prospective or intending parents, as well as for existing parents, society in the form of professionals, policy-makers and administrators concerned with children does have a duty to impart informed advice, and well-attested facts based on sound research evidence. A welcome move in this direction is discernible. For example, Burton White's book for parents (1978) called 'a detailed guide to the physical, emotional and mental development of young children' is firmly based on his own extensive, well-documented research over a number of years. Consequently, it presents far more detail about the roots and precursors of development and competence in various areas than do traditional counterparts that resort to rhetoric and exhortation. Burton White imparts ideas to his readers for the development of strategies to enhance parents' educative role in the development of their young children.

6. Parenthood: Preparation, Education and Support

It is only recently that serious attention has been given to preparation for parenthood and parent support programmes in terms of their availability, relevance and suitability. Course provision, as Pugh has pointed out (1980), has tended to be patchy and appears in several guises: under a 'health education' umbrella in schools; in clinic-based antenatal classes; in courses offered by adult education institutes.

The clearest call yet from an 'official' source for a concerted national effort to provide an educative and supportive service for present and future parents came from the government commissioned Court Report on Child Health Services (1976). The Committee cogently stated 'we have found no better way to raise a child than to reinforce the ability of his parent(s) whether natural or substitute, to do so' (p. 2). Mindful that 'even if there were an agreed body of knowledge about parenting to be transmitted (and there is not) and one could work on the assumption that knowledge always changes behaviour (which one cannot)' the Committee members urged 'that any programme of education for parenthood should be based on principles rather than prescriptions (p. 154, para. 10.34). Basically, they believed that

families could be better at bringing up their children if they were given the right information, support and relationships with the caring professions when it was needed and in a more acceptable way (p. 25).

Whitfield (1979) defines preparation for parenthood and parent education and conceptualises the major topics within the overall field of Education for Parenthood, which he presents in Venn diagram form (p. 64). A major initiative is under way at the National Children's Bureau to coordinate and disseminate the ideas and information, schemes and services in the fields of preparation and support for parents with young children (Pugh 1981a). A possible framework for action is beginning to emerge from the preparatory work for this project (Pugh 1981b) which tentatively presents a sequential approach that incorporates the age and developmental stages of children up to adulthood. This model proposes the stages in adulthood for education and support to be: 'during a committed relationship', 'pregnancy', 'as a parent with young children', 'as a parent of older children'. At each stage of childhood or adulthood, the aims and sources of support are mapped, so there is a pragmatic match between perceived individual needs (either as child or adult) and appropriate provision.

Workers in this field do not underestimate the skills required of parents, nor the present levels of competence shown by many parents, nor the complexity of the task of providing a comprehensive, nationally coordinated service 'based on principles rather than prescriptions'. The format and instructional methods of existing courses and programmes can vary from formal lecture inputs, discussions, visits, practical sessions, films, video-recordings, role play (Tizard 1974, Jackson 1978, National Children's Centre). The Open University is in a prime position with potentially unlimited access to thousands of parents, professionals and interested citizens, and since

1977, in conjunction with the London-based Health Education Council, its resources have been utilised via courses aimed at identifying the issue and problems and increasing the knowledge of skills open to parents.

But current developments such as the ones referred to above, have undoubtedly been hampered by the legacy of the past, characterised by a lack of policy and corresponding paucity of provision. Whitfield chronicles this erstwhile dismal scene, comparing the advanced thinking and range of provision for parent education offered by statutory and voluntary bodies in parts of Europe and in America (also see UNESCO Annotated Bibliography, and the International Federation for Parent Education (IFPE)).

Economic stringencies notwithstanding, the present does seem an opportune time to put into practice a policy coordinated amongst education (in schools and institutes), health (in clinics, health centres) social services and voluntary organisations (community-based training and support groups). Pringle (1980) envisages the expansion of resources for parent education as one part of comprehensive family services, which would include preventive and intervention techniques within a true realisation of parent–professional partnership. Pringle's conception, shared by a number of professionals and given expression in the Court Report's metaphor: 'The stage appears set for a concerted effort – if we have the will to do it' (p. 3), is nothing less than that children are seen as society's most precious commodity and that their parents can be restored to their prime position as participants and co-educators in their children's development and education.

7. The Educational Role of the Family

7.1. Functions and Change within the Family

The Court Report on Child Health Services referred to the 'family' as 'a social arrangement for the protection and rearing of children' (p. 26, para. 1.3). A UNESCO report (1980) perceives the family as a segment of society at large, and a setting in which society's cultural features are mirrored and represented.

It is the place both where myths are recounted and where the institutions regulating society as a whole and the values on which those institutions are based are recalled to the collective and individual consciousness (p. 5).

Within this microcosm, various functions are carried out mainly by the adults who create and sustain the unit. These include

provision of the security and stimulus needed by dependent and growing children, and the opportunity of education and enjoyment for children and parents alike, relationships for their protection and nurture, education for responsibility and mutual enjoyment (Court, p. 27, para. 1.4).

Kagan (1979) takes three perspectives in his consideration of the functions of the family, the State's, the parents', and the child's. From the parents' perspective, he asserts, the family can be a

locus of solace and psychic relief... it provides each adult with an opportunity to feel needed and useful... it offers parents an opportunity to validate the value system they brought to adulthood (p. 211).

For the child, the family offers a model for identification, a source of protection and target of attachment, a setting wherein he/she will be in receipt of information and guidance, a place in which skills can be gradually acquired and competence achieved.

Counterwise, from the perspective of family members, the family can be seen to fail on any or all of these criteria, and can be a *milieu* in which emotional needs are not met, positive, enduring attachments are not made, solace from external pressures is not found, and in which little constructive learning takes place. The countless case-histories in child guidance and psychiatric clinics in the 'advanced' countries of the world bear testimony to the fragility as well as strength of the family; these accounts are matched only in great literature by tales of family feuds and fracas, internecine strife which persists for generations, told incomparably by the world's novelists over hundreds of years, who tell, too, of great loves and cosmic unions that endure and propagate harmony and serenity.

Can today's behavioural scientists and social planners bring any newfound wisdoms or solutions to bear on the perennial and unresolved paradoxes that characterise family life?

It is evident that dramatic changes in family composition are taking place in many contemporary societies. (Court Report 1976, Doxiades, ed. 1979, Coussins and Coote 1981, Lefaucheur 1981,

Study Commission on the Family 1980). Trends are noted concerning changes in ages of marriage and childbearing, increasing numbers of one-parent families, unmarried mothers, teenage mothers, divorce rates, greater proportion of working women and working mothers, changes in family size.

Whether or not terms like 'alternative life styles' are used, as Klineberg does (1980) in partialling out typical and a-typical family styles, it remains evident that multi-angled permutations on jobs and roles within the home are becoming an integral feature of contemporary society. These trends are intimately bound up with profound changes in life-style to the point where, as the Study Commission on the Family report observes, there is now no typical or 'normal' family pattern prevalent.

The ideological debate rumbles on as to whether these changes are beneficial to people and society (Rutter and Madge 1976, Pringle, ed. 1980, Woodhead 1981). But whatever the philosophical stance and value-system protagonists choose to adopt, the factual acknowledgement has to be made by them that unlike past eras, behavioural scientists and social policy-makers have a bounden humanitarian and professional responsibility to continually predict and assess for change, in order that maximum resources and supports shall be made available to adults and their children in what is agreed to be a perplexing and unpredictable world scenario (Kahn and Wiener 1967) in which disasters could be rife (Rattray Taylor 1970).

8. Family Tasks and Society's Obligations: A Summary

Changes in family composition and life style have been accompanied by an articulated reappraisal on the part of many parents of traditional man–husband, woman–wife roles. An increasing number of men are now participant in household affairs and chores and child-rearing activities, in keeping with their wives/partners who are also wage earners. Research is now beginning to pay more attention to the actual and potential influence of fathers (McGurk 1978, Pilling and Pringle 1978, Whitfield 1979, Turner 1980, Parke 1981, Richards, Woollett et al. 1980).

It is clear, however, from a study of all the action-research and intervention projects described in previous chapters that it is fathers, who by virtue of work patterns as well as expectation, play least part in these collaborative ventures. If parent participation in all its facets is to become active practice, that balance has to be redressed some way to enable fathers to be and to feel free to contribute their equal share of interest, concern and expertise.

This brief focus on father involvement serves as an example to demonstrate the mutuality and complementarity of the tasks facing families and society institutions.

The current OECD/CERI research (1981 onwards) enquiry into *The Educational Role of the Family* in its initial (unpublished) draft papers captures the essence of the two-way 'contract' that could exist between parents and professionals. It regards the family as the most crucial agency of education; it 'may represent the most effective lever today for raising educational outcomes for the times ahead'. Initial evidence from the participating countries confirms that efforts in the field 'do not involve replacing parents but rather assisting them to realise their own parental resources – to foster for example, their own powerful intuitive processes – which are the fundamental resource available for the education of the young'. In societal terms, parental contributions to child development and education are seen as a central way of raising the efficiency of or 'return' on the investment in huge educational budgets of developed countries.

In an article which forecasts the family in the world of tomorrow, Klineberg (1980) asks rhetorically 'Can educators train parents and children to deal with the new, the unknown? Can they help develop the flexibility needed to face a world in constant and rapid change?'. His questions are asked in a spirit of 'high hopes for the future' for he perceives that the institution of the family and the members who comprise it can be flexible enough to anticipate and accommodate change.

Even the concepts of parenthood and parenting are undergoing change. There is evidence (Woodhead 1981, and in Doxiades, ed. 1979) that parenthood is coming to be regarded as a career and a phase of life rather than a closed permanent state. Increasing numbers of men and women have articulated aspirations to realise themselves fully as individuals, which involves occupations other than, though including, parenting. Again, this is an example of a two-way reciprocal responsiveness between individuals and wider society – for individuals to have the opportunities to meet these variegated personal needs, including untrammelled changes to be mothers or fathers, and for society to acknowledge and provide the circumstances, the career prospects, the childcare arrangements, the family support systems.

It is clear from weighing the evidence presented in this book, which in turn is representative of so much more evidence, that intervention into children's lives, and structuring of their experience, can take a multiplicity of forms.

Visionary variations, combining public resources for child and family benefit, come from highly respected academic sources. J. McVicker Hunt has long been associated with a compassion and concern for children's rights. He advocated (1969) Centres for Parents and Children which combine services for families on an 'open door' system, and aim to develop parental skills in child care. Marion Blank (in Tizard 1974) has suggested the development of 'shared rearing pre-schools' and 'academic pre-schools'. The former she envisages as

providing the parents of young children with services to aid them in the responsibilities of child care . . . to help them and the entire family to function in a more effective and enjoyable manner (p. 96).

'Academic pre-schools' would have formal education as the central goal.

This investment into childhood and a child-centred philosophy can be justified on the grounds that it is society's collective survival that is at stake. Whether or not this is so, undeniably, competence and adaptability are called for on the part of children and adults, i.e., 'we are all learners now' (Botkin *et al.*, see Chapter 2).

Machado (1980) asserts that each and every citizen has the 'right to be intelligent', consequently, 'the first human necessity is education'. Machado, now Minister of State for the Development of Human Intelligence in Venezuela would therefore be of the opinion that education begins in the home, and pace the quotation from Grotberg at the outset of this chapter, we could be confident that the delegation and sharing of this task to parents, with the proper support, is as appropriate now as it has ever been.

References

Ainsworth, M. D., Bell, S. and Stayton, D. (1974) 'Infant–mother attachment and social development: socialisation as a product of reciprocal responsiveness to signals', chapter 6 in Richards, M. (ed.) *The Integration of a Child into a Social World*, Cambridge University Press.

Aries, P. (1962) *Centuries of Childhood*, Harmondsworth, Middx: Penguin Education.

Bernal, J. (1974) 'Early language development: towards a communicational analysis', in Richards, M. (ed.) *The Integration of a Child into a Social World*, Cambridge University Press.

Blurton-Jones, N., Woodson, R. H., Chisholm, J. S. (1979) 'Cross-cultural perspectives on the significance of social relationships in infancy', Chapter 7 in Shaffer, D. and Dunn, J. (eds) *The First Year of Life*, Chichester, Sussex: John Wiley and Sons.

Bower, T. (1977) *A Primer of Infant Development*, Oxford: W. H. Freeman.

Bowlby, J. (1969) 'Attachment' *Attachment and Loss, Vol. I*, Harmondsworth, Middx: Penguin-Pelican.

Bruner, J. (1974). 'The organisation of early skilled action', Chapter 9 in Richards, M. (ed.) *The Integration of a Child into a Social World*, Cambridge University Press.

Bryans, T. and Wolfendale, S. (1981) 'Changing attitudes to children – a comparative chronicle', in *Early Childhood*, Vol. II, No. 1, October.

Burton, L. White (1978) The First Three Years of Life, London, W1 : W. H. Allen.

Burton, L. White (1979) 'Critical influences in the origins of competence', in Oates, J. (ed.) *Early Cognitive Development*, Open University Press (Milton Keynes) and Croom Helm (London, SW11).

Caldwell, B. (1975) 'What is the optimal learning environment for the young child?', Chapter 11 in Sants, J. and Butcher, H. (eds) *Developmental Psychology*, Harmondsworth, Middx: Penguin.

Challis, J. and Elliman, D. (1979) 'Child workers today', Antislavery Society, 56 Weymouth Street, London, W1.

Corter, C. (1974) 'Infant attachments', Chapter 5 in Foss, B. (ed.) *New Perspectives in Child Development*, Harmondsworth, Middx: Penguin.

Coussins, J. and Coote, A. (1981) *Family in the Firing Line*, NCCL and CPAG, 1 Macklin Street, London, WC2.

Court, D. (Chairman) (1976) *Fit for the Future*, Norwich: HMSO.

Davie, C., Vincent, E., Mason, M., Hutt, J. *Home Experience of Young Children*, Department of Psychology, University of Keele.

Doxiades, S. (ed.) (1979) *The Child in the World of Tomorrow*, Oxford: Pergammon.

Dunn, J. (1979) 'Mother–infant relations: continuities and discontinuities over the first 14 months', in Oates, J. (ed.) *Early Cognitive Developments*, Open University Press (Milton Keynes) and (London, SW11) Croom Helm.

Dunn, J. Medical Research Unit, University of Cambridge.

Grotberg, E. (1979) 'The parental role in education and child development' in Doxiades, S. (ed.) *The Child in the World of Tomorrow*, Oxford: Pergammon.

Hunt, J. McVicker (1969) *The Challenge of Incompetence and Poverty*, University Illinois Press.

IFPE (International Federation for Parent Education), 1 Avenue, Léon-Journault, Sèvres, France.

Jackson, T. (1978) 'A new look at parent education', *Adult Education*, Vol. 50, No. 5, January, pp. 294–297.

Jarman, D. (1980) 'Some implications for the child's educational potential of recent investigations into early childhood interaction' in *Early Child Development and Care*, Vol. 6, Nos. 3/4.

Kagan, J. (1979) *The Growth of the Child*, London, EC4: Methuen.

Kahn, H. and Wiener, N. (1967) *The Year 2000*, London, WC2: Macmillan.

Kennedy, D. (1971) *Children*, London, W1: Batsford.

Klineberg, O. (1980) *Futureology and the Family of Tomorrow*, IFPE Bulletin.

Lefaucheur, N. (1981) *The Emergence of New Family Styles*, IFPE Bulletin.

Macfarlane, A. (1977) *The Psychology of Childbirth*, Fontana (London SW1) and Open Books (Shepton Mallet, Somerset).

Machado, L. (1980) *The Right to be Intelligent*, Oxford: Pergammon.

de Mause, L. (ed.) (1976) *The History of Childhood*, London, WC1: Souvenir Press.

McGurk, H. (ed.) (1978) *Issues in Childhood Social Development*, London, EC4: Methuen.

Mead, M. and Wolfenstein, M. (1970) *Childhood in Contemporary Cultures*, University Chicago Press.

Metzl, M. (1980) 'Teaching parents a strategy for enhancing infant development', *Child Development*, Vol. 51, No. 2, June.

National Children's Centre *Preparation for Parenthood* courses, Longroyd Bridge, Huddersfield.

National Foundation for Educational Research (NFER) (1982)
1. *Continuity of Children's Experience in the Years 3–8.*
2. *Transition and Continuity in Early Education.*

Newson, J. and E. (1974) 'Cultural aspects of childrearing in the English-speaking world', Chapter 4 in Richards, M. (ed.) *The integration of a child into a social world*, Cambridge University Press.

OECD/CERI (1981) *The Educational Role of the Family*, Paris.

Parke, R. (1981) *Fathering*, Fontana (London, SW1) and Open Books (Shepton Mallet, Somerset).

Pilling, D. and Pringle, M. K. (1978) *Controversial Issues in Child Development*, Paul Elek and National Children's Bureau.

Pringle, M. K. (1975) *The Needs of Children*, London, N5: Hutchinson.

Pringle, M. K. (1980) *A Fairer Future for Children*, London, WC2: Macmillan.

Pugh, G. (1980) *Preparation for Parenthood*, National Children's Bureau.

Pugh, G. (1981a) 'Parenthood: towards a framework for education and support', in *Early Child Development and Care*, Vol. 7, Nos. 2 and 3.

Pugh, G. (1981b) *Parent Education and Support, a Framework*, draft paper, unpublished, National Children's Bureau.

Rattray Taylor, G. (1970) *The Doomsday Book*, London, WC1: Thames and Hudson.

Richards, M. *Theoretical Study of Ideologies of Parenthood*, Medical Psychology Unit, University of Cambridge.

Robin, M. (1980) 'Interaction process analysis of mothers with their newborn infants', in *Early child Development and Care*, Vol. 6, Nos. 3/4.

Rutter, M. (1972) *Maternal Deprivation Re-assessed*, Harmondsworth, Middx: Penguin.

Rutter, M. and Madge, N. (1976) *Cycles of Disadvantage*, London, WC1: Heinemann.

Ryan, J. (1974) 'Early language development: towards a communicational analysis', in Richards, M. (ed.) *The Integration of a Child into a Social World*, Cambridge University Press.

Schaffer, R. (1971) *The Growth of Sociability*, Harmondsworth, Middx: Penguin Education.

Schaffer, R. (1977) *Mothering*, Fontana (London, SW1) and Open Books Shepton Mallet, Somerset.

Schaffer, R. and Crook, C. (1978) 'The role of the mother in early social development', in McGurk, H. (ed.) '*Issues in Childhood Social Development*', London, EC4: Methuen.

Shaffer, D. and Dunn, J. (eds) (1979) *The First Year of Life – Psychological and Medical Implications of Early Experience*', Chichester, Sussex: John Wiley and Sons.

Stern, D. (1977) *The First Relationship: Infant and Mother*, Fontana (London SW1) and Open Books (Shepton Mallet, Somerset).

Study Commission on the Family (1980) *Happy Families*, 3 Park Road, London, NW1 6XN.

Tizard, B. (1974) *Early Childhood Education, a Review and Discussion of Research in Britain*', NFER.

Trevarthen, C. (1974) Conversations with a two month old, *New Scientist*, 2nd May.

Tucker, N. (1977) *What is a Child?*, Fontana (London, SW1) and Open Books (Shepton Mallet, Somerset).

Turner, J. (1980) *Made for Life*, London, EC4: Methuen.

UNESCO (1979) *Parent Education*, selective annotated bibliography compiled by M. Bekombo-Priso, 7 Place de Fonenoy, 75700 Paris.

UNESCO (1980) *The Role of Parents in the Education of Children of Pre-school age in tropical Africa, India and the Maghreb Countries*.

Villiers, P. and J. (1979) *Early Language*, Fontana (London, SW1) and Open Books (Shepton Mallet, Somerset).

Walkerdine, V. *Cognitive and Linguistic Operations in the Home and School Context*, Institute of Education, London University.

Wells, G. (1975) *The Language Development of Pre-school Children*, SSRC, Bristol University, School of Education.

Whitfield, R. (1979) *Education for Family Life*, Sevenoaks, Kent: Hodder and Stoughton.

Wolfendale, S. and Bryans, T. (1979) *Identification of Learning Difficulties – a Model for Intervention*, National Association for Remedial Education (NARE) 2 Lichfield Road, Stafford.

Woodhead, M. (1981) 'Cooperation in early education – what does it mean? Why does it matter?' in *Early Child Development and Care*, Vol. 7. Nos. 2 and 3.

Woollett, A. White, D. and Lyon M. L. (1980) *A Longitudinal Study of Family and Peer Interactions*, Child Study Unit, Department of Psychology, North East London Polytechnic.

Parental Partnership in Education – a Case for Policy

1. The Wider Context

One of the main purposes of this chapter is to present a case for a community-based parent/partnership model, within which the dominant component is educational.

A way of working towards this end is to effect a synthesis of the themes and elements. A synthesis is defined in Scott and Grimmett (eds 1977) as 'cumulative conclusions, not only *within* a single functional area' (e.g. child development research or special educational needs) 'but *across* functional areas as well' (e.g. between early child development, research and pre-school education or special educational needs and multi-disciplinary team approaches). In fact, Scott and Grimmett go on to quote from other sources in relation to child development theory and public policy, and since the point is relevant for the purposes of this chapter, the quotation is given here

Since theories are developed so that the world can be better understood, workable theories can have impact on social issues and actions. Without synthesis, without theories, it is almost impossible for child development research to keep up with social needs (in Scott and Grimmett p. 3).

And as Gordon in the same volume asserts 'a synthetic approach is one that ties together all the elements... requires a systematic not a piece-meal view' (p. 107).

It was suggested in Chapter 1 that a number of the content-areas shared 'common ideologies'. Hence reference throughout to British Government reports of the past fifteen years on education and child services[†] has intended to serve several purposes:

[†] Plowden 1967, Bullock 1975, Court 1976, Taylor 1977, Warnock 1978.

— to unify the themes via official, public perceptions and pronouncements

— to reiterate the point made initially in Chapter 2 that child practitioners and professionals, policy-makers and administrators could themselves unify perceptions and clarify practice for parental involvement in developmental and educational processes via the adoption of those relevant policy recommendations contained in each of several major government reports.

The time-span chosen for this enquiry is that of the Plowden Report and the post-Plowden era, and to some extent, therefore, an account has been given which charts developments during the last fifteen years or so regarding parent involvement in a variety of community and educational settings. Several conclusions emerge from this retrospective analysis:

1) In general there has been patchy local authority take up of Bullock and Court Report recommendations (Chapters 6, 8 and 9).

2) Regarding home-school links, evidence of surveys confirms inconsistent take-up. Some schools enthusiastically espouse and carry out a policy for parents coming into school, others pay lip-service to school-home cooperative links. The Plowden recommendations for 'a minimum programme' with suggestions for 'beyond the minimum' are still far from being standard policy in local education authorities, which is what the Plowden Committee, as well as bodies such as the Advisory Centre for Education, had hoped for.

3) Yet, several fundamental parents' rights, called for in the Plowden and Taylor Reports, are now enshrined in law via the Education Act 1980 (Chapter 4) and others, considered as of equal importance in the Warnock Report, are now incorporated in the 1981 Education Act which 'amends the law relating to special education (Chapter 7).

4) There is accumulating and possibly incontravertible evidence that parents, irrespective of socioeconomic background, are interested and concerned in their children's development and education; that apparent disinterest and remoteness arises from other factors (stress, anxieties, ignorance of educational processes, timidity – Chapter 4) which explain but do not cause. On those occasions where parental interest can be expressed (in situations

ranging from open evenings, classroom helping, assisting with 'home' work, attendance at support or self-help groups, involvement in child-training programmes) there is evidence of competence and potential for constructive participation.

5) Notwithstanding the erratic adoption of the Plowden Report's recommendations and some of the recommendations in the more recent reports, the signs are that a greater degree of conceptual and ideological sophistication is currently being brought to bear on issues relating to the participation by citizens in community activities; the functions of schools as community institutions; the parameters of social intervention into the lives of children and their families. In other words, the 'ecological' focus, cogently expressed by American writers (Chapters 2 and 5) is one that demands very careful thought and planning.

If this section of the chapter is to present a summary statement pertaining to the wider context in which the author has chosen to work, a number of underpinning queries have to be posed. It is proposed to deal wth these in the form of questions, with occasional reference back to the chapters in which evidence and argument were contained.

Question 1

Why is 'now' considered to be an opportune and appropriate time to assert the need for a policy for parental participation in children's development and education?
It is precisely because there are encouraging signs of progress, albeit slow in some respects. These signs are positive portents that there is not only the potential for further development, but that the will and motivation are present in a variety of educational and community settings. However, there is not one sub-area within the overall parent participation field in which Britain can claim to be ahead of any other 'western' or advanced country. Indeed, some of the proposals cited are standard practice in pockets of America and parts of Europe.
Now *is* the time to reappraise national goals and aspirations concerning the education of the young (Chapter 2). Even if the

continuance of human existence could be guaranteed, it remains glaringly evident that there are collective problems (the 'world problematique' discussed by Botkin *et al.*) in sectors of central concern to all mankind, such as energy, population, resources, and so on.

So a possibly contentious claim was made in Chapters 2 and 5 that education is now too important to be left to educationalists and schools. For all we know, the acknowledged problems teachers say they are faced with in what is generally regarded as a pluralist society – in which one-dimensional perceptions of human behaviour, values regarding correct modes for behaviour give way to a 'melting pot' model of society in which no one religion holds sway, no 'best' way of social and public conduct can be paraded, and where alternative family life-styles are all as viable (i.e., 'effective' and enjoyable) as one another – those teachers might actually welcome assistance and support from the community outside the school gates and not least from parents, who have vested interests in the harmonious running of schools, as well as being representative of a number of sub-community networks.

Question II

Is there the theoretical and humanitarian justification to evolve towards 'social engineering' intervention policies which by definition necessitate intrusion into family lives?

Chapters 3 and 5 were especially devoted to consideration of these issues. An attempt was made to present the evidence that appears to justify the continued investment by community 'agents of change' into forms of educational, community and family supports and redirection.

At this juncture in the short history of both compensatory and enrichment intervention strategies, a useful model to adopt might be the global, all-encompassing theoretical and conceptual approach refered to as the 'ecological approach' (Chapters 2 and 5). Within this holistic conception, it becomes possible to 'systems analyse' (see later in this chapter) both the constructive features of a situation as well as the postulated 'problems' inherent or emergent in any system. As analytic and problem-solving tools, these approaches seem to have techniques to offer.

In humanitarian terms, few people have yet quarrelled with the *raison d'être* of intervening in children and parents' lives. This is not to deny the very real problems that all 'interveners' must face. Raven (1980a) gives prominence to several of the inevitable sequiturs stemming from intervention programmes (also Raven 1980b, McCail 1981). Some of these are a possible increase in family stress, undue pressure place on the parent(s), paradoxes regarding 'true' parental participation in schools, the illusion of 'fate control', the risk of promoting an incompetent parent image.

But then it could be argued that both from professional and parental standpoints, we need, for the foreseeable future at least, to continue to explore the parameters and the sticking points of varieties of intervention technologies before we know simply 'what works, what does not', what is worth time and financial investment, what is welcomed by parents and practitioners alike, and so on.

Morrison (1978) succinctly states that as an alternative to the dilemmas and difficulties associated with 'the ethics of intrusion' we could 'do nothing – this policy of doing nothing is basically what has been done previously' (p. 4). He eschews the continued espousal of *laissez faire* policies, on the grounds that they are unproductive and finally, not people-centred. Morrison goes into all the pros and cons of parent involvement (in schools and in the community) and makes a powerful case for the adoption of parent participation policies and programmes.

Question III

Do parents want to be involved?

Surveys of parental participation in various settings confirm the existence of parental interest and concern and the potential remaining for involving parents to an even greater extent, based on their own expressed (and uncoerced!) willingness. It was pointed out in Chapter 4 that traditional assumptions made about parental attitudes by teachers, and by parents about teachers' attitudes need to be punctuated, not by further survey data but by action. That is, the assumptions have rested on untested hypotheses rather than on proven evidence regarding effective home–school policies.

As was also mentioned in Chapter 2 parents are not a homogeneous group or a collective force and it would behove professionals and practitioners to acknowledge the trite but not acted upon observation as to just how much parents represent *all* facets of society – how *all* skills, trades, expertise, specialisms are represented by the entity defined for the purposes of this report as 'parents'. Indeed, so many professionals are themselves parents that it is high time that parent–professional role divisions were blurred and defused and the mystiques cloaking some child-care professions exposed. Parental and professional experience and contributions to children's development and education could become refracted, if not through a fusion of roles (power, status, differential salary structures, hierarchies, role responsibilities being now too complexly organised for that degree of diffusion), then through an amalgamation. The nearest examples of conjoint responsibility/power sharing were examined in Chapter 7.

To quote him once more, Morrison (1978) claims, using US survey evidence to back him up, that parents do want involvement in educational processes, both as parents and as citizens.

Question IV

Are there models for parental participation in the development and education of children?

It is only possible in a summary section to give a 'surface' answer to this question, since the summary is of work and thought which has been examined in each of the previous chapters.

If the surface answer is 'yes' it is because a dissection of parent involvement and parent participation work demonstrates how different models are applicable to different settings. It was seen for example that empirical work with parents in the pre-school sector gave rise to various 'models' that could be tested and applied in the future. The brief for Head Start, EPA and post Education Priority Area collaborative projects gave the workers opportunities to apply and test a variety of learning-in-setting models. By common consent, it has been the uncertainty of what evaluative criteria to adopt that has rendered conclusions of some of this work ambiguous.

What could emerge from an across the board appraisal of much of this work could be rather more confident knowledge of the commonly successful features and elements of parent participation ventures.

G

Perhaps initial and tentative taxonomies could be evolved to use as a framework for conjoint hypothesis testing. In part B of this chapter an attempt is made to do that in the school/education context.

Question V

What would a policy for parental partnership in children's development and education amount to, in general terms?

The following assertions are based on as careful a review as was possible of the available literature, and are intended to apply as general principles to the settings which have been the focus of this report – namely schools, pre-school, multidisciplinary team work, the area of special educational needs, community *milieux*, and the home.

Such a policy, it is suggested, is neither the preserve nor the prerogative of particular local authority or community institutions or groupings: the philosophical elements in which the principles are embedded are applicable within and across settings. It would be up to participants in any sphere to combine or emphasise any or all of these principles into a format for practice (Chapters 7 and 8). This discussion presupposes the widest possible definition of service-delivery for families, but primarily for children and a presupposition that all participants will be willing agents of change.

1.1. A policy for Collaborative Parental Partnership

This could be based on and incorporate the following principles:

(a) Abandoning the client concept to evolve towards parents as partners in sharing exercises;

(b) Consulting of parents in the same way as professional views and specialist opinion are sought, and for parents to have a voice, a forum, or a means of expression – as professionals do.

(c) Mutual setting of objectives, for example, in curriculum process, learning programmes, special education provision, parent education programmes, aided self-groups.

(d) Central involvement of parents in the process (provision or 'treatment').

(e) Parents and professionals to take joint responsibility for out-comes, to be mutually accountable, as well as accountable to a wider public.

(f) Mutual and joint involvement in hypothesis-testing exercises and in-built evaluation.

These principles are, in turn, couched within the twin overriding principles of *reciprocity* and *advocacy*.

Reciprocity was defined at the conclusion to Chapter 2. *Advocacy*, or child advocacy, as a concept is less developed in this country than it is in America (see Mittler 1979) in which setting Rutherford and Edgar (1979) give this description of child advocacy:

Child advocacy has been employed... both on an individual and group basis to make child-serving agencies, institutions and systems more responsive to the rights, needs and desires of children (p. 168).

Further, the authors say 'child advocates believe that children should not be expected to adjust to the arbitrary demands and expectations of these (traditional) service systems. Rather, service delivery systems, which include schools, should be held accountable to children and must demonstrate that they are, in fact, fulfilling their duty' (p. 168). Child advocacy, which is evolving and being tested in North America settings is individual, child-centred and involves concerted efforts to guarantee that children receive a full measure of what is due to them by virtue of being members of society. Service systems must expect to be regularly monitored, and must be self-monitored, to ensure that they provide the services needed to meet children's needs effectively.

Rutherford and Edgar are certain that parents 'are the child's natural advocates'. Although child advocacy as a concept was originally designed to serve both children and their parents as consumers of service systems, Rutherford and Edgar suggest that 'wherever possible, parents become active advocates by encouraging others to assit them in generating services for their children' (p. 173).

From reading this, the misapprehension could arise that parents are urged to be only own-child centred, which could be a myopic line to take. In fact, supporters of active parental involvement in the development and education of children usually do include in the

process the development of collective and organised parents' groupings and united forces with which to challenge malpractice and sterile
procedures.

2. Policy into Practice in Schools

The grounds for a special focus on schools have been examined in
previous chapters and are perceived to be severalfold as follows:

— children spend so much of their time in school (Rutter *et al.* 1979)
  and schools are therefore in a position to be a main influencing
  medium;
— schools are a major community in the lives of children;
— schools can offer expertise and resources to children, families and
  communities;
— there is considerable potential for a greater complementarity
  between school and home, school and agencies, schools and their
  localities (Morrison 1978);
— there is a growing groundswell of opinion that with alleged rising
  levels of social unrest, it is encumbent upon schools to re-align
  with community institutions in order to effect relevant curriculum
  and adult preparation programmes for 'disaffected' youth. The
  disparate worlds for the child of school, home, the world of work
  have to effect a rapprochement (Bird *et al.* 1981, and Chapter 2);
— schools have a responsibility to address themselves directly to
  'world problematique' issues, to the extent that the definition of
  'education' may ultimately have to broaden.

It was argued in Chapter 2 that the development and education of
children should be the proper concerns of teachers *and* parents and
that 'the responsibility of equipping children with cognitive and
practical tools for personal competence and survival is a collective
one'.

The grounds for home-school links policies that invoke the parent
as partner model should, it is suggested, be appraised within the
overall guiding set of principles offered earlier in this chapter, and
particularly set within the two cardinal principles of *reciprocity* and
advocacy.

2.1. Objectives Setting for Home–School Policies

The main practical preoccupations ought to be with what the mutual objectives and purposes are for home–school collaboration, what the desired outcomes are, and by what criteria these can be assessed. The intended benefits to children, to parents and teachers could be used as the basis of negotiable contracts between parents and schools.

The tables below outline objectives and their intended outcomes which could be pre-formulated by schools' staff and parents, via working groups or representative committees (not necessarily or desirably via governing forums, but as offshoots or linked to these).

This hypothetical range of possible objectives and outcomes for children, schools and parents has precedent in actual practice as previous chapters have sought to demonstrate. Many small-scale experiments and projects would be amenable to replication, even generalisability, of some of their features at least. Furthermore, the outcomes could be measured and evaluated in a variety of ways (see later in this chapter).

There are so many possible combinations of a comprehensive home–school programme that a companion handbook would be required to do justice to all the practical possibilities. Many of these combinations have remained in the realm of speculation, contained in well-intentioned pamphlets for parents or visionary texts; others are known to have been tried out.

For example, The Advisory Centre for Education (ACE) produces a practical leaflet *How you can help your local school*. An article in Field (ed. 1977) proposes that schools should appoint advisers, in contrast with an earlier (1966) suggestion by ACE that local education authorities should appoint advisers with a brief for developing home–school contacts. Johnston (1977) puts forward a set of guidelines or questions for teachers to ask of themselves and each other to help them decide the extent to which they are responsive to parents' needs, and what further potential areas there are for fruitful contact. The Manchester branch of the National Association for Multicultural Education (NAME) includes in its document an *A–Z of good home/school relations*.

In a Scottish report (Macbeth *et al.* 1980) a list of schemes operating in various countries is provided which illustrates the many

TABLE 1

OBJECTIVES AND OUTCOMES – FOR CHILDREN

To enhance their cognitive development generally and to boost attainment (via parental involvement in curriculum and programme planning; parental participation in teacher-supervised 'home' learning).

To 'catch up' on skill-acquisition in traditional remedial senses (parental involvement as above).

To boost/train areas of developmental delay or handicap (parents involved in conjoint learning programmes as co-trainers; parents involved in 'treatment' process).

To resolve behaviour/emotional difficulties evident at home or in school (parents involved in problem definition and description, 'treatment' plans at school or at home).

To collaborate on career planning (meetings and information-seeking).

To feel a sense of well-being and ease that school and home share to the fullest possible extent, common concerns and aspirations for their welfare (home visiting by teachers, parents into school, forms of written communication).

TABLE 2

OBJECTIVES AND OUTCOMES – FOR SCHOOLS AND PARENTS

For schools	*For parents*
← Reciprocity →	
To gain knowledge and understanding of children's homes, families, interests and out-of-school activities.	To gain knowledge and understanding of function and aims of school, teachers' role and local education authority services.

Written and verbal exchange

←—————————————→

Increased accountability (via openness and access) of curriculum and provision.	To gain information regarding progress of children in main-stream and special education provision.
To gain parental interest, support and backing for schools' goals and activities.	To gain opportunities to discuss issues and formulate decisions: to become involved in curriculum process and learning programmes..

←——— Advocacy in action ———→

---

ways in which home–school partnership can work in practice in terms
of home liaison arrangements; traditional and innovatory forms of
verbal and written communication; novel ways of ensuring that
teachers and parents meet on a regular basis to discuss individual
children's progress; the appointment of 'key' parents to act as
catalysts and 'middlepersons' to facilitate other parents' responsiveness; collaborative teacher–parent planning and execution of work
programmes for which schools' and community resources are used.

One final example of 'good' or novel practice in this area comes
from recent reports that the West Midlands local education authority
of Walsall is planning to hold special training sessions to enable
parents systematically to evaluate schools and to help take decisions
about the school curriculum. This is in a locality which has a well-
developed policy of community schools.

3. Towards a Taxonomy of Home–School Partnership: A Basis for Reciprocity

A system of classification or taxonomy is offered below, which, it
is suggested could be used as a starting framework for the generation
and evolution of school and parent partnership policies. As with other
taxonomies (e.g. Bloom's 1956) this is divided into domains, two in
this case. These share a common format, but each has a different
emphasis.

Parents into School

This is intended to conceptualise the *areas* for involvement by
parents within the school context, with the main *types* of involvement
listed against each area and with the particular *focus* of the
involvement noted against each *type*. In this domain the perspective
and responsibilities of the schools are paramount.

School to Home

In this domain the tripartite conceptual framework is identical to
Parents Into Schools (i.e., with *area, type* and *focus*) but the
context and overall perspective is the environment outside the school,
i.e., the home and the wider community. Thus the taxonomic
approach here aims to emphasise the extension of schools into this
wider world.

From this presentation it can be seen that the initiatives are
intended to be two-way, that is, are beyond a Plowden conception.

TABLE 3
PARENTS INTO SCHOOLS

Area	Type	Focus
Concrete and practical	basic help with learning fund-raising and support; practical skills; social meetings	classroom and school
Pedagogical and problem-solving	syllabus design and planning, co-tutoring of school and home-based learning (general education, remedial, special education needs) school-based discussion of progress	curriculum
Policy and governing	educational decision-making; parents as governors	school as institution
Communal	groups for parents and children, (workshops, classes, courses, talks, demonstrations)	school and community

TABLE 4
SCHOOL TO HOME

Area	Type	Focus
Information	verbal, written communication – letters, reports, newsletters, booklets, check and recording systems	home and parents
Support	home visiting (enquiry, counselling, relations-fostering) imparting information, discussion of child progress	home and family
Instruction	educational home visitor/teaching brief (handicap, special educational needs disadvantage, preschool)	home, child and parents
Representation	input by schools into rest of community (resource sharing, resource loan, local meeting place, focal place for cooperative learning)	home and community

that schools are to 'allow' parents into schools. At worst this has meant far more accommodation by parents than schools themselves have been prepared to make.

It is on this basis of two-way initiative (home-community/school) that the principle of reciprocity rests. This was defined in Chapter 2 as 'mutual involvement, mutual accountability, mutual gain', and included these processes:

— the evolution of agreed aims;
— a stàtement of the means by which the contributions of parents and professionals can be made;
— concensus regarding the criteria for success or failure of the collaboration.

What is being called for in a 'new style' approach to home–school links is a re-examination by teachers of their professional self-concept.

4. Research and Evaluation

4.1. General Remarks

It was stated earlier in this chapter that any policy or programme adopted for try-out ought to have means of evaluation built in. The taxonomy presented above could be used as a framework, along with the principles outlined earlier which underlie such ventures. True, service-delivery systems need not necessarily be *research* focussed if the mandate is a pragmatic one to 'deliver the goods'. However, some of the research reported in previous chapters pertaining to parental participation needs to be replicated in other settings, especially those investigations which reported really positive outcomes.

A distinction should be made at this point between the *desirability* of research in the form of ideas hypothesis-testing being built into some parent partnership approaches, and the *necessity* for evaluative procedures to be part of any or all such approaches.

At an early stage of a policy, hypothesis testing might be considered to be essential; outcomes from these could determine whether or not certain features then become part of routine service-delivery and incorporated into routine programmes. Even continuing evaluation might cease eventually, once participants felt confident the pro-

H

cedures were worthwhile and working smoothly, although any venture needs some form of intermittent scrutiny.

It is hoped that the thesis of pedagogical conservatism and its antithesis of new suggestions from researchers will produce a synthesis incorporating the best of both worlds (Donarchy 1979, p. 144).

Thus Donachy promotes the desirability of a close cooperation between practitioners and researchers, in which all participants formulate as well as implement research proposals. Necessary distinctions are drawn by Brock-Utne (in Elliot and Whitehead, eds 1980) between 'traditional empirical–analytical research' with its particular ground rules, and 'educational action research' with its very different intentions, methodologies, instruments and requirements. The integral *raison d'être* of action research as epitomised in the EPA work of Halsey and his colleagues is described by Donachy as 'a multiplier releasing potentially educative forces in the community' (1979, p. 144). Educational action research takes place in direct cooperation with the educational practice that the research seeks to serve. So 'the research is intervening in the practice and has a say in changing it' (Brook-Utne in Elliott and Whitehead 1980, p. 10).

Nisbet (in Dockrell and Hamilton, eds 1980) has asserted that educational decisions are made without an adequate knowledge base, and Halsey himself (in Tizard 1974) taking the wider context of social and public policy on behalf of children urges 'new methods and new organisation if scholars, policy-makers and practitioners are to collaborate effectively in solving problems for themselves and each other' (p. 119). In the same vein and with equal concern for a coalescence of research and practice to effect viable policies for children and their families, Bruner (in Dockrell and Hamilton 1980) has called for the creation of 'educational task forces'. These he hopes could 'bring before the community for scrutiny the powerful factors that shape our decisions about schooling: economic, social, political, cultural, as well as the technical requirements of education itself' (p. 39).

The 'new methods' urged by Halsey are already becoming apparent and being explored in a variety of educational and social settings. Nisbet (in Dockrell and Hamilton 1980) juxtaposes 'older' traditional approaches to experimentation with 'newer style' open-ended enquiry, which may include participant observation and illuminative evaluation. Becher, too, provides a critique of traditional approaches (also in Dockrell and Hamilton 1980) and argues for a new role for the educational researcher in which the latter's function 'would more closely resemble that of a consultant, working alongside the teacher' (p. 60). This is not the fullest conception of the researcher as an essential participant, pace Brock-Utne (above) but one which brings the researcher from his/her erstwhile remote realm of impartial enquiry to one in which there is some identification on the researcher's part with the issues under scrutiny. In the same volume (Dockrell and Hamilton), Walker gives a detailed exposition of the case study approach, with its advantages and disadvantages.

Another theoretical approach with its developed methodologies is that of systems theory and systems analysis (Dalin 1978) which has been defined and discussed in Britain, particularly in relation to the work of educational psychologists and their brand of problem-solving activities (Burden in Gillham, ed. 1978, Burden in Gillham, ed. 1981, Burden in McPherson and Sutton, eds 1981, Miller 1980, Figg and Ross in Gillham, ed. 1981). Nevertheless, there could be much within the theory and the model(s) that would be applicable to parent–teacher, home–school collaborative work.

A research approach advocated by Burgess (1981) is that of diary-keeping, because, he says, in field research, systematic and useful documentary research evidence is often scanty. Burgess describes the substantive account, the methodological account, the analytic accounts – all of which descriptive data can be provided by researcher–participants in field or action–research.

The question of evaluating case-study work has been considered by Walker (in Dockrell and Hamilton 1980) who enumerates three types for the purpose. In the same volume, Stake describes well known and influential evaluation theories and methods, as well as his own modifications to these, which he has tried out in various settings, mostly educational.

Based largely on his experience as a researcher–evaluator for the Honeylands Project, Burden (see references under List B in Chapter 7) has examined the applicability of evaluation approaches to intervention projects, and described the format he adopted for evaluating one aspect of Honeylands' 'service delivery system'.

The essential point to be made here is that advocates of evaluation approaches usually stress how important it is to build in methods to measure the *process* of the project or programme (sometimes referred to as monitoring procedures) as well as their outcomes, or products.

4.2. Application of research techniques to parent-participation policies.

These various research and evaluation approaches should be relevant to the measurement and assessment of parent-participation policies. Some examples are:

1) *Exploratory, survey and information-gathering work* could focus around parents' and teachers' attitudes and aspirations, concrete suggestions as to how links should be fostered; practical ways in which participants can get together; what kind of meetings are suitable for what kind of purpose; what forms of accountability should exist; role and contribution of the support services – examples are legion.

2) *Hypothesis-testing and educational action research* could engage upon the setting up and follow-through of intervention projects, where the focus is school and/or home, both, or other milieux. The potential for 'home' learning where the parent is a co-educator under the supervision of the teacher is one area ripe for research activity.

3) *Evaluation* of rather more 'routine' apparently humdrum forms of collaboration would be a vital component. Meetings, working parties, the 'routine' presence of parents in schools, regular duties such as home visiting by teachers could all be subject to evaluation procedures carried out by participants to some extent, and researchers on funded secondment from local institutions of higher education.

5. Concluding Comment

As can be seen from a wide-ranging review of current literature, schools are being called upon from so many quarters to reappraise their role and function in today's world on behalf of tomorrow's adults. The CERI research enquiry, referred to in Chapter 9 in one of its unpublished draft discussion documents foresees changing school functions under several headings:

1) the scientific base for schooling
2) schools as the community's agents to support the family role
3) the 'human care' orientation of schools
4) 'family life' courses
5) school response to minority family cultures

In a discussion on education viewed from an evolutionary perspective, Martlew, Smith and Connolly (in Dockrell and Hamilton 1980) rework the definition of education as they perceive it juxtaposed between its traditional functions demanded by society and the requirements of a technological and fast-changing contemporary society, which call for different skills and competencies. Continued compartmentalism and educational separatism is not likely to guarantee optimisation of human potential, nor the ability to flexibly adapt to and cope with change.

Outmoded aspirations for conventional success in formal learning terms will have to give way to the need to develop different kinds of learning and coping skills. Wolfendale gave attention in an earlier publication (1980) to a curriculum which could include the necessary elements; her suggested list is reproduced here:

Social competence: self-care, daily problem-solving, skills of interrelating and empathy, community participation.

knowledge-based: knowledge of the world around us, current affairs at local and national level, basic history, origins of culture, literature.

performance-based: competence in numeracy, literacy, scientific and technological concepts, industrial and commercial procedures.

cognitive competence: problem-solving techniques; thinking and critical skills; anticipatory learning skills; decision-making; taking personal and altruistic responsibility.

No derogation of teachers' roles is envisaged in pleading for radical change; rather the teacher's contribution as organiser, catalyst, facilitator and expert is linchpin. For children's development to blossom, for their education to flourish, society's invitation to parents is for them to be partners in the educational and community enterprise.

From their perspective as lawyers, Coons and Sugarman (1978) argue a powerful and sensitive case for parental control over educational processes, concluding 'to treat education like childrearing generally would be to give the family the basic power to select the child's educational experiences, with the child protected from the

harmful exercise of that power through various judical and administrative mechanisms'. They say that they prefer 'families or familylike
units – supported by professionals – as the appropriate locus of the
authority over the child's education' (p. 223).

The last word comes from an extract from the United Nations
Declaration of the Rights of the Child:

The best interests of the child shall be the guiding principle of those responsible for his education
and guidance; that responsibility lies in the first place with his parents.

References

Bird, C., Chessum, R., Furlong, J., Johnson, D. (1981) *Disaffected Pupils*, Brunel
University, Department of Government, Educational Studies Unit.

Bloom, B. S. *et al.* (1956) *Taxonomy of Educational Objectives I: Cognitive Domain*,
London, W1: Longman.

Burgess, R. (1981) 'Keeping a research diary', *Cambridge Journal of Education*, Vol. II,
No. 1, Lent Term.

Coons, J. and Sugarman, S. (1978) *Education by Choice, the Case for Family Control*,
University of California Press.

Dalin, P. (1978) *Limits to Educational Change*, London, WC2: Macmillan.

Dockrell, W. E. and Hamilton, D. (eds) (1980) *Rethinking Educational Research*,
Sevenoaks, Kent: Hodder and Stoughton.

Donachy, W. (1979) 'Implications: Some Emergent Principles', Chapter 12 in
Clark, M. M. and Cheyne, W. N. (eds) *Studies in Pre-School Education*, Sevenoaks,
Kent: Hodder and Stoughton.

Elliott, J. and Whitehead, D. (eds) (1980) 'The theory and practice of educational
action research', *Classroom Action Research Project (CARN)*, *Bulletin No. 4*,
Cambridge Institute of Education, Shaftesbury Road, Cambridge.

Field, F. (ed.) (1977) *Education and the Urban Crisis*, London, WC1: Routledge and
Kegan Paul.

Gillham, B. (ed.) (1978) *Reconstructing Educational Psychology*, London, SW11: Croom
Helm.

Gillham, B. (ed.) (1981) *Problem Behaviour in the Secondary School*, London, SW11:
Croom Helm.

Johnston, S. (1977) 'Disadvantage in Education', *Journal of the Centre on Educational
Disadvantage*, Vol. 1, No. 2, January.

Macbeth, A., Mackenzie, M., Breckenridge, I. (1980) *Scottish School Councils: Policy-
making, Participation or Irrelevance*, Scottish Education Department, HMSO,
Edinburgh.

McCail, G. (1981) *Mother Start: an account of an educational home-visiting scheme for pre-
school children'*, Scottish Council for Research in Education.

McPherson, I. and Sutton, A. (eds) (1981) *Reconstructing Psychological Practice*,
London, SW11: Croom Helm.

Miller, A. (1980) 'Systems theory applied to the work of an educational psychologist', *Journal of the Association of Educational Psychologists*, Vol. 5, No. 3, Spring.

Mittler, P. (1979) *People not Patients*, London, EC4: Methuen.

Morrison, G. (1978) *Parent Involvement in the Home, School and Community*, Wembley, Middx: Charles E. Merrill.

National Association for Multicultural Education (NAME) Manchester Branch, *Home–school Liaison, a Multi-cultural Perspective*.

Raven, J. (1980a) *Parents, Teachers and Children*, Sevenoaks, Kent: Hodder and Stoughton.

Raven, J. (1980b) Intervention as interference', *Scottish Educational Review*, Vol. 12, No. 2, pp. 120–130, November.

Rutherford, R. and Edgar, E. (1979) *Teachers and Parents, a Guide to Interaction and Cooperation*, Boston, Mass: Allyn and Bacon.

Rutter, M., Maughan, B., Mortimore, P., Ouston, J. (1979) *Fifteen Thousand Hours*, Shepton Mallet, Somerset: Open Books.

Scott, M. and Grimmett, S. (eds) (1977) *Current Issues in Child Development*, National Association for the Education of Young Children, Washington, D.C.

Tizard, B. (1974) *Early Child Education, a Review and Discussion of Research in Britain'*, NFER.

Wolfendale, S. (1980) 'Learning difficulties; a re-appraisal', editorial article in *Remedial Education, Journal of the National Association for Remedial Education*, Vol. 1, No. 3, August.

Children of Multi-Ethnic Origin and Home–School Links

The title of this book suggests that is is *all* children who have been the focus, and all children who are intended to be in receipt of the assumed benefits of closer home–school links. The lines of argument are intended to support the contention that a policy for parent-professional partnership would be the umbrella for all children and their families, irrespective of defined or designated groups within the overall child population.

The 'defined' and 'designated' groups were seen to be children with an evident variety of mild or severe problems and handicaps, ranging from alleged material and experiential deprivation with its concomitant educational disadvantage, to physical and/or mental handicap, to emotional, behaviour and learning problems. The general and special educational needs of these groups of children were assessed with a view to examining how partnership policies between parents, professionals and practitioners could best bring about desired change and assist children and their families.

It is in this spirit, and with the same concern, that this section devotes attention to numbers of children from multi-ethnic backgrounds. It is debatable as to whether this numerical minority of all the children in Britain should be singled out at this point, because ethnic minority children are represented in each of the 'defined and designated' groups, as well as within the overall child population. Thus all remarks made and data presented in previous chapters applies to them equally and parent partnership policies are intended to be universally relevant.

The justification for this appendix is based on the latent concern felt by some, and manifest anxiety now expressed by many, that ethnic minority children have – in addition to often requiring temporary or long-lasting special educational needs – *distinctive* needs, especially at this point in Britain's social history.

Concern prior to legislation on race relations centred around the existence and effects of racial prejudice and discrimination. Since the Acts outlawing racial prejudice, concern on the part of those with ethnic minority interests and responsibilities has continued to be focussed on:

— persisting and pervasive effects of discrimination in housing, in jobs and in social community affairs (White paper 1975, Commission for Racial Equality (CRE) 1977, CRE 1974/1979, Home Office 1981, House of Commons Paper 1981);

— alleged and apparent underachievement by ethnic minority children and especially it seems by West Indian children (CRE 1974/1979, interim report Rampton Committee now the Swann Committee, *Times Educational Supplement*, May 1981; proposed Department of Education and Science funded research at Lancaster University/Policy Studies Institute)

— the extent of 'disaffection' by black youth and their sense of alienation from the education process and 'mainstream' society (Ratcliffe 1981);

— those areas of the school curriculum that appear to be irrelevant to ethnic minority children and topics perceived to be relevant for inclusion into the school curriculum (Select Committee 1974, Little and Willey 1981, Stone 1981).

These areas of concern have thus been delineated and examined in a spate of official reports. A number of survey and research reports are at pains to come up with general and specific recommendations for measures to alleviate or resolve the problems on behalf of ethnic minority children and their families. Within the terms of reference outlined in Chapter 7 for general and special educational needs, ethnic minority children at present growing up in Britain have acknowledged *distinctive* needs. The measures proposed in various reports are designed to meet these needs.

Resources have been created and provision has expanded to meet these needs. As the School Council Pamphlet (Little and Willey 1981) confirms, local education authorities now provide advisers and advisory teachers with a multi-cultural brief, English as a second language and supplementary teams; there are posts in schools with designated multi-cultural and multi-ethnic responsibilities, many in-service teacher training programmes, and elements in pre-service training. A number of the home visiting programmes and parents' support groups described in Chapters 3 and 5 of this report as well as others were either explicitly intended for recently-arrived immigrant families and their children, or include 'minority' families.

Within the defined group of children seen as having distinctive needs by virtue of their or their parents' recent (in the last few years) arrival in the UK, there are of course so many differences that it is really invidious, even injurious to talk of a multi-ethnic collective entity. Differential attention has been given to the cultural history, language, customs, religious of all the nations of origin represented in the numbers of British citizens who have settled in Britain in the post Second World War years (e.g. 'The West Indian Community' 1978, also see Bell 1976). The sub-minority groups have been regarded overall as target groups for the receipt of social and educational services, and legislation has been aimed at their protection.

Little (in CRE 1978a) identifies a number of issues and addresses himself to what he sees as the task and responsibility of schools in tackling these issues. One is the particular concentration of minority communities in some geographical areas; another is the strong link between ethnic minority groups and socioeconomic disadvantage; yet another is latent and expressed racial prejudice. The fourth issue is 'the fact of underachievement' in school by minority background children.

The general consensus of opinion from survey and research reports is that British educationalists have a duty to propagate concepts of multi-cultural education and to ensure the full adoption of multi-cultural syllabuses throughout the school system. Watkins (1978) asserts that the fact has to be recognised that we live in a multiracial society and 'accurate knowledge provided through the school curriculum about the origins and present situation of our multiracial society would seen to be an essential element in the education of the attitudes of the nation's future leaders' (p. 3). Furthermore, teachers have a key responsibility to disseminate understanding, acceptance and tolerance of ways of life other than a supposed norm.

Overtly, teachers' attitudes would appear to be endorsing of the need to 'preach and teach' understanding and promote racial harmony. But reports refer to covert attitudes, hidden prejudices, negative stereotyping by teachers towards ethnic minority groups of children, or a deliberate suppression or denial of the issues by adopting what is termed as 'colour blind' policies (Fitzherbert *et al.* 1972).

One example of 'negative stereotyping' is an assumption often made by teachers based on surface 'evidence' that ethnic minority parents, for example, West Indian or Asian are not interested in their children's schooling. This 'myth' is being exposed as evidence is coming in to refute it (Tomlinson in Craft *et al.* 1980). Stone (1981) in her discussion of the well-meaning but failing attempts to introduce relevant curriculum elements on behalf of the black child makes it quite clear that parents are concerned about their children's education, to the extent that a number of them, in conjunction often with church or voluntary organisations, set up Saturday or supplementary schools and classes. These teach skills and subjects that, the parents claim, are either not being covered in schools, or are not being taught in such a way or with the right emphasis for their children to benefit. A group of parents in North London was so concerned over the ways in which the state education system seems to be failing the black child that they set up a pressure and action group called Black Educational Advance (BEA) which takes up individual problems as well as general issues.

1. Towards the Fostering of Home—School Links and Parent Participation Policies for Ethnic Minority Children

There seem to be enough grounds for concern and anxiety on the part of public policy makers, as well as parents of ethnic minority children, to warrant some attention being paid to ways in which parent-professional partnership can promote positive multiracial relations in general, and bring special benefits to school children in particular.

The taxonomy and main principles for parent partnership policy put forward in Chapter 10 would be equally applicable to approaches which explicitly concentrated on links with ethnic-minority families and which have a specified set of objectives. The reader is reminded (Chapter 10) that one of the changing functions or duties of schools as envisaged in the preliminary documents of the CERI research project, *The Educational Role of the Family*, is the 'school response to minority family cultures'. Regarding the language teaching dilemma, the CERI project sets out the 'choices' of maintaining two languages, developing the 'mother tongue' first as a bridge to literacy, or immersion in the dominant (?host) language.

ESL (English as a second language) teaching has been available in schools for a few years, but mother-tongue teaching is seen as more of a controversial issue, that is to say, opinion is divided as to whether the emphasis should be on developing then enhancing competence to speak in the majority language and dominant registers, or on maintaining and developing competence to speak the 'mother' tongue or first language (Moon and Reid 1979).

Differences of opinion are exacerbated at present by what is seen as a laggardly even indifferent official Britain response to the European Economic Community (EEC) Directive on the Education of Children of Migrant Workers. This directive, now in force, demands of member nations that they shall provide 'teaching of the mother tongue and culture of the country of origin' as well as the language of the 'host' country. Britain is regarded as vacillating on a definite commitment to this principles, except in the area of funding (via the Department of Education and Science and Schools Council) exploratory and action-research.

The CRE considered the implications of the directive on the education of children from ethnic minority groups in the United Kingdom (CRE 1980) and came up with a list of recommendations for the effective implementation of the policy. A programme for mother-tongue teaching, if it were to be fully comprehensive, could involve parents directly in curriculum planning, in some teaching/tutoring, and in the facilitation of school-community links. Tizard et al. (1981) discuss the implications for parent involvement of mother-tongue teaching in nursery and infant schools.

Every single recent report on the educational needs of multi-ethnic children and on multicultural education has stressed the importance of developing home–school links. In nearly every report the deliberate institution of a partnership policy with parents is advocated.

Moon and Reid (1979) talk of 'home bridging schemes', two CRE reports (1977 and 1974/1979) call for extended schemes of 'educational home visits' and 'measures . . . to increase effective home/school contact in multiracial schools and . . . encouraging experiments by head teachers in bringing parents into the school'. In a section

entitled *School and the Community*, a CRE memorandum (1978b) states
'we believe it is of great importance that teachers and the parents of
ethnic-minority pupils should meet and learn from each other about
the children, their progress and their needs as perceived both by
parents and the school'. The memorandum asserts that despite
manifest difficulties of communication, schools and local education
authorities in cooperation with statutory, voluntary and community
organisations 'should make positive efforts to contact and involve
ethnic minority parents as far as possible' (p. 6).

The Schools Council report (Little and Willey 1981) pays due
tribute to the innovative programmes initiated in a number of local
authority areas in regard to home—school liaison, via home visiting,
reference to local community relations councils, and communicating
to parents in written form in minority groups languages. One of the
suggestions in section B *Action by LEAs* in the Schools Council report
is for the 'development and resourcing of ways of encouraging
home/school links among minority ethnic groups' (p. 33); in section
C *Action by Schools*, 'development of a *framework* for encouraging
home—school links . . .'

It is laudable to express 'official' public policy in terms of abstract
ideals. But in order that these abstractions do not remain in the realm
of nebulous exhortation, schools and the families and communities
they serve have to translate these into action, first specifying aims and
objectives and knowing precisely what outcomes are intended (see
Chapter 10).

Tizard *et al.* (1981) discuss the evident communication problems,
misunderstanding, mismatches in aspirations that lie in the way of
easy progress towards home—school cooperations, and come up with
constructive suggestions partly based on their experience during their
project (see Chapter 6). As a starting point, they advocate setting
aims. These are to facilitate the contribution of minority group
parents to the life of the school by adopting a multi-cultural
approach; to enable minority group parents to contribute their
knowledge of their children and their culture to the teachers; to
enable teachers to consult minority group parents about their
children's education and discuss educational issues with them; to help
teachers to explain their aims and methods to minority group parents
(p. 227).

It can be seen that these aims are compatible with the objectives and outcomes list given in Chapter 10 as well as fitting into the taxonomic framework also offered in Chapter 10.

The concrete back-up to the work of Tizard *et al.* comes via their description of their interviews and their attempts to facilitate school–home relations. Their suggestions cover curriculum, home visiting, parental contributions in school. Finally, they feel that teachers working with minority group parents and children should be in possession of basic information pertaining to family details, language and cultural background, family and cultural and religious customs, some geographical and ethnic knowledge, and details of community provision.

The Manchester branch of the National Association for Multi-cultural Education (NAME) has produced a booklet which combines discussion about a 'philosophy' of home–school liaison with a practical A–Z guide on how to develop and maintain home–school relationships.

Lightfoot (1978) does not minimise the conflicts teachers and parents have to resolve as they attempt to 'bridge the chasm'. A first requisite she says is that 'parents and teachers recognise the critical importance of each other's participation in the life of the child' (p. 220) and then explore the differences of attitudes, aspirations, social class and ethnicity which exist between them.

Schools will only become comfortable and productive environments for learning when the cultural and historical presence of black families and communities are infused into the daily interactions and educational process of children (Lightfoot, p. 175).

Lightfoot's accounts of some US collaborative ventures between schools and ethnic minority parents where 'the essence of education was transformed by the presence of families within the school' (p. 175) could provide positive and inspiring examples to guide future British experience.

At a time when economic and job prospects for the young are uncertain and at a time therefore when they need maximum support from their parents and their teachers – preferably in tandem – the onus for the realisation of public policy is on the schools to instigate and maintain a partnership with parents.

References

Bell, L. (1976) *Underprivileged Underfives*, London, W1: Ward Lock Education.

CRE (1977) *Urban Deprivation, Racial Inequality and Social Policy: a Report*, Commission for Racial Equality, Elliott House, 10–12 Allington Street, London, SWIE SEH.

CRE (1978) *Five Views of Multiracial Britain*.

CRE (1978) *Schools and Ethnic Minorities, Comments on 'Education in Schools: a consultative document'*, issued by DES, February.

CRE (1974/1979) *Educational Needs of Children from Minority Groups*.

CRE (1980) *The EEC's Directive on the Education of Children of Migrant Workers*.

Fitzherbert, K. *et al.* (1972) *Report on the Relationship Between School and Parents*, Home/school project, West London Institute of Higher Education.

Home Office Report (1981) *Ethnic Minorities in Britain*, HMSO.

House of Commons (1981) *Racial Disadvantage*, 424–1, HMSO.

Lightfoot, S. L. (1978) *Worlds Apart, Relationships Between Families and Schools*, London, WC2: Basic Books.

Little, A., and Willey, R. (1981) 'Multi-ethnic education: the way forward', *Schools Council Pamphlet 18*, Schools Council, 160 Great Portland St, London, W1.

Moon, J. and Reid, D. (1979) 'Some considerations in social policy for the underfives in a multiracial Britain', *Early Child Development and Care*, Vol. 6, Nos. 1/2.

NAME Manchester branch, *Home–School Liaison*.

Rampton Committee interim report (unpublished), see *Times Educational Supplement* (29.5.1981) 'Why failure is skin-deep', p. 8 (Rampton Committee is the Committee of Inquiry into the Education of Children from minority ethnic groups, changed in 1981 to the Swann Committee).

Ratcliffe, P. (1981) *Racism and reaction, a Profit of Handworth'*, London, WC1: Routledge and Kegan Paul.

Select Committee (1974) 'Educational disadvantage and the educational needs of immigrants', *Command 5720*, HMSO.

Stone, M. (1981) *The Education of the Black Child in Britain*, London, SW1: Fontana.

Tizard, B., Mortimore, J., Burchell, B. (1981) *Involving Parents in Nursery and Infant Schools*, London WC1: Grant McIntyre.

Tomlinson, S. (1980) 'Ethnic minority parents and education', Chapter 12 in Craft, M. Raynor, R. Cohen, L. (eds) *Linking Home and School*, 3rd Edition, London, WC1: Harper and Row.

Watkins, R. (1978) 'Celebrating difference', in *Disadvantage in Education*, CED No. 10, July/August.

The West Indian Community (1978) Observations on the Report of the Select Committee on Race Relations and Immigration, Command 7186, HMSO.

White Paper on Racial Discrimination (1975), Command 6234, HMSO.

Glossary

1. Explanation of British Educational Terminology Used in the Text.

Infant school Many local education authorities operate schools catering for an age-range from five years (sometimes 'rising five', i.e., from four and a half years) which is the statutory starting-age, to seven plus years.

Junior school In local education authorities with infant schools, the junior stage is from seven plus to eleven years.

Junior mixed and infant school Sometimes infant and junior schools are on the same campus site and may be operated jointly, in which case they are called JMI schools. Otherwise, infant and junior schools are separately organised and administered.

Nursery education Many local education authorities provide nursery schools, or nursery classes attached to infant schools, catering, on a parental option basis, for three to five year olds.

Primary education Local educational provision catering for nursery age (three to five years) and five to eleven year olds is referred to as primary education.

Secondary school Caters for eleven to sixteen year olds (or eighteen years if a child wishes to remain at school beyond the statutory leaving age of sixteen years). See Comprehensive education below. A number of local education authorities operate an educational system organised around these age-groups:

First school Caters for children aged from five to eight/nine years

Middle school Caters for children aged from nine to thirteen/fourteen years

High School Caters for children aged from fourteen to sixteen (or eighteen years).

Comprehensive education Refers to the national system of education introduced in the 1960's whereby, in the vast majority of local education authorities, old divisions of grammar, secondary modern, technical schools have been abandoned. Now most British children attend a neighbourhood school which accepts children from a range of socio-economic backgrounds, abilities and attainments.

Local education authority (LEA) The administration, oversight and financial responsibility for local services are carried out by local authorities organised on a district or regional basis. The LEA is part of the local authority and therefore has responsibility for providing education locally.

2. Government Reports on Education and Child Services Referred to and Discussed

The titles and terms of reference are given in order of publication.

Plowden Report Plowden, Lady B (Chairman) (1967) Children and their Primary Schools, a report of the Central Advisory Council for Education, Vol. I, HMSO.

to consider the whole subject of primary education and the transition to secondary education.

Bullock Report Bullock, Lord A (Chairman) (1975) *A Language for Life*, Report of the Committee of Enquiry, HMSO.
to consider in relation to schools:

a) all aspects of teaching the use of English, including reading, writing and speech;

b) How present practice might be improved and the role that initial and in-service training might play;

c) to what extent arrangements for monitoring the general level of attainment in these skills can be introduced or improved;

d) and to make recommendations.

Court Report Court, D. Prof. (Chairman) (1976) Fit for the Future, the Report of the Committee on Child Health Services, Vol. I, HMSO.

our task has been to review the existing health services for children, judge how effective they are for the child and his parents and to propose what the new integrated child health service should try to achieve and how it should be organised and staffed.

Taylor Report   Taylor, T. (Chairman) (1977) *A New Partnership for our Schools*, Report of the Committee on School Management and Government, HMSO.

to review the arrangements for the management and government of maintained primary and secondary schools in England and Wales, including the composition and functions of bodies of managers and governors, and their relationships with local education authorities, with headteachers and staffs of schools, with parents of pupils and with the local community at large; and to make recommendations.

Warnock Report   Warnock, M. (Chairman) (1978) *Special Educational Needs*, Report of the Committee of Enquiry into the Education of Handicapped Children and Young People, HMSO.

to review educational provision in England, Scotland and Wales for children and young people handicapped by disabilities of body or mind, taking account of the medical aspects of their needs, together with arrangements to prepare them for entry into employment; to consider the most effective use of resources for these purposes; and to make recommendations.

3. Institutions, Government Departments, Associations

The full name and address are given in alphabetical order, and where appropriate, a brief explanation or description.

Advisory Centre for Education (ACE)   18 Victoria Park Square, London, E2 9PE. ACE provides essential information and advice for all those involved in the maintained education service. It publishes a monthly magazine. Where, information sheets, and handbooks on the education system and educational topics.

Centre on Educational Disadvantage (CED)   11 Anson Road, Manchester. The CED was set up as a unit for a five year period from 1976 to 1981 by the government to act as an information centre and clearing-house on educational disadvantage. The CED sponsored and organised a number of conferences and seminars on the education of minority group children and children with a variety of special educational needs.

Commission for Racial Equality (CRE)   Elliott House, 10/12 Allington Street, London, S.W.I. CRE was set up to support the Race Relations Act of 1976. It has a wide range of useful publications, many of them free, concerning education from pre-school to adult education.

Department of Education and Science (DES) Elizabeth House, York Road, London, S.E.I. This government department oversees British education, monitors educational standards and developments, via Her Majesty's Inspectors (HMI) who have been professionals within education, and civil servants.

Department of Health and Social Security (D.H.S.S.) Alexander Fleming House, Elephant and Castle, London, S.E.I. This government department oversees health provision and care and social (personal) services for children and adults.

Education Act 1980 This deals with school governing bodies; parents' choice of school; information to be given to parents; procedures for establishing, choosing or altering schools, awards, grants.

Education Act 1981 This amends the law relating to special education. Due to come into force during 1983. It establishes new procedures for assessing and helping children designated as having special educational needs and handicapping conditions. It extends the rights of parents to be involved with the assessment and formulation of their children's needs and subsequent educational decision-making; it endorses the principle of integration into ordinary schools of handicapped children.

Educational Priority Areas (EPA) The Plowden Committee (see part 2 of this glossary) asked for 'positive discrimination' in favour of schools in deprived areas, and for the children in them. It recommended the designation of EPAs, which were to be provided with extra resources for education. A number of action research and evaluative projects developed directly or indirectly out of this proposal.

Health Education Council 78 New Oxford Street, London, W.C.1A 1AH. The HEC is 'the body responsible for promoting better health in England, Wales and Northern Ireland'. Funded by government and local government, it runs national and regional campaigns, school curriculum development projects, community education programmes; it produces information and publications catalogues; it has a library and resources centre open to visitors.

Home and School Council 81 Rustlings Road, Sheffield, S11 7AB. Formed in 1967, in order to foster good home–school relations. It is concerned with disseminating information about good practice and helping parents to understand their children's educational needs.

The three parent organisations of the Home and School Council are A.C.E. (see this glossary), the Campaign for the Advancement of State Education (43 Little Heath, London S.E7 8EB) and NCPTA (see glossary).

International Federation For Parent Education (IFPE) 1 av. Léon Journault, 92310 Sèvres, France. The main objective of the Federation is the study of the problems experienced by families in various civilizations in attempting to adjust to changing ideas and ways of life. It is concerned to help parents in their educational task. The Federation sponsors conferences, seminars, and publishes journals and bibliographies.

National Confederation of Parent–Teacher Associations 43 Stonebridge Road, Northfleet, Gravesend, Kent. An organisation which is the umbrella body for school-based parent–teacher associations. It publishes a newsletter, gives advice on starting PTAs, and supports initiatives at local level.

National Children's Bureau 8 Wakley Street, London E.C.IV 7 E. The NCB receives grants from central and local government and other agencies to carry out research into all aspects of early child development, and the development, education and problems of young people. It has produced much seminal research, a considerable amount of which has important practical implications. The Bureau staff publish many books, articles and papers, and the Bureau runs an information and clearing-house service.

National Foundation for Educational Research (NFER) The Mere, Upton Park, Slough, Berkshire SL1 2DG. NFER is the main national body which instigates, carries out research within education, and is responsible for disseminating the results to people working in education. It is funded by government and local education authorities.

Organisation for Economic Cooperation and Development (OECD) and the Centre for Educational Research and Innovation (C.E.R.I.), 2 rue Andre-Pascal, 75775, Paris, Cedex, 16, France.

Open University Bletchley, Milton Keynes, MK7 6AA. This was founded during 1960s. It offers opportunities for adults to study for diplomas and degrees part-time. Entry requirements are less stringent and more flexible than with conventional universities and colleges. Courses are linked to the national television and radio network run by the British Broadcasting Corporation (BBC). Students can therefore study at home, and there are regional Open

University centres, via which students can be in contact with academic and pastoral tutors.

Schools Council 160 Great Portland Street, London, W.1. This government and local educational authority funded national forum represents views of educationalists and representatives from industry. It stimulates and instigates educational research, monitors developments in curriculum areas and educational practice. At present the government is planning to reorganise the Schools Council.

Swann Committee (formerly Rampton Committee). This was set up by the government to look into all aspects of the education of children from ethnic minority groups. By mid 1982, the Committee was still considering the evidence.

United Nations Educational, Scientific and Cultural Organisation (UNESCO), 7 Place de Fontenoy, 75700, Paris, France.

Author Index

Subject Index